Freda Briggs, formerly a teacher an
of Child Development at the Univer:
also the author of *From Victim t*
Developing Personal Safety Skills in C
Children Safe and *Child Sexual Abuse: Confronting the problem*.
Russell Hawkins is a psychologist in private practice and a senior
lecturer in Psychology at the University of South Australia.

CHILD PROTECTION

*A guide for teachers and
child care professionals*

Freda Briggs and Russell Hawkins

ALLEN & UNWIN

First published in 1997 by
Allen & Unwin Pty Ltd
9 Atchison Street, St Leonards, NSW 2065 Australia
Phone: (61 2) 9901 4088
Fax: (61 2) 9906 2218
E-mail: frontdesk@allen-unwin.com.au

National Library of Australia
Cataloguing-in-Publication entry:

Briggs, Freda.
  Child protection: a guide for teachers and child care professionals.

  Includes index.
  ISBN 1 86448 221 4.

  1. Child abuse—Prevention. 2. Child sexual abuse—Prevention. I. Hawkins, R.M.F. (Russell Martin Francis). II. Title.

362.7672

Set in 10/11.5 pt Garamond by DOCUPRO, Sydney
Printed by Southwood Press Pty Ltd, Sydney

10 9 8 7 6 5 4 3 2 1

CONTENTS

PREFACE

Child abuse and neglect have become government policy issues which most countries are forced to address. International debate was first triggered by an article entitled 'The battered child syndrome' by Henry C. Kempe and colleagues, published in the *Journal of the American Medical Association* (1962). This revealed that physical abuse was more common than previously acknowledged.

In the early 1980s, the focus of attention moved to child sexual abuse. The size and nature of this problem were brought to media attention by the women's movement in North America. In New Zealand, the Mental Health Foundation disclosed that half of all female clients in need of counselling, for whatever reason, had been sexually abused in childhood. Australian Rape Crisis phone-ins confirmed that most sexual offences against children were committed by known and trusted adults, not strangers.

The publication of report statistics led to the demand for realistic child protection curriculum in schools and preschools which would help children to identify, avoid and report sexual misbehaviour. The early programmes were written by women with information provided by adult female victims of sexual abuse. The vulnerability of boys was not identified until the early 1990s and many parents and professionals continue to underestimate the risks to males.

All of the American states, all of the Canadian provinces and territories except the Yukon, and all Australian states and territories except the Australian Capital Territory and Western Australia acknowledged the importance of schools and early childhood centres in child protection legislation relating to the reporting of cases of child maltreatment. These governments recognised that it was inappropriate for professionals responsible for the care of children to be given the choice of whether to report child maltreatment or ignore it and let it continue. They removed the uncertainty relating to who should be responsible for investigating reports and managing cases of abuse. They also protected notifiers from civil action if their suspicions were not confirmed by the authorities responsible for the assessment of abuse cases.

Although governments, through their legislation and guidelines, have long recognised the importance of school and preschool personnel in child protection, tertiary education has been slow to recognise and respond to the pre-service educational needs of professionals who work with children. This book has been written in response to those needs.

The authors utilised current international research findings and anecdotal material from teachers and child care personnel. Each chapter was circulated for comment to experienced practitioners and child protection experts in Australia, New Zealand, the United Kingdom and the United States. Their suggestions were incorporated into the text. We are grateful to Professor Sonia Jackson, University of Swansea; Janet Moyles, University of Leicester; Jim Ennis, University of Dundee; the NSPCC and ISPCC for information relating to the United Kingdom and Ireland; and to Jeremy Robertson from the office of the Commissioner for Children (New Zealand) and Nicholas Robinson (UK) for data on child homelessness.

Special thanks must also go to Dr Maris O'Rourke, Secretary for Education, New Zealand, for granting permission to reproduce and adapt *Prevent Child Abuse: Guidelines for Early Childhood Services* (Ministry of Education 1993) which provided the basis for chapter 14 of this book. Thanks are also due to Michael McVeity, Louise Ward and Wendy Ashenden of the South Australian Department of Education and Children's Services and Owen Sanders, New Zealand Police, who read the manuscript and provided valuable feedback.

At the end of most chapters we have included tasks for students. These tasks are intended for use in pre-service or in-service courses and ideally should be moderated by a leader or instructor.

Freda Briggs and Russell Hawkins, 1996

1

CHILD PROTECTION IS EVERYBODY'S BUSINESS

Child abuse and neglect are triggered by a combination of forces at work in the individual, the family, the community and the culture. Such complex causes require a multiprofessional response that is sensitive to cultural diversity and other special needs. Thus, the prevention and treatment of child abuse have become shared responsibilities between government agencies and services involved with children, families and the community. Most important on the list of 'human services' are the teaching and child care professions.

STATE OBLIGATIONS: CONVENTION ON THE RIGHTS OF THE CHILD

On 20 November 1989, the United Nations General Assembly adopted the UN Convention on the Rights of the Child. Within a year, 141 countries had either signed the Convention or had become State Parties to it by ratification or accession. Australia became a State Party by ratification. New Zealand, Canada and the United Kingdom became signatories without ratification and the United States became neither (Alston & Brennan 1991).

By signing the Convention, countries agreed that 'The child shall be protected against all form of neglect, cruelty and exploitation. He shall not be the subject of traffic in any form' (Principle 9).

Furthermore, under Article 19 it was agreed that:

1

1 State Parties shall take all appropriate legislative, administrative, social and educational measures to protect the child from all forms of physical or mental violence, injury or abuse or negligent treatment, maltreatment or exploitation including sexual abuse while in the care of parent(s), legal guardian(s) or any other person who has the care of the child.

2 Such protective measures should, as appropriate, include effective procedures for the establishment of social programmes to provide necessary support for the child and for those who have the care of the child, as well as for other forms of prevention and for the identification, reporting, referral, investigation, treatment and follow-up of instances of child maltreatment described heretofore, and, as appropriate, for judicial involvement.

Article 34 requires that:

Children shall be protected from all forms of sexual exploitation and sexual abuse. Governments shall take appropriate measures to prevent:

a the inducement or coercion of a child to engage in any sexual activity;
b the exploitative use of children in prostitution or other unlawful sexual practices;
c the exploitative use of children in pornographic performances and materials.

Article 39 states that:

Governments shall take all appropriate measures to promote physical and psychological recovery and social reintegration of child victims of any form of neglect, exploitation, abuse, torture or any other form of cruel, inhuman or degrading treatment or punishment.

CHILDREN'S RIGHTS VERSUS ADULTS' RIGHTS: SOCIETY'S CONFLICTING VALUES

Although child protection is a worldwide concern, Western society is the most vociferous in condemning child abuse. The sincerity of that commitment must be doubted, however, when we examine our dual sets of values and the public outcries that occur when children's rights are promoted.

Society concedes that children should have some rights but

only when those rights don't diminish or impinge on adults' rights, parental authority or the right to maintain traditional parenting practices. As we approach the 21st century, there is still a lingering notion that 'what happens behind closed doors is no-one else's business'. Crime reports in daily newspapers confirm that some men still perceive themselves as having total ownership and control over their wives and children. 'I will do what I like with my kids and nobody is going to stop me' is a statement often heard in criminal and family courts. Although several European countries have adopted legislation to ban the use of corporal punishment, the same proposals have met with strong public opposition in Australia and the United Kingdom. Peter Newell, a promoter of British children's rights, commented on the irony that we don't condone hurting animals but we protect parents who decide to hurt their children. In British and Australian society, children form the only group that is not protected from violence (Newell 1995).

It is worrying that, although half of all cases of serious physical abuse that reach the courts start out as 'punishment', the Australian Family Society maintains that parents 'know best' and should have the right to 'bring up children' and 'discipline' them as they see fit without government intervention and legislation (Bastick 1995).

Although child protection experts have long known that family privacy facilitates child maltreatment, policy makers throughout the Western world are being urged to introduce privacy legislation to stop state intrusion into cultural mores and family life. Furthermore, in many states and countries, professionals are given a choice as to whether they acknowledge and report child abuse or collude with the offender and ignore it.

DEFINING CHILD ABUSE IN A MULTICULTURAL SOCIETY

Although legal and operational variations are found in definitions of child abuse and neglect, all refer to the protection of children from emotional, physical and sexual harm. Current debate in multicultural societies revolves around what parameters should be included in those definitions.

One of the problems is that techniques used to socialise children differ within groups and cultures and what is regarded as normal adult behaviour in one context may be viewed as abusive in another. If we lack a cross-cultural perspective, we are apt to view our own practices and standards as the only 'right' ones. On the other hand, if we value cultural interests more highly than the humane treatment of children, we may ignore evidence of child abuse and condone or even justify lower standards of care for children from other cultures.

Korbin identified three levels of abuse, the first of which encompasses practices which are considered to be acceptable in the culture in which they occur but are viewed as abusive by outsiders (Korbin 1977, p. 9). Migrants often protest that some long-established Western practices are detrimental. They cite such examples as the isolation of young children for punishment, placing them in separate bedrooms and allowing infants to cry themselves to sleep.

The second level of abuse identified by Korbin (1991, p. 66) encompasses individual abuse or neglect which exceeds the boundaries of behavioural standards set by the abuser's 'own community'. While Australia, New Zealand and the United Kingdom are reconsidering the legitimacy of smacking children, it remains a very common form of punishment in all three countries. The Department of Health report (England and Wales), *Child protection: Messages from research,* noted that 75 per cent of British infants are hit by their parents during their first year of life which, 'statistically speaking', confirms that hitting babies constitutes 'normal' British parenting behaviour (Department of Health 1995).

Similarly, Rosalie Duke's Australian survey (1995) showed that 97 per cent of parents and 94 per cent of children were smacked in childhood and although the children hated it, most intended to use smacking for punishment when they became parents. It was even more disconcerting to find that 60 per cent of teachers who were trained to use positive child management techniques in their professional work believed that it was acceptable for parents to smack their children.

The third level of abuse defined by Korbin (1991, p. 67) relates to societal conditions which may be beyond the parents' control, such as poverty, poor housing or lack of sanitation.

Arguments continue as to when authorities should step in to stop harmful cultural practices and to what extent migrants should have to conform to the legal requirements of the host country when they conflict with their traditional parenting practices. Should we, for example, ignore the fact that our child labour laws are being flouted because the families are migrants from countries where children are expected to contribute to the family income? Should we ignore the fact that young migrant children are left in charge of younger siblings because these responsibilities were accepted as 'normal' in their homelands? Should we permit East African parents to submit children for facial scarification or allow Sudanese Muslims to infibulate their daughters when they live in London, Sydney, Toronto or Auckland? Should governments allow migrant adults to import child brides because such arrangements are acceptable in the bridegroom's birthplace?

In recent times, there have been heated arguments between child advocates and proponents of multiculturalism. There is, for example, a division of opinion relating to female genital mutilation. Multiculturalists (of both sexes) argue that this is an established cultural practice which should be tolerated in multicultural societies. Child advocates insist that it be banned as a barbaric form of child sexual, emotional and physical abuse and an unacceptable method of controlling females. Some Western medical practitioners have entered the debate, publicly defending their participation in genital mutilation on the grounds that, if parents insist on subjecting their daughters to this form of surgery, it is better undertaken by doctors than left in the hands of grandmothers using razorblades.

Significantly, female genital mutilation was 'wholly condemned' as a 'vicious' and 'harmful practice' in a joint statement made by religious leaders from Islam and Coptic Christian faiths, Imam Tajaddine Al-Hillaly in Australia and Sheik Mansour Leghaei, representative of the Shi'ite tradition of Islam in Iran. They proclaimed that 'All prophetic traditions which support this practice are fabricated' (Ceresa 1995). Unfortunately, this welcome statement is unlikely to end the practice or the debate.

In the meantime, while Western society condemns genital mutilation and harsh initiation rites, it turns a blind eye to the circumcision of baby boys, often undertaken for no better reason than that 'his dad was circumcised'.

In their report, *Culture: No excuse,* the New South Wales Child Protection Council makes it absolutely clear that educators and child care workers must never excuse or ignore evidence of child abuse or neglect on cultural grounds. The Council is concerned that physical abuse and neglect are often discounted as 'cultural practice, leaving children from non-English-speaking backgrounds at high risk of abuse' (NSWCPC undated, p. 4). The Council noted that physical abuse is most likely to be ignored when fathers proclaim that, as 'head of the household', they have both a right and a duty to inflict physical pain on children 'for their own good'.

While a knowledge of the cultural framework in which abusive behaviour occurs is vital for guiding professionals on when and how to intervene, intervention itself 'on the grounds of suspected abuse should never be inhibited or delayed by cultural considerations' (NSWCPC undated, p. 5).

REPORTS OF CHILD ABUSE AND NEGLECT

During the year ending 30 June 1994, there were 74 436 reports of child abuse and neglect made to statutory authorities in Australia, that is, approximately 1.2 per cent of the child population. This represents a 26 per cent increase over the previous year. Of the fully investigated cases, 44 per cent of reports were substantiated (Angus & Woodward 1995).

Boys and girls were represented almost equally at all ages in substantiated cases of physical and emotional abuse and neglect but sexual offences against girls were reported three times more frequently than offences against boys. This should not be interpreted as evidence that boys are at less risk than girls but rather that they are less likely than girls to disclose offences. Reasons for under-reporting are discussed in chapter 8. The most frequent reporters were:

- friends and neighbours;
- school personnel;
- parents and guardians;
- police (Angus & Woodward 1995).

In Tasmania and South Australia, teaching is the profession responsible for making the most reports.

In the twelve months to 30 June 1994, the New Zealand Department of Social Welfare received 30 552 complaints of child maltreatment, an increase of 10 per cent on the previous year. For a small country with only 900 000 young people under the age of 17, New Zealand's Commissioner for Children cites some chilling statistics (Barber 1995).

- Child abuse reports are made at the rate of 500 a week and the nature of abuse has become increasingly serious.
- New Zealand has the highest youth suicide rate in the world.

- New Zealand has the sixth highest infant death rate from child abuse in the world.
- New Zealand has the second highest percentage of single parent families which UNICEF describes as having 'a close and consistent connection' with children growing up in poverty.
- In a survey, teachers had identified 22 600 undernourished school children and more than a third of schools provided free food for hungry children.

In England, the National Society for the Prevention of Cruelty to Children (NSPCC) estimates that three or four children die each week following child abuse and neglect (NSPCC Annual Report 1993a, p.1). This charitable organisation, which has accepted responsibility for child protection since 1883, spent an astonishing £35.4 million on protection projects during the year 1992–3. Ninety per cent of this money was donated by the public. They responded to 48 136 calls for help, 87 per cent of which came via their Child Protection Telephone Helpline.

With a child population of about 10.9 million (0–17 years) in England, there were 24 700 new substantiated cases of abuse during the year ending 31 March 1993. Although this may seem to be a very high number of reports, it is actually less than the number of substantiated cases in Australia where the child population was less than 4.3 million. This suggests that child abuse cases in England are under-reported. The lack of emphasis on the teacher's role in child protection is further confirmed by the fact that schools and preschools were responsible for initiating only 8 per cent of cases in England over a five-year period (Creighton & Noyes 1989, p. 52). By comparison, teachers were responsible for making 26 per cent of reports in South Australia (Angus, Wilkinson & Zabar 1994, p. 24).

In the year ending 1994, there were 1610 children (or 24.1 per 10 000 population) on child abuse registers in Wales (Welsh Office 1994).

Irish data show a steady increase in reports over recent years. In 1993 there were 4110 cases of child abuse and neglect reported by Health Boards in Ireland (ISPCC 1996). A survey undertaken for the ISPCC (1993) showed that there were substantial, unde-tected problems. Only 2 per cent of victims reported sexual abuse. Others remained silent because of shame (24 per cent), fear (24 per cent) and ignorance (18 per cent), while 35 per cent did not know where to go for help. Only 51 per cent of Irish interviewees realised that child abuse should be reported to the authorities

(ISPCC Irish Marketing Surveys 1993) and many people believed that families should be left to resolve their problems.

ABUSE PREVENTION

Prevention is usually divided into primary, secondary and tertiary categories. Primary prevention includes preschool, school and parent education programmes aimed at stopping child maltreatment before it starts. In preschools and schools it includes the provision of:

- positive (non-violent) child management techniques and effective communication/listening skills which can enhance parent–child interactions in and outside the centre or classroom;
- curriculum to develop children's self-confidence, self-esteem and appropriate assertiveness skills;
- personal safety curriculum and opportunities to practise safety skills (with parent involvement for optimum effectiveness);
- opportunities for parent education encompassing topics such as child development, children's emotional needs, child protection, nutrition, budgeting and discipline;
- opportunities for parents to develop self-help and mutual support schemes when they live in areas with high levels of poverty and unemployment;
- parent-organised, school-based used clothing 'boutiques' and similar facilities to benefit families;
- secondary school courses in child care, family and life skills and sex education;
- emergency child care, before and after school care and holiday programmes.

Secondary prevention programmes focus specifically on children and/or families 'at risk'. In schools and preschool centres they often include:

- early intervention such as placing young children in day care centres either for safety reasons or to provide respite for parents who are overwhelmed by problems. Early childhood education is often used to enhance victims' development and help parents caring for children with serious disabilities;
- intervention and family centre programmes to improve deficient parenting skills;

- homeless youth support programmes in secondary schools.

Tertiary prevention involves direct intervention to stop abuse, prevent its recurrence and help abused children. Early childhood professionals play a major role in centres used by courts and social welfare services for the protection of children.

LEGISLATION RELATING TO THE REPORTING OF ABUSE

In most Australian and American states and Canadian provinces, people whose professional role involves contact with children are charged with a special responsibility for reporting suspicions of child abuse and neglect (McClare 1990). In the United States, teachers and early childhood professionals have been required by law to make such reports since the early 1970s. Compulsory reporting legislation has been successfully resisted in the United Kingdom and the Republic of Ireland, New Zealand, the state of Western Australia and the Australian Capital Territory.

In England and Wales, all schools are required to have a 'designated teacher' (usually the head teacher in primary schools) who communicates with the relevant social services department. Head teachers in schools or principals of colleges are responsible for child protection and they make the decision whether to report child abuse. Designated teachers are expected to ensure that all employees are aware of the procedures and of signs of abuse. Awareness of procedures becomes part of ordinary and regular inductions and in-service training. The degree of confidentiality is governed by the need to protect the child. It will not be maintained if withholding information will prejudice a child's welfare. Schools are relatively autonomous and as a consequence there are problems controlling dissemination of information which is disadvantageous for child protection (Jackson, Sanders & Thomas 1994).

In the Republic of Ireland teachers 'should' report suspicions of abuse to one of a number of people (the Principal, the Chair of the Board of Management, the School Manager or the Chief Officer of the Vocational Education Committee) who should in turn report to the local Director of Community Care or Medical Officer of Health and Department of Education. People are protected by law when they report in good faith.

New Zealand child protection legislation makes it clear that all adults have a *moral* but not a legal obligation to report suspicions of child maltreatment.

In Australia, different levels of resistance are apparent in the legislation of the eight states and territories.

South Australia

The government of South Australia was years ahead of other Australian states when it introduced mandatory reporting in 1969. Only doctors and dentists were required to report until 1976 when the legislation was modified to include teachers, nurses and the police. At first, teachers had to report suspicions of abuse to their administrators who, in turn, were expected to pass reports to the statutory authority. This proved to be unsatisfactory. Some teachers were told, 'Leave it with me, dear. I'll handle it', only to find that no report had been made and the victim was still being victimised. Contract staff sometimes feared that their contracts might be terminated if they persisted in making a fuss. As a consequence, procedures were changed so that individuals who suspect abuse are the ones charged with the task of reporting it.

Over the years, the range of professionals mandated to report child maltreatment was expanded to include anyone who has contact with children in health, legal, child care or educational services. This included parents and other voluntary helpers, cleaners, students on field experience and even school gardeners.

New South Wales

In New South Wales, medical practitioners have been required to report child maltreatment since 1977. However, it was not until 1987 that teachers, school administrators, social workers and school counsellors were required by law to report suspicions of child *sexual* abuse. Strangely, there is no penalty for failing to report physical abuse, emotional abuse or neglect but teachers are expected by the Department of Community Services policy to notify suspected cases.

Queensland

In Queensland, medical practitioners and Family Court staff are required by legislation to report suspected cases of child maltreatment to the Departments of Family Services and Aboriginal and Torres Strait Islander Affairs but there is no legislation or policy that requires teachers or child care personnel to make reports.

Education Department guidelines merely expect teachers to advise senior staff of suspected cases.

Tasmania

In Tasmania, it is mandatory for school principals or 'teachers in charge' (in other words, not classroom teachers), child welfare officers, registered nurses, doctors, guidance and child welfare officers and psychologists to report suspected cases to the Child Abuse Protection Board. It is hard to imagine why child care personnel were not included on the list.

Victoria

As a result of a public outcry following the deaths of many children while they were under the supervision of state authorities, the state government of Victoria introduced mandatory reporting in June 1993. The professions obliged to report to the Department of Health and Community Services are: doctors, teachers, police, youth and care workers, social workers, welfare workers and others in health, education, community and welfare fields.

Western Australia

Reporting child abuse in Western Australia is not mandatory but there are policies to educate selected professionals, including teachers and health workers, on how and when to report to the Department for Community Development.

Australian Capital Territory

The ACT legislation provides for the voluntary notification of child maltreatment to the Community Advocate. In practice, the majority of notifications are received and investigated by the Family Services Branch working with the federal police.

Northern Territory

Happily, there is no scope for confusion in the Northern Territory. It is mandatory for anyone who believes that a child may be abused or neglected to make a report to either a delegated officer of the Department of Health and Community Services or police.

Given these wide differences in state legislation, it is easy to see why Australian advocates for children are seeking federal legislation and a Commissioner for Children to protect the nation's most important assets.

WHEN SHOULD CHILD ABUSE AND NEGLECT BE REPORTED?

Most states and Western countries expect teachers and early childhood professionals to report *suspicions* of abuse. A 'suspicion' in this context means that the reporter has reasonable cause to believe or suspect that abusive behaviour has occurred or is likely to occur and that the child's physical or emotional health will be or has been harmed. Reporters do not have to provide evidence that the abuse actually happened; to the contrary, most legislation requires teachers and child care personnel to make reports of conditions that could result in future sexual or physical abuse or psychological harm. It is also important to remember that it is the responsibility of the social worker (*not* the teacher or child care professional) to investigate a suspicion and make the decision as to whether the child has been abused or is at risk of abuse.

WHY WE NEED LAWS TO ENFORCE THE REPORTING OF CHILD ABUSE AND NEGLECT

Mandatory (compulsory) reporting was first introduced in recognition of the fact that child protection is a community concern and that professionals have a responsibility to protect the children in their care. Mandatory legislation also protects reporters from being sued for damages by suspected offenders if reports are made in good faith and suspicions are not confirmed.

Some countries have long and sorry histories of child deaths which occurred under the very noses of the professionals employed to protect them, that is, police, doctors, the NSPCC (UK), teachers, general practitioners, and local authority health and social workers. Many British inquiries into such deaths consistently confirm the dangers of having parallel and overlapping services involved in the investigation and management of cases (DHSS 1982).

The first example was revealed at the inquiry into the death of seven-year-old Maria Colwell (DHSS 1974). One of a family of nine children, Maria spent most of her life in foster care. When her mother and violent stepfather sought her return, social workers acceded to their request. Although reports about the child's rapidly worsening state were made by teachers and neighbours and a variety of child protection workers visited the home, Maria was systematically starved, neglected and battered to death by her stepfather within a short time of leaving foster care. Her death caused a national scandal, first because she was removed inappropriately from a caring, long-term foster placement to satisfy the whim of her mother and, second, because a succession of professionals either ignored signs of abuse or accepted the mother's explanation that the child was not at home when, in fact, she was lying bruised and battered in her bedroom.

The Colwell Inquiry and eighteen subsequent inquiries into the deaths of British children resulted in pages of recommendations relating to omissions, mistakes and misjudgements by different workers, compounding failures and serious cumulative effects (DHSS 1982).

Unfortunately, this succession of expensive inquiries did not protect others from similar deaths. Three-year-old Heidi Koseda was locked by her stepfather in a damp, dark, unheated room as a punishment for taking sweets. No-one knows how many months she remained imprisoned but she eventually died of starvation and her body remained in the room for a further eight weeks. The inquest heard that the child's grandmother and a neighbour made a succession of reports between 1983 and 1985. Social services and health authorities were alerted to the child's disappearance but they left responsibility to the NSPCC, whose investigator submitted a false report claiming that he had visited the home and found Heidi alive and well within a caring family (*Times*, 26 September 1985, pp. 1, 4).

On separate occasions, four different social workers and a health visitor accepted the stepfather's explanation that Heidi was visiting friends. Similarly, when police and social workers arrived with a search warrant, they accepted his story that Heidi was on holiday and that the foul stench from the child's decomposing body was a damp-proofing chemical which made it dangerous to enter the room. Four months elapsed between the first notification of Heidi's disappearance and the implementation of emergency procedures involving a search of the house.

Subsequent child deaths, inquiries and recommendations have continued to emphasise the need for one authority to take responsibility for the assessment and management of cases.

Nevertheless, the British system remains uncoordinated and provincial compared with its North American, Australian and New Zealand counterparts.

The Australian exception is the state of Victoria where, in recent years, more than forty young children have died while supposedly in the care of the authorities. It was the brutal murder of two-year-old Daniel Valerio by his mother's partner (8 September 1990) which galvanised public opinion and led to legislative changes.

A Melbourne court learned that Daniel's body had 104 bruises, two new and several untreated old fractures, a ruptured duodenum and tears to the membrane anchoring the intestines to the abdomen. These injuries were inflicted over a four-month period when Daniel was thrown against a wall, punched on the head, beaten on the penis and had his face rubbed in faeces. They gave the impression that the child had been in a severe car crash (Goddard & Liddell 1993; O'Neill 1994).

At the trial, it was reported that the teachers of Daniel's siblings had reported serious concerns to state community services. A succession of doctors noted his injuries and admitted the child to hospital (but only briefly). Further abuse was reported within a week of his release. One week later, a visiting plumber reported that Daniel had shocking injuries. The child was examined by a police surgeon. Again he was sent home. Daniel was seen by the family doctor on four subsequent occasions and yet, within a week, the toddler was dead. Once again, no organisation had taken responsibility for protecting the child.

On 26 February 1993, the perpetrator was sentenced to 22 years jail. On 3 March 1993, the news headline was 'Child abuse win: Law to change'. The state government of Victoria had introduced mandatory reporting.

THE PENALTIES FOR NOT REPORTING ABUSE

State laws in the United States, Canada and Australia impose liability on mandated reporters who fail to notify statutory authorities of their suspicions of child maltreatment. In the United States, penalties include short jail sentences. In addition, those who fail to report child maltreatment may be charged with the negligent performance of their duties in the civil court and subjected to both legal and administrative penalties. A teacher who receives a disclosure of abuse and takes no action may be sued by victims and their (non-offending) parents. The teacher may also be dismissed by the employing authority.

In South Australia, mandated reporters can be fined $2000 for failing to report abuse. This is regarded as helpful to junior teachers and child care workers who wish to report a suspicion of abuse and are constrained by administrators. The member of staff can confidently say, 'I have to report it because if I don't, I can be fined'.

THE RIGHTS (AND RESPONSIBILITIES) OF MANDATED NOTIFIERS

It is usually the right and responsibility of the individual to report his or her suspicions of abuse or neglect. In practice most employees tell their supervisors of their concerns, but the supervisor does not have to approve the reporting. It is also important to note that you are not breaching any code of professional ethics when you make a report in the sincere belief that a child may be at risk.

WHY THERE IS RESISTANCE TO MANDATORY REPORTING

When legislation for mandatory notification was first suggested, there was a great deal of resistance from the medical profession because of its commitment to client confidentiality.

Successive New Zealand governments have resisted pressures to introduce such legislation, supported by senior staff in the Department of Social Welfare. They argue that in the United States, the introduction of mandatory reporting brought a substantial increase in the number of reports with no comparable increase in resources. Administrators believe that, without a substantial increase in funding (which the government will not provide), there would be insufficient staff to investigate the influx of reports. In other words, 'We know that a large number of child abuse cases go unreported in New Zealand but we prefer to keep the lid on the problem and let the victims suffer rather than risk a staff overload'.

In the United Kingdom, education authorities and academics argue that they cannot afford to train teachers to identify and report cases of child abuse. Arguments relating to cost are very short-sighted because the cost of protection is minuscule compared with the bill that society pays for the long-term effects of untreated abuse.

CHILD PROTECTION IS A POLITICAL CONCERN

Any country or state which has statute-based responsibility for the investigation and management of child abuse has a distinct advantage over others because the legislation places child protection in a special category and gives it priority among the range of health and welfare problems. However, for laws to be effective there must be:

- confidence in the child protection system by those required to report;
- a clear understanding of what has to be reported;
- the capacity of authorised interveners to respond quickly to reports;
- the willingness of child protection officers to provide feedback to the professionals who report;
- the capability of support networks to assist the family and child involved in the report (Swain 1993).

Every judgement about what is in the child's best interests is dependent on the knowledge, professional experience and skills of individual social workers and the judiciary, none of whom is a specialist in child development, children's communications, their understanding of safety issues or their emotional needs.

It must also be recognised that regardless of how concerned the directors of child protection services may be about the abuse problem, politicians make funding arrangements based on their own pragmatic perceptions of public expectations. Although it should not deter concerned adults from complaining to their Members of Parliament and responsible Ministers, some politicians would prefer to spend taxpayers' money on sports and entertainment centres (which are clearly visible and can be enjoyed by everyone) than on less visible child protection services. Child protection is not a vote-catching issue because few voters understand the cost of child abuse to the taxpayer and the fact that prevention is cheaper than the investigation of cases, the treatment and fostering of victims and the prosecution and imprisonment of offenders.

IMPORTANCE OF TEACHERS AND EARLY CHILDHOOD PROFESSIONALS IN CHILD PROTECTION

Teachers and early childhood professionals play a vital role in both the primary and secondary prevention of child abuse. No other professionals have such close, continuous, daily contact with child abuse victims on a day-to-day, long-term basis or have such an extensive knowledge of the children in their care. Their knowledge of families has sometimes been built up over many years and no other professionals are exposed on a regular basis to the warning signals given by both children and their parents.

Some children attend early childhood centres for up to ten hours a day on five days of the week for fifty weeks of the year. Centres are also used increasingly by courts and social services to provide safe havens for 'high-risk' children.

Teachers and early childhood professionals are in a unique position to identify and help children to stop abuse. Their importance can be viewed in perspective when we consider that, in countries with compulsory education, most child abuse victims in the 5–16 year age group attend school. Furthermore, schools have long accepted that their role is not limited to academic achievement; it involves the development and well-being of the whole child. Staff in preschools and primary schools are (or should be) trained to observe children, to note changes in their appearance, their self-esteem, concentration, socialisation, behaviour and progress. They are also expected to seek specialist help for troubled children who exhibit developmental problems, emotionally disturbed behaviours or learning difficulties. It is widely recognised that children who live in abusive environments are less able to benefit from the learning experiences available to them. For those who are depressed about what is happening outside school and those who, because of abuse, are sexually obsessed, lessons on the voyages of Captain Cook or the feeding habits of earthworms may seem totally irrelevant.

Teachers and early childhood professionals are vitally important in the identification and reporting of child maltreatment and the support of child victims after reports have been made. Schools and preschools undertake a valuable role in supporting the parents of children 'at risk' of maltreatment. In family centres, early childhood professionals help parents to develop new parenting skills. Unfortunately, when teachers are inadequately trained for their role in child protection, they misinterpret or fail to see the signs of maltreatment or, in cases of neglect, some try to compensate for the deficiencies of parents without taking action that will improve the child's circumstances at home.

TASKS FOR STUDENTS

1 Contact your local office of the government department responsible for family and community welfare services for copies of guidelines and publications about laws and procedures relating to the prevention and reporting of child abuse and neglect.

2 Request leaflets relating to other family services provided by the department.

3 Familiarise yourself with the definitions of child abuse in the child protection legislation: emotional (or psychological), physical and sexual abuse as well as emotional and physical neglect.

4 Check the age of childhood and the definition of 'child' in the child protection legislation.

5 If you work in a school or centre, ask your employer for a copy of the policy document relating to child protection.

6 Investigate which non-government services offer support for families in your community: for example, Smith Family (Australia); Catholic Welfare; Lutheran Community Care; Anglican Community Services; Salvation Army; Barnados (UK, New Zealand and New South Wales), NCH; NSPCC and Family Service Units; Children's Society (UK); Help Foundation Centres; Parent Help and Parentline (NZ).

7 Investigate the child protection information and services available for families of non-English-speaking backgrounds and obtain leaflets.

8 If you are working with children and/or families, display child protection and family support services information on noticeboards for parents and distribute copies to other staff.

9 Investigate the whereabouts and aims of groups and organisations which focus on children's rights and child protection.

10 You have reason to believe that a child under your care is at risk of abuse from a parent who will shortly arrive to collect her from school. Do you have any right to withhold the child from the parent? What should you do?

11 Does your school or centre have a person designated to disseminate information and receive reports about child abuse? If so, make this person's acquaintance.

12 You are at a party when one of the male guests tells everybody that he and his wife have sex with their four-year-old son on his back and that the little boy plays 'having sex' with the little girl next door. Everyone laughs, including the mother. What, if anything, would you say or do? Why?

CASE STUDIES

1 Xue-wei, aged five, reveals that when she returns home from school each day, she is cared for by her older sister Lan Xian, aged nine. Lan Xian supervises their evening meal and puts Xue-wei to bed. Another staff member tells you that the parents are new migrants who own a Chinese restaurant. Because they had to take out a huge loan, both parents work long hours. Your colleagues assure you that 'the kids are okay, they're sensible, and anyway, its none of our business'. Discuss.

2 Emma (aged ten) is the daughter of the chairman of the school council. Her parents are both lawyers. She indicates that her parents are just about to leave on a two-week P&O cruise. They have given her thirteen-year-old brother a large sum of money for entertainment and the freezer is full. You establish that there are no other adults in the house.

   a What, if anything, would you do? Give your reasons.

   b Emma later reveals that her brother is planning a party for his friends and that alcohol will be consumed. Does this information change your earlier decision (part a)? Why? What factors would inhibit you from reporting this? Discuss.

2

EMOTIONAL ABUSE

The little girl was about two years old. She rocked backwards and forwards with the movement of the bus, the pompom on her knitted hat swinging like a pendulum across her face. She began to sing a song about the grandfather clock that goes 'tick tock' and the passengers smiled. She smiled back but her mother was not amused. She pulled the child towards her and smacked her across the head. 'Be a good girl, sit still and shut up,' she said, and ignored the child's tears.

Andrew tripped up the steps as he ran into school. The cuts to his forehead were deep and clearly needed stitches. The school secretary contacted Andrew's father at home and asked him to take his son to the hospital. When the father collected the distressed boy, he complained that Andrew's clumsiness had interfered with his viewing of cricket on television. The father took one glance at his son's head and said, 'He'll be right. He doesn't need stitches. He just makes a fuss about nothing.'

Neither of these parents are likely to feature in social workers' reports on child abuse but you only need to walk around a market, travel on a bus or watch children join their parents at the end of the day to realise that these damaging behaviours are not uncommon.

Yule (1985) observed families in public places and found that while the adults smiled and talked to each other, many ignored their children. They disregarded children's tears or smacked them for crying. They adjusted their clothes without speaking. They yanked them across roads. They discouraged normal curiosity. Yule noted that only one parent in eighty-five holds conversations with children on outings: 'The most typical adult–child couple consisted of a woman staring ahead with a sombre face as if tuned to some dumb misery of her own', while the child sat, walked or was carried 'with a blank expression on its face'.

Yule noted that most parents are 'hair-trigger irritable' and impatient, offensively rude and incapable of coping with the slightest manifestation of children's ignorance or curiosity, least of all when it diverts them from their primary objective.

The emotional abuse of children is widespread. Most of us have been recipients at some time during childhood and most of us survived with no long-term, serious harm. By the very nature of adult–child relationships and cultural influences, most adults will have inflicted emotional abuse on children, probably without realising it.

Emotional abuse is inherent in some cultures. In the industrial north of England, for example, traditional values concentrated on modesty and sincerity. The widely accepted 'putting down' of children was linked to the perception that conceit and dishonesty were the worst character defects that children could have. Parents reared with such values are unlikely to understand the importance of developing children's self-esteem. Some never show affection. Some ignore children's talents and achievements and criticise their perceived inadequacies with the mistaken notion that the expression of their displeasure will motivate children to overcome their weaknesses. Damage occurs when carping criticism becomes a pattern of behaviour.

Emotional abuse differs from physical abuse and neglect in that there are no unique consequences. In other words, many of the signs and symptoms could be caused by other conditions. As a result, emotional abuse is often given a low priority for investigation and action.

While emotional abuse occurs in isolation, it is important to remember that it is involved in all forms of child abuse. Adults who were physically or sexually abused in childhood often describe the emotional aspects as the ones responsible for long-term damage. Children can recover from physical pain but they may never recover from such examples of emotional abuse as the terror, emotional hurt, constant degradation, humiliation and breach of trust which are involved in sexual abuse. This was confirmed in recent revelations by men who were allegedly physically, psychologically and sexually abused daily by many caregivers while residents in cottage homes and Christian Brothers boarding schools in Western Australia (Davies 1994; Welsh 1990; Briggs 1995b).

DEFINITIONS OF EMOTIONAL ABUSE

Less has been published about emotional abuse than about any other form of child maltreatment. It is the abuse least reported and the one most difficult to define and prove. O'Hagan (1993, p. 28) discusses the differences between psychological abuse, emotional abuse, emotional deprivation and emotional neglect. However, emotional abuse is the term most frequently used to describe sustained, repetitive, inappropriate responses to a child's expression of emotion and emotional needs.

Emotional abuse can involve a passive, neglectful state involving acts of omission as well as involving the deliberately cruel, active rejection of children. In England, Scotland and Wales, children are placed on Child Abuse Registers when it is established that their behaviour or emotional development has been severely affected and there is evidence of either persistent or severe emotional neglect or rejection (Gilmour 1988). However, most authorities expect teachers and early childhood professionals to report abuse long before children have been 'severely affected' so that family support systems and parent re-education can be introduced. Unfortunately, professionals in children's services become disillusioned and postpone reporting when they find that the authorities do not respond to non-urgent cases.

It should be remembered that parents who emotionally abuse children are not happy with their parenting, not least because they tend to have fretful, unhappy, clinging children. Many respond to helpful intervention when they realise that, with guidance and a little cooperation on their part, life can become more rewarding.

Garbarino and Gilliam (1980), Garbarino, Guttman and Seeley (1986) and Broadhurst (1986) identified several types of behaviour as constituting emotional abuse, all of which are included in the following list.

Rejection of a child

The caregiver or other influential adult refuses to acknowledge a child's worth and the legitimacy of a child's needs. Abusive caregivers tend to distance themselves emotionally from dependent children.

Punishing positive, normal social behaviour

Children are punished for exploring the environment, talking, laughing, seeking affection and being sociable. Research has shown that punishing children for displaying normal social competencies causes serious damage to essential building blocks in their development.

Lacking and/or discouraging caregiver–infant attachment

Attachment emerged as a central issue in child development as a result of the work on maternal deprivation undertaken by John Bowlby (1953), Klaus and Kennell (1976) and others. Although some aspects of Bowlby's work have been challenged, major disruption in infant–caregiver attachment has long been linked to physical abuse, failure to thrive and a variety of deficits in children's well-being. Premature babies separated from their mothers were thought to be particularly vulnerable to attachment problems and subsequent emotional neglect or abuse. Hospitals now endeavour to increase mother–infant contact to develop bonding and reduce the long-term risks of abuse to premature children.

Discouraging children's self-esteem

Constant scapegoating, carping, putting down, deriding, belittling, using sarcasm or telling children that they are stupid, lazy, worthless, clumsy, ugly, fat, unloved and unlovable all combine to damage a fundamental component of growth towards self-sufficiency. Some children are constantly told that they have the same traits as a relative who is obviously disliked. They come to accept their labels and behave according to adults' expectations.

Punishing and preventing the child from developing interpersonal skills

The child is deprived of skills necessary for adequate performance in school, peer groups and other situations outside the family. Abusive families fail to provide positive reinforcement for important social skills.

Isolating a child

The victim is cut off from social relationships. Friendships are discouraged and parents denigrate the child's choice of companions.

Depriving children of security

Some children are terrorised and live in perpetual fear. Some parents fail to provide a safe environment with continuity of care. The latter is sometimes very obvious in dysfunctional families where the parenting role is thrust on a variety of sexual partners, lodgers and acquaintances who accept responsibility (intermittently) for the physical care of children but in an affectionless, resentful manner.

Exhibiting indifference to or ignoring a child

The child is deprived of essential stimulation and responsiveness. This usually results in deficiencies in communication skills.

Corrupting a child

The adult mis-socialises the child, stimulating antisocial behaviour, reinforcing deviance and making the child unfit for formal social experience (Garbarino et al. 1986, p. 8). Some parents take children shoplifting, telling them what to steal. Some force children to sell drugs in school. Some children are controlled by 'Fagins' who use them for thieving and breaking into premises. One of the reasons for using young children is, of course, that current legislation in Western society does not punish child criminals for their offences.

Unfortunately, many parents allow children to watch pornographic videos. Some engage in sexual activity in view of their children. These are totally unacceptable methods of introducing children to human sexuality and they should be reported.

Depriving children of opportunities to develop as individuals

Authoritarian parents do not seek children's views or grant choices. They impose excessive demands, rigid rules, discipline or controls. Children may be punished for expressing opinions. Their likes, needs and feelings are ignored. It is often suggested that the pressures placed on some gifted and talented children are emotionally abusive.

BEHAVIOURAL INDICATORS OF PARENTS WHO EMOTIONALLY ABUSE THEIR CHILDREN

The emotionally abusive caretaker may persistently:

- penalise the child for normal, positive, developmentally appropriate behaviour such as showing normal curiosity and initiative;
- show low tolerance to frustration and blame or 'take it out on' the child when things go wrong;
- lack an understanding of developmental norms and set unrealistic goals and expectations leading to the child's failure and everyone's dissatisfaction;
- make excessive demands on the child for the caretaker's own emotional satisfaction;
- complain that the child is a nuisance, ugly, unlovable and different from other children or that the victim was unwanted from birth (or conception);
- belittle, deride, taunt or scapegoat the child;
- ignore the child or behave coldly in circumstances when empathy might be expected (for example, when the child is sick or injured);
- leave the child unsupervised in or outside the house, in a car, outside hotels, casinos and so on, for prolonged periods of time;
- reverse roles by making children responsible for protecting the caretaker from punishment and/or for 'keeping the family together'; for example, in cases of child sexual abuse and other adult crimes, perpetrators often tell victims that if they reveal the adults' behaviour 'I'll be sent to jail and then we'll have no money and nowhere to live' or 'your mother will leave home', or 'the police will come and take you away and it will be all your fault';
- exhibit extreme swings of mood resulting in inconsistent handling of the child: what is acceptable today may be punished tomorrow;
- dominate, direct and restrict the child, depriving the child of the opportunity to make choices and develop independence;
- threaten to abandon or kill the child.

Because of taunting by peers, a mother transferred her two sons to a new school. The gender of the boys was often mistaken because they were dressed in frilly blouses and their waist-length

hair was worn in feminine styles decorated with baubles and ribbons. Although the boys were called Tim (aged eight) and James (aged nine), children referred to them as 'she' and 'her'. Because they were perceived as girls, boys denied them admission to male toilets and male groups playing football and cricket. The teacher decided to 'talk to the mother' when the younger boy, Tim, became depressed and drew self-portraits labelled, 'Everyone thinks I'm a monster. That's because I am one.'

Tim indicated that he had resigned himself to rejection: 'I suppose I shall just have to get used to it'.

The mother, a professional in human services, proclaimed that the boys' appearance was her own private business and that the school should teach children to accept individual differences. The teacher enquired whether the boys had been given a choice in their mode of dress or whether it had been imposed on them.

She found that the parent was unable (or unwilling) to differentiate between adults' rights and children's needs. The matter was reported to the child protection authority and the problem was only resolved when the boys went to live with their father.

The abusive parents most frequently encountered by teachers and early childhood professionals are the ones who are completely preoccupied with their own problems, often involving unemployment, financial problems or discordant relationships.

Investigators often find that emotional abuse has featured in a family for several generations. The indifference, lack of empathy and understanding and the emotional deadness that parents experienced in childhood are passed on to the next generation. It is difficult to give or receive love if our own childhood was affectionless.

Professionals are often confused by the fact that victims of emotional abuse often cling to their mothers: the greater the abuse, the more they cling. These children are caught in the dilemma of needing a reliable parent-figure to shield them from harm when the very source of that harm is the parent. Paradoxically, the more that emotionally abused children need and seek attention, the more they 'get on the parent's nerves', leading to further rejection and verbal abuse if not a smack for 'being a pest'. Similarly, professionals often find themselves disliking abused children because of the intensity with which they demand attention.

There is little doubt that some children are easier to love than others. Some infants are colicky, fractious and difficult to please from birth. It is also difficult to assess how selectively children's personalities play a part in precipitating emotional abuse or, for that matter, how they will respond to their experiences in the long term (Szur 1987).

In the end, when all else fails, affectionless children will seek negative attention at home, preschool and school. This is when positive child management techniques are most needed.

BEHAVIOURAL INDICATORS OF EMOTIONALLY ABUSED CHILDREN

Obviously, not everyone is permanently damaged by emotional abuse; it is the repetition that causes the damage. The extent of the damage will depend on the child's personality and whether alternative forms of support are available. Some children will accept that they are worthless and sink into a depressed state; others will think 'I'm going to show you that I can succeed without your support or approval'.

When abuse detrimentally affects children's development, the consequences gradually become apparent to the people engaged in their care and education.

Behavioural indicators at ages 0–2 years:

There may be:

- failure to thrive;
- poor general health;
- delay in growth and/or social and motor development;
- apathy and listlessness;
- fretfulness;
- no smiles;
- no language response;
- rocking or head banging;
- frozen watchfulness;
- pervasive unhappiness.

Behavioural indicators at ages 2–6 years

There may be any of the above and/or:

- aggression;
- unresponsiveness: does not communicate with the educator/caregiver or other children;
- attention-seeking behaviour;
- excessively clinging behaviour;
- affection-seeking behaviour (often misinterpreted as over-affectionate);
- poor appetite;
- poor sleeping patterns;
- fears failure and lacks self-confidence for tackling new learning tasks; chooses 'safe' activities with no risk of failure such as water and sand play; repeats the same jigsaw; resists tackling new words in reading;
- behavioural extremes: being overly compliant, passive, fearful, demanding or aggressive;
- habit disorders such as sucking, biting, enuresis;

- lagging in emotional, speech and intellectual development;
- psychoneurotic reactions including hysteria, obsessions, compulsions, phobias and hypochondria;
- evidence of depression or low self-esteem;
- no tears or complaints when hurt or distressed in circumstances where emotional expressions would be normal;
- overly adaptive behaviours which are either inappropriately adult (parenting other children, for example) or inappropriately infantile (head banging, rocking, thumb sucking).

Behavioral indicators at age 6+ years

There may be any of the above and/or:

- poor school attendance;
- theft (to draw attention to unhappiness);
- substance abuse such as the inhalation of adhesives, white correction fluid (Twink, Tippex, Liquid Paper), felt-tipped markers, petrol, Ventolin, alcohol abuse (including alcohol-based essences) and tobacco or marijuana smoking;
- irritatingly submissive, crushed or rebellious behaviour resulting from excessively rigid discipline;
- inability to play freely, laugh and enjoy themselves;
- worldly wise, pseudomature or promiscuous behaviour, possibly accompanied by an intense search for approval;
- distrust of others (especially if the child has been with multiple caregivers or foster-parents); there is an undercurrent of anxiety as the child tests teachers and caregivers, expecting rejection; relates to peers in a superficial way with a lack of genuine interaction;
- self-destructive behaviour and attempted suicide.

Not all children who show these indicators have been emotionally abused. There are strong similarities between the behaviour of emotionally maltreated and emotionally disturbed children. Parental behaviour may help to distinguish disturbance from maltreatment. The parents of emotionally disturbed children generally accept the existence of a problem. They are concerned about their children's welfare and they actively seek help. By contrast, the parents of emotionally abused children often blame victims for their problems. Some ignore their existence and dismiss the concerns of professionals.

Over time, emotionally abused children fail to develop the capacity to empathise with others. This is a precursor to trouble with peers, poor sexual relationships and inadequate parenting skills. Serious damage leads to antisocial behaviour with the offender showing no sign of conscience where a conscience would normally be expected; for example, inflicting cruelty on young, old, disabled or otherwise less powerful people 'just for fun'.

Not all emotionally abused children suffer long-term damage. The common factor in survival cases is the availability of another close, supportive person to whom the child can turn. This positive figure helps to 'develop a more secure capacity for making decisions and to establish a relatively healthier and more reality-based split between good and bad, positive and negative' (Szur 1987, p. 105).

Positive handling by a close relative or caregiver can help children to detach themselves emotionally from the abusive parent and respond to other relationships. It follows that children reared in isolated families are more vulnerable to damage from emotional abuse than those in extended families where a supportive relative is often available. Grandparents and aunts frequently intercede on behalf of vulnerable children, creating vital bonds of affection.

NON-ORGANIC FAILURE TO THRIVE

Every year, a significant number of young children are examined in hospitals because, despite there being no signs of illness, they are not developing on normal lines. When they are in hospital, these children usually gain weight, begin to smile and communicate. When they return home, the failure to thrive syndrome occurs again and they are re-admitted to hospital to regain the lost weight. The high frequency of this phenomenon was discussed by Oates (1982, 1985). The mothers of these children were identified as those who:

- are deficient in parenting skills; they were often deprived of affection and care in childhood;
- have a knowledge of parenting skills but don't use them because they are overwhelmed by personal, financial and health problems;
- have significant psychological problems with/without drug or alcohol abuse;
- are immature and depressed but responsive to help;

- are immature and chronically deprived or impulsive to the extent that they cannot cope with social systems or social relationships;
- are deprived, leading a chaotic lifestyle and in need of a great deal of structured support;
- are angry and hostile to the world at large and difficult to help;
- are temporarily overwhelmed by a rapid series of events which undermine their basic capacity to be good mothers, but they respond well to help;
- have wholly negative perceptions of their babies and accuse them of being deliberately naughty to annoy them (Oates 1982, 1985).

In all cases, the common feature is that the primary caregiver is not emotionally responsive to the child. Regardless of their education or social class, mothers of 'failure-to-thrive' children perceive them negatively, slap them frequently and withdraw from them emotionally. They are less likely to kiss, cuddle and praise victims but, as the children are less 'cuddly' than most, it is difficult to distinguish between cause and effect and where the vicious circle starts. These children frequently present as depressed, tearful, whiny, withdrawn, lethargic and anxious (Iwaniec, Herbert & McNeish 1985). The relationships between mothers and children often seem fraught and unhappy (Iwaniec, Herbert & Sluckin 1988). Over two-thirds of the mothers in Oates' sample perceived themselves as nervous or depressed.

CHARACTERISTICS OF CHILDREN WHO FAIL TO THRIVE

The babies are often reported as having feeding problems from the first week of life. The difficulties include refusing the nipple, poor appetite, falling asleep during feeds, frequent vomiting and struggling against the person giving the feed.

Drotar et al. (1990) showed that mothers of failure-to-thrive infants of six months showed less positive affective behaviour and more arbitrary termination of feedings than other mothers.

Oates (1985, p. 123) found that the syndrome usually involved only one child in the family and the child most vulnerable was born within 18 months of an older sibling.

Infants who fail to thrive differ from sick children in that they seldom respond to being cuddled. They sometimes stare in a watchful, distrustful way with no hint of liveliness in their eyes. They rarely smile or communicate. They have often been described as sad, waif-like, apathetic, having cold hands and feet (Hopwood & Becker 1979; Oates 1985, p. 25). Deprived of nutrition, they sometimes appear to have large heads. Muscle wasting occurs and skin can be 'floppy' on the thighs and buttocks. Quite obviously, infants with these difficulties will provide little satisfaction to their primary caregivers.

Regardless of whether it starts with the child or the parent, once the cycle is set in motion, it is difficult to stop. Because of poor parent–child relationships, these children are often also subjected to physical abuse resulting in re-admission to hospital with fractures and other non-accidental injuries.

EFFECTS OF THE SYNDROME ON CHILDREN'S LATER DEVELOPMENT

Oates (1982, 1985) shows that, even when physical growth improves, child victims suffer from intellectual and behavioural problems consistent with emotional abuse. A third of the children in the Sydney study were described by their teachers as deficient in language development and two-thirds were retarded in reading skills (in other words, 50 per cent were two years behind their chronological reading age). On a personality assessment, half scored in the abnormal range.

All of the children were perceived as 'different' by their mothers. Oates argued that, if mothers perceive their children as difficult, unrewarding and even unpleasant, this could partly account for their emotional and nutritional deprivation early in childhood. It might also partly explain the delay in language skills and the personality problems which persisted in later childhood, when physical growth became normal.

The mothers also reported high levels of emotional symptoms in these children, such as temper tantrums, nervousness, bed wetting, attention-seeking behaviour and socially undesirable characteristics including lying and stealing.

Twelve years after their initial presentation at the hospital, the children were compared with a control group matched for education, socioeconomic status and other factors. The failure-to-thrive children were still conspicuous by their poor performance in most tests but the greatest difference was in teacher-assessed behaviour where they appeared as predominantly antisocial and neurotic. Oates concluded that although non-organic failure-to-thrive children may recover growth, there are likely to be serious long-term problems in the development of language, literacy and numeracy. Clearly, hospital treatment does not provide the solution for the individual child if, when that child returns home, nothing has changed. If there has been no intervention to improve the mother–child relationship, deterioration is inevitable. When this deterioration becomes apparent to the mother, it reinforces her low self-esteem and negative feelings about parenting. Recognition of the problem necessitates a family treatment approach in which the mothers of failure-to-thrive children are admitted to hospital and are involved in their total care, supported by expert staff. The mothers are praised for effort and given credit for all evidence of progress (Oates 1985, pp. 31–2).

TASKS FOR STUDENTS

1 When you visit a supermarket or market or travel on public transport, observe a parent and child for five minutes. During that time, note how the child tries to attract the parent's attention (and why) and how the parent responds.

2 At what stage would you feel justified in reporting suspicions that a child is suffering emotional abuse at home?

3 Observe parents and children leaving your school or centre. Note which parents greet children fondly and listen to them attentively. Note which parents appear to be preoccupied or irritable. Which parents walk away, leaving their children trailing behind?

4 Which children do you like and dislike? Account for your feelings.

5 Which children in the group exhibit behavioural signs suggesting that they may be suffering from emotional abuse? Observe these children closely and plan strategies to help them in the centre or classroom.

6 Offer informal workshops for parents including discussion of the children's emotional needs and opportunities for parents to share their problems and ideas for solutions.

7 Encourage parents of 'at risk' children to spend time with you in the classroom or centre.

3

EMOTIONAL ABUSE IN CARE AND EDUCATION SETTINGS

No-one wants to abuse a child but it occurs; no-one plans to become a bad teacher but it seems to happen (Harper 1980, p. 321).

Kids who are the victims of persistent put-downs don't walk around with bruises on their arms and legs but often they're damaged just as much as if they've been physically assaulted (Brown, 1979, in Hart et al. 1987, p. 225).

Ignorance of children's emotional needs and emotional maltreatment are, unfortunately, not the sole prerogative of parents. Although child maltreatment and neglect are usually conceptualised and dealt with by teachers as if they only occur elsewhere, studies have shown that teachers commonly use emotional maltreatment along with punitive practices to 'discipline' and punish children for unwanted behaviour, control them and convince them of their inability to learn. In their comprehensive chapter, 'Psychological maltreatment in education and schooling', Hart et al. refer to a large number of studies which show the extent of this problem (Brassard et al. 1987, pp. 223–8).

While physical punishment is banned in most educational establishments, emotional abuse by individual members often goes unchallenged. It leaves no visible scars and is difficult to prove but it has long-lasting consequences. In recent interviews with New Zealand parents, many told the authors that they avoided school meetings because, although they liked the staff as individuals, whenever they 'set foot inside the building', they experienced the same feelings of fear and inadequacy that they felt in childhood at the hands of their emotionally abusive teachers (Briggs & Hawkins 1996a).

MANY TEACHERS IGNORE CHILD ABUSE AND NEGLECT

Despite teachers' apparent concern for children, James Garbarino (1979) found that teachers tolerated child abuse and physical neglect in particular. Although they were in loco parentis, that is, in the role of responsible parents with children in their care, teachers distanced themselves from children's problems, denied their pastoral role and maintained a narrow academic perspective. (In some places, such as South Australia, courts have determined that teachers are expected to act more responsibly than parents because of superior training and knowledge. Teachers are expected to demonstrate a higher level of care and regard for safety.)

Despite mandatory reporting legislation, researchers have found that few teachers report evidence of child abuse. The school often allows victims to return home day after day to be further victimised. Levin (1983, p. 15) found that teachers not only failed to report abuse but they mishandled suspected cases. This is tragic because for some children the school may offer the only defence against maltreatment in the family.

Other reasons for not reporting include:

- a reluctance to interfere in family privacy;
- the belief that parents own their children and have the right to treat and punish them as they wish;
- distrust of the community welfare agency's capacity to handle cases sensitively following previous unsatisfactory experiences (such as breaches of confidentiality, lack of action or inadequate feedback from social workers);
- inadequate training and uncertainty about the signs, symptoms or definitions of abuse;
- lack of confidence and fear of making a mistake;
- fear of repercussions from parents;
- a narrow perception of the role of teacher and resistance to any form of widening of that role: 'I'm only employed to teach my academic subject. I'm not a social worker. It's nothing to do with me';
- lack of support from school administrators.

Teachers in middle-class and fee-paying schools are the ones most likely to 'turn a blind eye' to signs of child abuse, thereby helping to perpetuate the myth that the problem only occurs in poor and criminal classes.

Garbarino cited the poor record of schools as reporting agents as visual testimony to the fact that teachers behave as accessories to the fact of maltreatment (1979, p. 200). He concluded that head teachers set the tone and define the norms for the whole school; if senior staff accept the school's responsibility for child protection, staff follow the lead.

Hart and colleagues warned that civil court cases have been won by victims and parents against American teachers who failed to report child abuse (Hart et al. 1987, p. 221).

ABUSE THROUGH THE USE OF PUNITIVE DISCIPLINARY PRACTICES

Although physical punishment is now banned in most schools, forms of physical abuse are still used in conjunction with emotional abuse to control and punish children, for example, by pushing them into line and forcibly moving them from one place to another.

Krugman and Krugman (1984) in their study of third and fourth grade teachers and Hyman (1985) in a study of psychological abuse in schools found that teachers emotionally abused children by:

- overly limiting the very young in their use of the toilet and imposing penalties on those who asked to go outside approved times;
- threatening to tell parents of children's misbehaviour and unsatisfactory work;
- rejecting them and/or their work;
- using verbal put-downs;
- harassing and allowing some children to harass and belittle others;
- labelling children as ineducable using descriptions such as 'clumsy', 'stupid' and 'dummy';
- screaming at children until they cried;
- pinching, shaking and pulling them by their ears;
- using fear-inducing techniques to control children, for example, throwing unsatisfactory workbooks across the room to hit their

owners, tipping or pulling chairs from under seated children to make them fall;

- providing continuous experience of failure by setting unrealistic academic goals and giving children tasks that are inappropriate for their stages of development.

A recent example of the latter is the teacher who, on Friday afternoons, routinely gave a spelling test to the whole class. Every Friday afternoon, six-year old Andrew took home his marked test paper and presented it to his mother, as directed. Because he could neither read nor write, every Friday afternoon Andrew received a score of 0/20 for spelling. Fortunately, his mother was a preschool teacher who realised that it was not her son but the teacher who had a problem.

REJECTION AND SCAPEGOATING

Sarcasm, derision and humiliation, scapegoating and rejection have long been used as child management strategies by inadequate and frustrated teachers, caregivers and early childhood professionals. Children are subjected to emotional abuse when they fail to conform to the teacher's expectations.

Sometimes, abusive punishments are given spontaneously in a moment of panic. For example, an inexperienced teacher on playground duty failed in her efforts to stop Wilhelm, aged six, from chasing girls into their outdoor toilet block. The reprimands were to no avail and, in desperation, she grabbed the culprit by the collar and said, 'If you want to be a girl, you can dress as a girl'. She frog-marched the boy into the classroom, took a dress from the 'dressing-up box' and forced him to wear it for the rest of the afternoon. He responded to the taunts of peers with aggression and bravado. The headmaster ignored her behaviour because the child's parents did not complain.

Scapegoating occurs when the adult implies that a child's inattention or lack of conformity is part of a deliberate plot to deprive the whole group of pleasurable activities or experiences. Visitors to classrooms sometimes hear remarks such as, 'Someone is stopping *us* from having *our* nice story. I wonder who it is? Oh, not you again Marietta! We might have guessed!' These remarks aim to change behaviour by making the child feel guilty, antisocial and fearful of rejection by peers.

Teachers and caregivers blame individual children for their

own decisions to punish the whole group. They make statements such as, 'We can't go out to play until everyone has tidied up. Rick is dawdling. He obviously doesn't want us to go outside. What a pity. We're missing all that lovely sunshine.' What is happening here is that the adult perceives Rick's tardiness as an unacceptable challenge to authority. The adult becomes vindictive, punishing the whole group because one member is perceived as disobedient. The adult knows that the offence is trivial, that group punishment is unjust and that it will be resented by those who conformed to the instruction. Because the adult does not want to be disliked for making an unpopular and unfair decision, the miscreant is blamed for the group's loss of privileges. By transferring responsibility to Rick, the adult then directs the inevitable wave of resentment to the child. This transfer is achieved very subtly by using the words 'we' and 'us' instead of the direct 'I'.

Oblique, emotionally damaging methods of control are commonly used by teachers of young children. Instead of asking the nonconformist to change behaviour, the teacher addresses the whole class as if the targeted child is not present; for example, the question, 'Do you think that Sarah intends to get her book out today?' is addressed to the whole class specifically to humiliate the child who did not give the required response to a command. In addition, teachers sometimes maintain control by talking about miscreants as if they were not present: 'I don't think that Sarah intends to get her book out today. Maybe we ought to continue without her.'

Educators and caregivers sometimes use jokes to change children's behaviour. They are especially effective when laughter is directed to the individual child, causing humiliation and a sense of isolation. Victims smile or laugh along with everyone else but the laughter often conceals their hurt.

CHILDREN KNOW WHEN TEACHERS REJECT THEM

In his classic work on the management of children aged 5–8 years, King (1978) found that, in the second year of school, children knew that they were labelled in dichotomous ways. Quiet conformists were approved and judged to be sensible, good, nice, an asset to the class and worthy of emulation. Noisy or rough behaviour resulted in children being identified as naughty, disruptive, uncooperative and unwanted. Class members knew who was valued by teachers and who was not. Teachers' faces brightened when favoured children gave the expected responses.

Good and Brophy (1978) also found that teachers use differential verbal stimuli as a powerful tool in shaping pupil behaviour and self-concept, for example, they tend not to expect or wait for responses from 'poor' students. Furthermore, when children give responses other than the one that the teacher wishes to hear, the teacher often ignores the speaker and points to another child who has raised a hand. The silent movement from child to child continues until the desired response is given. Then, there is often praise on the lines of, 'Good! I knew I could rely on you, Sophie, to give me the correct answer'.

SCHOOLS FAIL TO PROVIDE A HIGH QUANTITY AND QUALITY OF INTERACTION

Hart and colleagues (1987, p. 227) point out that, for their satisfactory development, children need a social support network that incorporates frequent, dependable and caring interactions with others. They show that few schools (least of all, schools for older children) provide opportunities for these relationships. Secondary schools are often vast, subject orientated and depersonalised. There are often no opportunities for children to have one-to-one contact with teachers. Hart and colleagues concluded that the teacher's withdrawal of communication constitutes emotional maltreatment. These conditions increase reliance on peer and sibling relationships which may limit children's intellectual development.

The growing use of electronic media in schools suggests that social support will decline even further in the future. Hart commented that: 'This might not be so bad if it were not for the evidence that students experience little in the way of supportive human reactions with adults in their homes' (Hart et al. 1987, p. 227).

EFFECTS OF EMOTIONAL ABUSE BY TEACHERS

Teacher disapproval has powerful effects on children's attitudes, behaviour and self-esteem. Krugman and Krugman (1984) and Hyman (1985) noted the following effects of teacher rejection on children. In addition to the symptoms already noted, children:

- change from positive to negative perceptions of self, school and their own performance;
- verbalise fears that the teacher might hurt children in their class;
- cry excessively about school;
- complain of headaches, ear-ache, nausea and stomach-ache. Some vomit when it is time to leave home;
- decrease functioning in social situations outside school;
- exhibit hyperactive/anxious behaviours;
- have high levels of absenteeism.

Krugman and Krugman (1984, pp. 284–5) found that conditions in abusive classrooms had often been known to school administrators and staff for many years but no-one had intervened. School administrators avoided taking action even when confronted with the evidence. The Krugmans suspected that administrators underestimated the seriousness of the abuse because, being afraid of their teachers and unwilling to risk antagonising their unpredictable and erratic personalities, they remained fearfully silent. A quiet class was regarded by school principals as evidence that the teachers were managing their classes well and 'doing a good job'.

Emotionally abusive methods of control have been around for a long time. They are effective in persuading children to cooperate with adults' wishes and, on the surface, some may seem to be quite harmless. When examined closely, however, the messages that teachers give and children receive are often quite insidious.

WHY SOME TEACHERS ARE ABUSIVE

Because child abuse is the result of the interaction of specific environmental and personal factors, we are all capable of becoming abusive parents or abusive professionals involved in the care and education of children. Harper's (1980) premise is that bad teaching and emotional abuse arise from the same dynamics as abuse by parents. Ignorance of child development creates an aura of incomprehensibility around children. This sometimes results in near-hysterical responses to children's normal behaviour. Abusive parents overreact to thumb-sucking, playing with genitals and regression in toilet training. Teachers often overreact to children talking and their mischievous behaviour that arises from boredom. Inadequate teachers seldom relate unwanted behaviour to their own failure to provide appropriate, challenging curriculum which caters for children's abilities and developmental levels. The resultant chaos is then attributed to deliberate naughtiness, low intelligence (referred to derogatorily as being 'as thick as a brick', 'dumb' or 'stupid'), the family environment or antisocial tendencies when the biggest problem is the inadequate teacher.

In a study of emotionally abusive teachers, Harper (1980) confirmed that, whenever a staff member spends an inordinate amount of time disciplining, controlling and punishing children, whether verbally or by the removal of privileges, emotional abuse is likely to occur. The dynamics identified by Harper as conducive to abuse are included in the following list:

- a sense of isolation, perceptions of struggling alone, unappreciated and inadequately rewarded by peers, parents or unsupportive management;
- anger and resentment towards children in general and/or some children in particular; the attribution of bad motives to specific children—those who remind us of children who bullied us are particularly vulnerable;
- serious financial, career, health or relationship problems—the teacher's preoccupation with his or her own needs brings insensitivity to children's needs;
- disinterest in children, for example, the teachers who joined the profession to satisfy their own parents' wishes or because working conditions seemed attractive or because there seemed to be no alternatives at the time;
- inadequate pre-service and in-service education;
- a lack of social sanction of control applied to the abusive teacher;
- the abuser experienced an abusive role model in childhood and/or on teaching practice/field experience;
- the abuser is still striving to meet his or her own emotional needs for affection and self-esteem and expects children to meet those needs;
- inadequate understanding of developmental norms; this is commonly found when teachers are assigned unwillingly to age groups for which they have not been trained; they may conclude that individuals with learning or behaviour problems act maliciously to wreck their activities or lessons.

When feeling inadequate, there is always a risk that teachers will resort to the extreme but effective methods of control that were used in the same circumstances by their own school teachers.

For example, when a difficult six-year-old used an obscenity, his teacher ordered him to 'Go to the cloakroom and wash your mouth out with soap'. Embarrassed, she explained to onlookers that this instruction had taken her completely by surprise. 'It came off the top of my head. It's what the nuns in my convent school did to kids accused of lying, swearing and spitting.'

ABUSIVE TEACHERS ARE READILY IDENTIFIED

Bad teachers and bad caregivers can be readily identified. Because they do not know that they are bad, they emotionally abuse children in the presence of parents, visitors, researchers and other staff. Some try to involve their colleagues by inviting them to confirm publicly that they have never seen such appalling work or such terrible behaviour (and maybe the culprit should be sent back to the first class to work with the five-year-olds).

Emotionally abusive behaviour is habitual. Culprits have no idea how frequently they use punitive methods and how infrequently they use praise and encouragement until faced with the findings of researchers. Because of their lack of awareness, abusive teachers need a great deal of support and re-education to change their child management techniques and improve their knowledge of child development.

It is important that all professionals employed with children regularly scrutinise their control methods to ensure that they do not rely on subtle or overt humiliation, social isolation and damage to self-esteem to maintain order in their classes and activity groups. All staff should be encouraged to make a conscious effort to avoid situations that lead to insecurity, unkindness and an unhappy environment.

EMOTIONAL ABUSE BY BULLIES AT SCHOOL

International studies confirm that bullying is a problem in most schools. It invariably leads to a deterioration in the victim's emotional and psychological health (O'Hagan 1993, p. 50).

Interviews with New Zealand children (Briggs & Hawkins 1996a) confirmed that bullying is particularly prevalent in the 9–11 year age group. Victims are perceived as different to the majority, either by race, disability, physical appearance, clothing worn, or stature. Since spectacles were first worn by children, the wearers have been taunted and belittled. Some New Zealand parents disclosed that they had bought expensive contact lenses to protect children from deliberate spectacle breakage. Some children are victimised if they don't wear the approved 'designer label' clothes.

Some parents transferred children to other schools when excessive bullying resulted in feigned sickness and school refusal. Bullying involves belittling, name calling, rejecting, pushing, shoving, tripping, hitting, isolating and tormenting. It commonly involves the removal and hiding of victims' clothing, school bags or essential equipment.

New Zealand girls aged 8+ years revealed that male bullies now threaten to rape them to gain control of them or playground equipment. Parents confirmed that the fear of rape inhibited girls' lives and resulted in night fears.

Bullies isolate their victims by recruiting their targets' friends as allies. This recruitment is usually achieved through fear. Bullies gain satisfaction from their capacity to manipulate others and the accomplices are blamed when they carry out instructions and are reported by victims.

Bullying has a major impact on the education and school life of victims. The Ministry of Education in New Zealand has introduced a school programme specifically to discourage bullying. Parents described this as effective but they made it clear that a great deal of work needs to be done to diminish the power of bullies and peer group pressure. A survey of New Zealand children aged 11–12 years, their parents and teachers showed that, despite children's fears of retribution, reporting bullying to parents and teachers is effective (Briggs & Hawkins, 1996a).

HELPING THE EMOTIONALLY ABUSED CHILD IN THE EARLY CHILDHOOD CENTRE AND SCHOOL

Teachers and early childhood professionals are in a unique position to identify the signs and symptoms of emotional abuse. Sometimes the school or early childhood centre provides the only stable aspect of a child's life. Sometimes staff or other children are responsible for the abuse.

Emotionally abused children need the same stable, predictable environments as children who are emotionally disturbed for other reasons. They need warmth of affection, consistent handling, a curriculum that provides opportunities for success, praise for effort and the knowledge that the teacher or caregiver is a reliable friend and supporter. Valuable one-to-one attention can be provided by student teachers or parent helpers.

Brassard, Germain and Hart (1987) and Maher (1987) offered many suggestions for how schools and preschools can help emotionally abused children and their parents. They note that child victims require a curriculum to meet their special needs, that parent education programmes to reduce stress and develop parents' competencies are desirable and that everyone benefits from friendly visits to homes for assessment and support. Underlying their recommendations is the idea that the school can be used as a centre for family support services.

The curriculum

The special curriculum referred to should attempt to enhance victims' self-esteem and confidence levels and should offer emotionally abused children opportunities and encouragement to express their needs and feelings in socially acceptable ways, for example, with the provision of therapeutic activities such as water, clay, finger painting, paint, dramatic play and woodwork.

In extreme cases, when children exhibit emotional or behavioural problems which place their behaviour outside the norms for age-peers and demonstrate severe personal and social maladjustment, professional psychological help may be required, but the amount of positive good that can be done by teaching staff should not be underestimated.

Parent participation in the programme

Parents who emotionally abuse their children are often lonely, socially isolated people who have more than their share of problems. Early childhood centres and schools can help to offset the sense of isolation by developing good staff–parent rapport and offering a supportive environment.

Parent–child–staff relationships are usually enhanced if parents can be persuaded to participate in the school or centre's educational programme. Attention should be given to the provision of challenging and worthwhile activities with clear information about what is expected and how children will benefit. Some schools encourage parent groups to meet in unused classrooms or the staff room. Programmes usually offer opportunities for socialisation, self-help, mutual help and parent education.

Education for parenting is likely to support good child care practice, including information on children's emotional needs, the norms of development, discipline and positive child management techniques and helping children to learn.

A needs analysis in South Australia showed that the top six topics wanted by parents were 'Drugs and teenagers', 'Lying/stealing', 'Dealing with disobedient children', 'Accident prevention/first aid', 'Child abuse' and 'Sex and teenagers' (Hunt, Hawkins & Goodlet 1992).

Some schools and family centres have been very successful in creating support groups for unemployed parents. With help from community workers, these have provided opportunities to gain work skills, training and further education, increasing parents' self-image and confidence.

Home visits

Some early childhood centres and schools adopt an open-door policy which includes home visits. Attention should be given to visiting and maintaining contact with high-risk families. Visits enable staff to provide feedback to parents about their children's well-being and progress. Staff benefit from their insights into children's home environments and parent–child interactions. When socially isolated parents realise that staff care about them, they are more likely to talk about their problems, enabling the professionals to assess the need for referral to support services.

Discussing a child's problems with the parents requires tact and skill. Teachers should not, for example, disclose children's confidences to parents. The careful balance between communicating concern for child and parent must be achieved while keeping the relationship professional.

Staff should not ask parents for explanations for their behaviour, nor should they interview parents for 'evidence' to prove maltreatment. If an explanation is given, it is appropriate for the professional to sympathise with the parents' problems and feelings but staff should never express shock, apportion blame or make judgements. Even though initial concern may be for a child, it may be very helpful to focus on helping the parent.

The decision to report becomes more difficult when professionals have worked hard to create a rapport with the parents, perceiving themselves as 'a friend of the family'. In his article on dangerous professionals, Peter Dale (1984) noted the frequency with which professionals failed to report signs of child abuse 'for fear of losing our relationship with the family'. He points out that there is, in reality, no relationship if the adults cannot acknowledge realistic concerns; it is only 'an avoidance of conflict and difference' (Dale 1984, p. 21).

When we attempt to overapply a nurturing model, we are at risk of becoming too enmeshed with the family's problems. In abusive families, this often results in the professional becoming 'sucked in' by the overwhelming power of the adults to the extent that they 'can't see the wood for the trees' (Dale 1984, p. 21).

TASKS FOR STUDENTS

1   Conduct an informal survey of your colleagues to determine what proportion can recall incidents of emotional abuse which occurred in both primary and secondary schools. Discuss the consequences of examples cited.

2   Does your school or centre have a formal antiharassment (bullying) policy? If so, familiarise yourself with it.

3   Consider your own interactions with children and assess, for example, to what extent you:

   a   make comparisons that humiliate or embarrass (use mistakes as class examples or return tests in rank order);

   b   in a child's presence, discuss the child's problems with others as if the child was not there;

   c   find that a child's intellectual ability negatively influences your interaction with the child;

   d   insist that students answer questions even when it is clear that they do not know the answer (examples based on Nesbitt 1991).

4   Observe the different methods of control used by teachers and early childhood professionals to gain children's compliance and note the circumstances in which humiliation, scapegoating or rejection were used. Which positive management methods would have been just as effective?

5   Describe the emotionally abusive behaviours that would justify reporting a colleague.

6   Which children does the teacher like and dislike? How can you tell?
7   Who are the bullies in the group? What steps are being taken to curb bullying?

4

INSTITUTIONAL AND SYSTEM ABUSE

Child abuse is not wholly the consequence of behaviour by individual caregivers. It has also been perpetuated throughout history by institutions and political forces. Paradoxically, victims of institutional abuse in Western society are usually the children who have already been abused by others and the abusive institutions are usually the ones specifically set up to take responsibility for their care and protection.

EMOTIONAL ABUSE OF CHILDREN BY THE JUSTICE SYSTEM

The abuse which has caused most concern in recent times has been the emotional abuse of child sexual abuse victims by the justice system. Until comparatively recently, there were rules which prevented children from giving evidence in criminal courts below a certain age. In some states and countries, the age limit was fourteen years. Although the rules have changed, criminal courts continue to discourage prosecutions involving young victims, those with disabilities and those who lack the sophisticated communication skills needed to respond to the (deliberately) complex, confusing and often insensitive questions put by defence lawyers. This, in effect, gives sex offenders a licence to victimise disabled and young children, providing of course that they commit offences in private.

Children's advocates who have struggled to create changes to the justice system have encountered strong opposition from lawmakers, the judiciary and the legal profession. Criminal courts were designed by adults with adults in mind. They work on the principle that all parties are equal when, of course, children can never be equal in a system devised by adults for adults. Furthermore, the court sees its primary roles as protecting the rights of the accused and allocating appropriate punishment; it is not there to protect victims.

The emotional abuse of child witnesses occurs when the adults responsible for the justice system are unwilling to adapt court procedures, practices and questioning techniques to meet the needs of children. In some courts, victims are still required to face their abusers while they testify, often without the presence of a supportive parent.

Long delays and adjournments are always advantageous to offenders and disadvantageous to children. In the meantime, neither victims nor their families can put the abuse behind them and get on with their lives. The longer the delay, the greater the opportunities for defence lawyers to confuse child witnesses about the dates, times and nature of offences.

Although many British, Australian and New Zealand courts now have facilities for interviewing children by video link from an adjacent room, their use is usually at the discretion of the judge. The reason frequently given for the prosecution's failure to use the facility was the belief that distressed children create the greatest impact on juries. Defence lawyers also resist video evidence because they perceive it as being advantageous to the victims.

Sadly, child sexual abuse victims in the British judicial system (and systems inherited from Westminster) often conclude that the assessment and justice process caused more trauma than the abuse itself and, had they known what was in store, they would not have reported the offences.

EMOTIONAL ABUSE OF CHILDREN INVOLVED IN FAMILY COURT DISPUTES

Anyone who has contact with families engaged in Family Court disputes relating to children will know that the children frequently suffer emotional abuse during this process. Victims are usually children who have either been abused by a parent or their parents have failed to take account of their children's psychological well-being in making their determinations. For example, parents in faraway places sometimes gain the custody of children they have never nurtured and scarcely know, for reasons which have nothing to do with children's needs. Some courts follow the advice of counsellors, many of whom lack expertise in early childhood development and make bizarre recommendations for children's living arrangements, such as that children must live with their embattled parents on alternate weeks, necessitating two homes, two lots of toys, two lots of friends and disruption to school learning. Some children are forced to maintain visits to parents and parent figures who have sexually abused them and, when allegations are before the Family Court, victims are often deprived of therapy pending the outcome of cases.

The problem is, of course, that parents in the Family Court system are usually preoccupied with their own needs. Hurt by former partners, they often use their children as pawns to hurt each other. Children rarely have the opportunity to talk to Family Court judges who make the decisions which affect their future lives. Their views are often ignored because of the belief that their choices would be strongly influenced by the most dominant parent.

CHILDREN VICTIMISED WHILE IN THE CARE OF THE CHURCH AND STATE

In Australia, current concerns revolve around past abuse such as the removal of Aboriginal children from their parents by the state. The aim of this damaging exercise was to teach them European values in the hope that they would be assimilated by the dominant white society.

The abuse of British child migrants has only recently come to notice. In the meantime, publications by Bean and Melville (1989) and Margaret Humphreys (1994) tell the stories of the shipment of 130 000 British children, some as young as three or four, to Australia and Canada. Philanthropists responsible for migration schemes built up dreams of a new life in new lands. For the English authorities, these schemes were beneficial because they emptied orphanages and populated the colonies with British stock. Roman Catholic agencies promoted the scheme as a means of Catholicising the state of Western Australia. They expanded the intake of boys by attracting Catholics from the island of Malta. Parents were led to believe that their sons would receive a sound education and training to become engineers and other professionals (Welsh 1990).

In practice, life for many of the 90 000 British children exported to Canada and the 40 000 sent to Australia was often one of slave labour, beatings, sexual and psychological abuse and unremitting hardship. Descriptions of the cruelties inflicted on boys sent to Christian Brothers schools in Australia would be beyond belief but for the consistency of victims' statements and photographic evidence.

Victims of Institutionalised Cruelty, Exploitation and Supporters (VOICES) is the driving force behind a class action which resulted in writs being served against the Christian Brothers Catholic organisation, claiming compensation for the multiple abuse of some 250 boys who, until the 1960s, were placed in residential schools, often as wards of the state (Davies 1994). There is evidence to suggest that social workers ignored evidence of sexual abuse, possibly to protect the Catholic Church from shame.

The big shock to recent researchers was the finding that child migration continued after World War II and some 10 000 young children were shipped to Australia between 1945 and the late 1960s. Most of these children never heard from their families again. Abuse and deception characterised the Australian schemes. Parents were told that their children had been adopted while the children in Australia were led to believe that they were orphans. For many, the search for their families became a lifelong crusade. Because of the withholding of information, men in their fifties have only recently been reunited with relatives they thought were dead—a reunion of happiness and confusion on one side and guilt and disbelief on the other (Bean & Melville 1989).

Recognition of the emotional damage inflicted on children by orphanages led to the creation of cottage homes managed by husband and wife teams to replicate the normal, albeit large family. Research is now beginning to show that child abuse continued in these supposedly homely environments. For example, there is evidence that boys residing in seven separate cottage homes at Mittagong, New South Wales, were subjected to all forms of abuse with the knowledge and participation of a paedophile superintendent (Briggs 1995b).

SYSTEM ABUSE

In recent times, there have been allegations of children being emotionally abused by overzealous professionals (Fitzpatrick & Briggs in Briggs ed. 1994, p. 97).

As children's services have become aware of their own capacity to inflict emotional damage on children, some have tried to change policies and practices to safeguard children's interests. Nevertheless, there are still major concerns about foster children who experience multiple placements and victims of child sexual abuse whose abusers remain in the family home supported by their mothers.

American authorities have tried to find ways of avoiding the further abuse of sexual abuse victims by the child protection system. Whenever possible, they remove offenders and leave the children in their homes. In Australia, New Zealand and the United Kingdom, victims in these circumstances are the ones most likely to be removed and placed in family substitute care. This tends to occur when the mother has other children to support, is unaware of the emotional consequences for the victim and is emotionally and/or financially dependent on the offender. It is especially hurtful and emotionally damaging to victims when the offender is not their own father but he is allowed to remain in the family home while they have to leave. Emotional damage is greatest, however, when offenders are not punished for their offences while their victims are placed in foster care. They blame themselves for being stupid and reporting their abuse. Self-blame is greatest when they were warned by offenders that reporting would result in being 'taken away and put in a place for bad kids'. When that prediction proves to be correct, victims often refuse to cooperate with police and withdraw their statements, accepting that sexual abuse is the price they have to pay to remain in their own homes.

Unfortunately, some child victims of abuse suffer further abuse in foster families. Although physical punishment is usually banned by foster agencies, there is a risk of physical abuse if foster parents have not been taught how to handle children's emotionally disturbed, difficult behaviours.

Sexual abuse victims are also at risk of re-abuse if they unwittingly exhibit the learned sexual behaviours and members of the foster family do not understand why this happens or know how to deal with it. Although it is no excuse for sexual abuse, adolescent males and uneducated foster parents sometimes misinterpret the behaviour as a sign that the foster child wants sex, is experienced and willing to participate.

When a child victim is re-abused in foster care this adds to the sense of helplessness and confusion. 'Why does it keep happening to me? Why am I different? Why did the welfare people put me there when they were supposed to protect me?' are the questions often asked.

Children are sometimes abused by 'the system' when they cannot be cared for by their own dysfunctional families and social workers lack other means of keeping them safe. Children may be taken into emergency foster care when the caregiving parent is suddenly hospitalised, imprisoned, abandons them or refuses to accept responsibility for them and there are no suitable relatives willing and able to provide a home. Emergency foster placements are highly traumatic because there is no time for preparing the child.

What must it be like to be a child removed from your home and family without warning in the middle of the night by an unknown adult?

What must it be like when the strange adult takes you in a strange car to a strange bed in a strange house occupied by people you have never seen before?

What must it be like (when you are too young to understand) to be suddenly deprived of all contact with your family, your school, teachers, pets and favourite toys?

When children are removed from their homes in this way, they go into a state of grief. First there is shock, then denial, anger, depression and self-blame. Children create their own faulty explanations and blame themselves for what happened: 'I was sent away because my mum didn't want me. If she loved me she wouldn't have let them take me away. She doesn't love me because I'm not worth loving. I'm not worth loving because I'm bad.'

Emergency foster care is only temporary. If family problems are not resolved, children may move into longer term placements. They experience abuse by 'the system' when they are sent home at the whim of unreliable, immature parents who quickly change their minds and demand that the children be returned to foster care. The children can rarely return to the same placement and, as a result, are passed from foster parent to foster parent until, eventually, their angry, disruptive, destructive, attention-seeking or withdrawn behaviour makes them unfosterable. One of the authors of this book has encountered adolescents in day care centres who have been in forty different foster placements.

When abused by the system, children learn to distrust all adults and they experience difficulties in creating relationships. Expecting to be rejected, they often put new foster parents, teachers and group leaders to the test until they reach the limit of their endurance. When this behaviour occurs, it may be helpful to empathise with the child: 'I understand why you're doing this. You've had a rotten time. You're angry about being moved again and it's okay to be angry. I want you to know that although your behaviour is unacceptable, I care about you and am not giving up on you . . . so you might as well stop right now.'

It is always helpful to teach foster children how to express their feelings in acceptable, healthy ways.

Institutional abuse occurs when:

- rigid procedures and systems matter more than the emotional needs of children;
- children lack a long-term regular case worker;
- case workers fail to understand and respond sensitively to children's needs, resulting in mismatching children and foster parents or the separation of siblings, either of which may result in the subsequent breakdown of placements;
- case workers are inexperienced, lack a sound knowledge of children's development, fail to communicate effectively with children but have a need to please and be accepted. They are then likely to listen to the (more articulate and forceful) parents and return children to their care long before they are capable of caring for them, resulting in insecurity, instability and multiple placements.

HELPING FOSTER CHILDREN TO ADAPT TO NEW SCHOOLS AND EARLY CHILDHOOD CENTRES

Insufficient recognition is given to the important role that schools and preschool centres play in supporting foster children who have been damaged by the system. Teachers often complain that they receive no information from case workers while foster parents complain of poor communications with schools. Case workers give education a low priority while teachers seldom see that children in care are a discrete category in need of a special, negotiated curriculum. In Scotland, social work departments must inform schools when children are placed in care. In turn, schools must closely monitor the development and attendance of those children and pass information to the responsible service. Each school appoints a member of staff to act as liaison officer with social work departments (Scottish Office 1989).

Foster children are severely disadvantaged by disruptions to their education. As time goes on, school seems to become less and less relevant to them. There are often lengthy periods of no schooling due to delays incurred in finding foster placements.

After multiple placements and multiple schools, some foster children face the humiliation of being rejected by staff who fear that they will bring disruption and behaviour problems and few rewards. The result is that foster children often suffer failure, leaving school illiterate, innumerate and unemployable (Carey 1986).

When staff are not informed of the needs and problems of foster children, they are unlikely to respond appropriately to their emotionally disturbed behaviours. In ignorance, they may add to the emotional abuse heaped upon them by their abusers and the system. In ignorance, some staff blame the foster parents for the children's unacceptable behaviour in class. With inadequate knowledge, teachers and caregivers often expect foster children to show gratitude for the provision of food, clothes and a bed because, after all, their own parents don't care enough about them to provide a home. The reality is that foster children are seldom grateful for these material benefits. However abusive or inadequate their parents may be, children long for a loving home with their own relatives and if those are unattainable, they create their imaginary families, talking of imaginary outings with parents, imaginary birthday parties and gifts.

Foster children, especially those who have experienced multiple placements, need special support in the school system. The greater the discontinuities in educational provision, the more severely damaged are their opportunities for achievement (Berridge & Cleaver 1987; Jackson 1989). How can these children be supported?

First, there should be regular communications and informal meetings between teachers, case workers and foster parents.

Second, when foster children have enrolled at a new school, it is important to contact previous teachers for information that will help provide continuity in the curriculum. If the foster child left friends behind at the previous school, the teacher can encourage communications between the child and the former class. This is especially important if the child is likely to return to that school.

When children move on to another school, teachers should forward their workbooks and information that will ease the transition process either directly to the school or through the case worker.

Whenever possible, one-to-one tutoring should be made available to foster children. In a South Australian study of 808 children in foster care, it was found that over half of the children achieved a test age score four or more years below their chronological age in reading, comprehension and maths tests (Carey 1986). Minimal intervention involving one-to-one tutoring produced dramatic improvements (Johns & Baxter 1986). In Australia, the Commonwealth Department of Education has set up funds for tutoring but improvements can be achieved with the help of trained parent-volunteers.

Because children in multiple foster placements often have no memories of their past, it is helpful if schools and preschools collect photographs of the class, the staff and the child's activities to create a pictorial life history. Case workers will usually accept responsibility for putting this together.

If the parent did not commit any offence against the child, or if family reunification is planned and the case worker approves, teachers can help the child to maintain contact by writing letters and sending drawings from school.

CASE STUDY

Winston is transferred to your class in the middle of term when social groups are well established. You learn that he has been taken into emergency foster care because his mother is seriously ill. His brothers and sisters are in different placements because none of the foster homes with vacancies could accommodate five children.

a Discuss the emotional issues for Winston.
b Plan how you might help to reduce the trauma.
c Plan curriculum, bearing in mind that an emergency foster home is unlikely to become long term.

5

CHILD NEGLECT IS NEGLECTED

While the physical neglect of children is the most common and obvious form of child maltreatment, it is also the most tolerated and the most ignored. Cases of neglect are known to be under-reported in the United States and in the United Kingdom (National Centre for Child Abuse and Neglect 1988; Minty & Pattinson 1994). Neglect involves an act of omission or commission which jeopardises or impairs the child's social, psychological, intellectual or physical development. This includes instances where a parent or guardian has failed to take adequate precautions to ensure the child's safety or has failed to provide food, clothing, shelter or necessary medical care. The most frequently reported forms of physical neglect involve abandonment or forcing children to leave home. In most cases, emotional abuse is implicit in physical neglect.

Neglect is often associated with physical and sexual abuse. Farmer and Owen (1995) reported that in the United Kingdom one-third of neglect cases also involved physical abuse and one-quarter of sexual abuse cases also involved neglect. With the rapid increase in notifications of child sexual abuse and the way in which cases are prioritised, the problem of neglect is sometimes neglected by the authorities charged with the task of protecting children.

POVERTY, NEGLIGENCE AND SCHOOL PERFORMANCE

Despite the apparent affluence of Western countries, the problem of child neglect remains a cause for serious concern. In the

English-speaking world, we have seen 'the rich get richer and the poor get poorer', regardless of whether socialist or conservative governments have been in power. Although impoverishment does not necessarily lead to neglect, the two are often interrelated.

Various authors have suggested that neglect is neglected even by social workers because of perceptions that it is a consequence of poverty and, since the fundamental causes of poverty are difficult to address, very little can be done about it (Birchall 1989; Wolock & Horowitz 1984; Minty & Pattinson 1994).

'There is no reason for families to be so impoverished,' you might say. 'Social security benefits are adequate. And the Salvation Army will provide clothing.' The Salvation Army (along with other charitable organisations) does help needy families but the very act of seeking help involves effort, an acceptance of helplessness and a loss of pride. While middle-class shoppers brag about bargains they bought from charity shops, parents feel ashamed and depressed when they can only afford other people's discarded clothing.

Poor families are not always negligent. Many poor parents are good managers who grow their own food, make their own clothes, cook inexpensive, nutritious meals and budget carefully. But these skills require tools, training, energy, determination, knowledge and sound health, all of which are conspicuously missing in negligent families.

Negligent families often complain that poverty is the problem but their shopping trolleys show that they spend their money differently from middle-class families. The National Institute of Economic and Industry Research 'Spend Info' (1994) showed that in the Australian suburbs with the highest number of social security recipients, households spent the largest amount of money on gambling ($8.88 per week), tobacco ($14.20 per week) and beer ($10.00 per week) (*Advertiser*, 19 November 1994, p. 21). In other words, the poorest parents turned to alcohol and cigarettes to relieve stress and they gambled in the hope that their luck would change.

Poor parents usually delineate some non-essentials that they are 'not prepared to do without'. Cigarettes or alcohol may be valued more highly than food. Parents also create a 'bottom line' for their children, declaring, for example, that no matter what else is crossed off the shopping list, their children will not be deprived of cordial or a similar non-essential. One of the first tasks for family services workers is to help parents to budget and shop more sensibly, purchasing their indulgences when essentials have been paid for.

The material circumstances of parents play a large part in determining the life chances of children. The impoverished are the ones least likely to succeed in the education system. A New Zealand study by Wilson and Dupuis (1994) confirmed Douglas' British findings thirty years earlier (1964) that poor children live in the largest families where bedrooms are shared and there is no quiet place for homework. Poor homes offer few opportunities for educational activities; poor parents cannot afford to buy expensive educational toys, paints, paper, crayons, books, maths games or computers. As a result, children from disadvantaged environments often start school lacking the skills that other children already possess. Because they cannot participate in activities requiring money, poor children are deprived of access to sports and activities which require tuition or club membership. They often miss school excursions and lessons which require special clothing, materials or equipment.

At home, there was a strong mother–daughter dependency; girls in poor families spent 12 hours a week on domestic chores which included babysitting. This enabled the New Zealand mothers to work outside the home, usually for long hours and little money. The households were authoritarian-male dominated, with child rearing and household tasks clearly designated as the responsibility of females.

Wilson and Dupuis found that poor fathers were characterised by powerlessness outside their homes and dominance within them. Relationships were strained and families were marked by instability. In addition, half of the women and girls in the New Zealand study 'had to contend with some measure of domestic violence or sexual abuse'.

A number of studies have dispensed with the myth that parents in disadvantaged environments 'don't care about their kids'. Fifty-nine per cent of parents in the New Zealand study were sufficiently concerned to talk to teachers about their children's lack of progress but only one felt that she received assistance. The remaining 41 per cent of parents felt too ashamed to approach the school, sensing that they would be blamed for their children's problems. In conversations with parents, teachers slipped easily into the 'expert' role and used educational jargon which added to the parents' sense of inadequacy.

The education system has changed markedly in the last three decades, especially in the early years of schooling. The New Zealand study suggests that the attitudes and behaviour of individual teachers still contribute to the alienation of disadvantaged children. Some teachers were unapproachable, if not blatantly rude and offensive to disadvantaged parents.

Wilson and Dupuis (1994) believe that it is the school's responsibility to recognise and respond to the multiple problems experienced by children in disadvantaged families. They confirm the importance of using the school as a community resource. They stress the need for a less competitive, more supportive environment with a relevant and stimulating curriculum. However, the utilitarian aspects should not be neglected; they emphasis that children need basic numeracy and literacy skills along with social and survival skills for their everyday lives. They call for teachers to be specially selected for their sensitivity towards the lives of children in disadvantaged families.

'Teachers who cannot appreciate the fact that these students are not inherently stupid and lazy have no place in teaching [them]. The life circumstances of the children must be understood and appreciated' (Wilson & Dupuis 1994, p. 2).

MIDDLE-CLASS NEGLIGENCE

Teachers in private schools and early childhood centres often assume that, because parents pay fees, they do not maltreat their children. When middle-class children suffer from neglect, it is often much less obvious than in poor families. Wealthy parents who wish to escape from their children can usually pay for substitute care. The parents' lives are less likely to be marked by chaos than by self-indulgence and disinterest. They provide money in lieu of meals and material gifts in lieu of attention. Their children will never starve but their emotional deprivation can leave lifelong scars.

DIRTY CHILDREN IN THE CLASSROOM

The teacher's responsibility towards dirty, neglected children is a subject of controversy. Some arrive at school so dirty and malodorous that they are belittled, ridiculed and ostracised by their peers.

Although early childhood professionals accept the caring role readily, the older the child and the more middle-class the school, the more resistant teachers seem to be to the suggestion that schools can or should do anything to improve the physical well-being of neglected children in their classrooms.

'Cleanliness is the parents' job,' teachers say. 'Parents should be made to accept their responsibilities. If we start cleaning up their kids, parents will never do it.' Interestingly, schools in disadvantaged areas which employ counsellors or home visitors now have fewer problems of this kind than previously. This is because they have a policy of early intervention and a community culture of protecting and supporting. They build up relationships with troubled parents when children are young and help them to use available services.

A common, well-meant but unhelpful teacher response to an offensive child is to place responsibility for family cleanliness on the child by providing a class lesson on hygiene. The teacher expects the neglected child to 'take the hint'. This assumes, unfairly and unrealistically, that young children can instruct depressed parents to launder their clothes, provide baths and clean up a dirty household. All that happens, of course, is that the lesson draws everyone's attention to the fact that someone in the group is not conforming to minimal expectations. This gives clean children the confidence to harass the neglected ones with state-ments such as, 'I don't want to sit by you. You stink!' Some assertive parents insist that their children are removed to tables far away from the offenders. Who can blame them? Why should they have to tolerate bad smells or risk the unpleasantness of infestation by vermin?

When teachers do nothing to help dirty children to become socially acceptable, the most disadvantaged members of society become more disadvantaged. Sitting, working and playing alone, they are left in no doubt that they are pariahs. School then becomes a very unhappy place.

The effects of poor hygiene on children's development are far reaching. Children's perceptions of themselves are gained from how others behave towards them. If their peers avoid them, they are deprived of opportunities to develop social skills, language, communication skills and self-esteem. If they feel inadequate, they fail to develop confidence. Without confidence, they are unlikely to learn to read. Deprived of opportunities for success, they lose interest. In other words, dirty children are unlikely to achieve their potential in intellectual or social development if there is no helpful intervention.

With a little imagination, most early childhood centres and junior schools can improvise baths for small children. In hot climates, early childhood centres usually provide showers for use during the course of the day. Showers are available in most secondary schools but neglected children need help to use them in private. Group showers cause embarrassment for many teenagers and neglected teenagers often avoid activities followed by group showers because they are afraid of hurtful comments about their underwear. Neglected children in secondary schools need toiletries to shampoo hair and make themselves look and feel attractive.

The problem of dirty clothing is harder to resolve. Most primary schools and early childhood centres have a supply of clothing ready for 'accidents'. The considerate teacher starts the day with messy activities such as painting and finger paint which, with a little imagination, can provide a reason for washing dirty children and foul-smelling clothes. A neglected six-year-old who liked to be clean asked at ten minute intervals, 'Am I dirty enough to have a bath now?'

If the problem persists, teachers can help by using a four-pronged approach.

- First, take steps to ensure that children are made comfortable without drawing attention to their condition or damaging their self-esteem or alienating their parents.
- Develop a relationship with parents through home visits by an experienced member of staff or school counsellor.
- Refer parents to the needed services.
- Ensure that child protection authorities are notified of the problem and your actions.

CHILDREN LOCKED IN, LOCKED OUT OR LEFT TO THEIR OWN DEVICES

Young children are sometimes locked inside or outside their homes while parents go shopping, go to work or seek entertainment. Especially vulnerable are children whose unsupported parents work late at night. The children's plight is often revealed by neighbours who see them alone out of doors late at night. Tired, their parents are unlikely to get up in the morning to prepare them for school. Without adequate supervision, the children arrive too soon or too late and sometimes they are distracted and do not arrive at all. They often go to school without lunch or money for food.

Some parents spend their evenings in clubs or hotels, taking their children with them. The children provide lively descriptions of their escapades in class 'news time': they disclose what they drank, whose dad was drunk and whose fathers engaged in fights.

> I knocked Kevin's dad's beer over and it spilt all down him and his dad said to my dad, 'Why don't you leave your bloody kid at home. He's just spilt my beer.' And my dad said, 'Don't talk to me like that. I have a right to bring my kids here. If you don't like it, you can piss off.' Then his dad hit mine and then they had a fight and all the beer got spilt.

It is not unusual for early childhood professionals to find that young children arrive at school slightly drunk, either because they were at a family party the previous night or because their parents gave them alcohol in lieu of a babysitter. Some parents find young children's drunken behaviour amusing.

The questions for teachers and caregivers revolve around whether the child's health or safety are at risk and whether the child's development or school progress is impaired as a result of the parents' behaviour. If the child is likely to be disadvantaged, a report should be made to child protection authorities so that parents can be made aware of the long-term consequences of their actions.

Children locked inside the home can be as unsafe as those locked outside it. While one of the authors of this book watched a group of children playing in a sand-pit at the base of a high-rise block of flats, milk bottles suddenly descended from an open window on the tenth floor. The caretaker used his master key to enter the flat where he found that four-year-old twin boys were locked in the bathroom while their unsupported mother went to work for the day. She had given them two bottles of milk and packets of corn chips to eat for their lunch.

Some working parents, desperate for affordable child care, resolve their problems by drugging children to ensure that they sleep during the parents' absence. When children are sedated, there is less risk that they will injure themselves or burn the house down but there is a high risk that their physical development will be retarded for want of fresh air, exercise and appetite. Sedation also deprives them of opportunities for curiosity, exploration, intellectual stimulation, play, language development, numeracy, literacy and opportunities to develop social skills. When they eventually attend an early childhood centre or school, these children are undersized, pale, malnourished and retarded in all aspects of their development.

Child imprisonment of this kind is most prevalent in poor migrant areas where impoverished women work long hours in 'sweat shops' for little pay.

In the late nineteenth century, there were concerns throughout the English-speaking world that working mothers kept young children at home from school to care for siblings. This problem is still a concern in developing countries and, unfortunately, it has re-emerged in Western society. Children as young as six are designated as childminders. Babies and toddlers left alone or with immature caregivers are at risk of injury. In cold weather, poor families use inexpensive kerosene stoves which, if knocked over, quickly engulf a house in flames.

Clearly, neglect of this kind must be reported to child protection authorities so that parents can be helped to make safe arrangements for their children. Migrant mothers, especially those with little or no English, are seldom aware of 'before and after school care' and holiday programmes or the childminding services which provide supervised, flexible care in private homes with registered minders. It is helpful if shopping and medical centres, schools and early childhood centres display notices about such services in the languages used by parents. Some parents are illiterate, however, and the messages must also be transmitted by community media and word of mouth.

A not uncommon problem for staff in child care centres is the unsupported parent, usually the mother, who fails to collect her children at closing time on Fridays. Staff wait an extra half-hour before they send for emergency services. Another hour may go by before the distressed children are taken to emergency foster care for the weekend. Empathy for the children increases when parents return and abuse the staff for involving 'the welfare'. With no sign of conscience and no apology, two mothers explained that they 'met this bunch of guys' and accepted the invitation to go away for the weekend. This kind of negligence makes staff very angry because, of course, the children are subjected to enormous trauma while their mothers are pursuing a 'good time'.

Neglected middle-class children often receive material benefits in lieu of adult attention. Australian student counsellors in secondary schools report that children are given exorbitant sums of money to amuse themselves while parents go away for weekends. In large houses equipped for entertainment, they hold parties, abuse alcohol and experiment with drugs, alcohol and sex.

64

CHILDREN SUFFERING FROM POOR NUTRITION

Many children are so inadequately fed that they cannot concentrate on tasks involving literacy and numeracy. Staff at a South Australian primary school found that children were fractious, tired and restless from mid-morning onwards. A community health study undertaken by the local hospital showed that some children had not eaten a meal or had anything to drink since leaving school the previous day. Many others had missed breakfast and some children were given money in lieu of food. With that, they purchased sweet foods which produced short bursts of energy followed by a rapid decline. The researchers found a relationship between low energy levels and negative views of themselves and school in general (Briggs & Potter 1995).

The problems for the children and staff were largely resolved by changing the curriculum. The morning session was given over to Learning Centres, one of which was a breakfast centre. At any time during the morning, hungry children could visit the centre and prepare and eat cereals, boil an egg, fry bacon or serve baked beans on toast (under supervision). Attendance was voluntary and carried no stigma. Associated learning tasks included counting, weighing, measuring, timing and recording. The effects of the breakfast programme were carefully monitored. Rapid improvements were noted in children's concentration, skill development and learning and teachers noted a marked reduction in behaviour problems.

The breakfast programme is now available during activity time throughout the school and it has become part of the school's culture. Unfortunately, increasing poverty in Australia resulted in enormous pressures being placed on businesses for gifts of milk, cereals and other breakfast foods. A prominent international cereal manufacturer found it necessary to issue a statement to the effect that the company could no longer make charitable donations to schools because requests were arriving at a rate of thirty a day. As a consequence, although breakfast programmes are now widely available in the less affluent suburbs, they are dependent on the financial support of charities such as Save the Children.

WHEN PARENTS ARE UNSUPPORTED AND DEPRESSED

When parents are depressed, they are often incapable of normal activity. Unable to face another awful day, seriously depressed mothers stay in bed. They can't make the effort to shower, get dressed, make a meal or take children to school. At best, they escape from the wretchedness of their lives by entering the fantasy world of television 'soapies'. Their children come to the school's notice because of their erratic or late attendance, accidents or their unkempt appearance.

Teachers and school counsellors in deprived areas have found that large numbers of unsupported mothers are addicted to drugs legally prescribed by general practitioners. As a result, many young children are admitted to hospital suffering from accidental poisoning by these, as well as by alcohol and household substances. Tired, depressed, drugged or alcoholic parents fail to take elementary precautions to ensure their children's safety.

PARENTS WITH DRUG OR ALCOHOL PROBLEMS

Sometimes, at the end of the day, parents arrive at centres too 'spaced out' to be given responsibility for their children. Sometimes, when staff take children home, they find that parents are too drugged or too drunk to realise that the children have returned. Staff have to make a quick decision whether to leave the children with their parents or take them back to the centre and call emergency services.

As child care centres are increasingly used by courts to protect children from drug-addicted parents, it is not surprising that early childhood centres are encountering more cases of neglect than ever before. Children often reveal that they have had no food since leaving the centre the previous day. In the morning, staff often find that babies and toddlers are wearing the same nappies that they fitted sixteen hours earlier. Nappy rashes and blisters are a common problem for these children.

Drug counsellors are often reluctant to remove children from their parents' care when they have joined Alcoholics Anonymous or methadone programmes and seem to be genuinely trying to overcome their addictions. Teachers and child care personnel have to ensure that, while meeting the parents' needs, social workers and counsellors do not overlook children's needs.

WHEN CHILDREN ARE GIVEN TOO MUCH RESPONSIBILITY TOO SOON

One of the common forms of child maltreatment is that which results in children being treated as mini-adults. Children of all social classes are given both freedom and responsibility long before they are ready for it.

As a result of family breakdown, large numbers of young, unaccompanied children travel vast distances by air, train and coach to visit their non-custodial parents. The authors have heard Family Court judges, ignoring protestations from mothers, declare that children as young as five are sufficiently mature to use cross-country bus services to visit their fathers in other counties and states. Airline staff are overwhelmed by these children at the beginning and end of school holidays. Some young passengers enjoy being alone. Others are in tears throughout the flight and neither of their parents is aware of their distress.

Children's needs for security are sometimes secondary to parents' emotional and material needs. Some children are 'turned out into the street' when parents are 'partying' or entertaining new partners for the weekend. The children make for city centres in search of similarly neglected children, convinced (often with good reason) that their parents neither know nor care about where they are, whom they are with or what they are doing. The parents' attitude is perceived as, 'I don't care where you go so long as you get out of my way'. These children are highly vulnerable to seduction by paedophiles who frequent the amusement arcades and cafes which attract lonely and neglected children (Briggs 1995b). They are often perceived as kindly, caring men who listen sympathetically to children's problems, buy them food, give them money for video games and fill a gap in their affectionless lives. When sexual conversation and sexual touching are introduced, few can resist these people on whom they have become emotionally dependent.

CHARACTERISTICS OF MARGINALLY NEGLIGENT PARENTS

Negligent parents are often childlike in their needs and responses as they search for the love and attention that they missed in childhood. They expect children to love them, not make demands on them. When they lacked a loving, responsible parent model in their formative years, they are unlikely to know how to give loving care to their own children. They may be fond of them in their own way and they seldom abandon them completely but they may see nothing wrong in going out for the evening and returning a day later. They are oblivious of their children's fears, needs and the risks to their safety. They assume that children will feed themselves even when the fridge is empty.

While serious neglect can have life-threatening consequences, marginal neglect is much less traumatic. The house may be dirty, the lifestyle chaotic, but children are fed, albeit irregularly from a restricted and unhealthy diet. Parents tend to be poor and uneducated rather than cruel or indifferent. And whereas seriously negligent parents tend to be disorganised in every aspect of their lives, the marginally negligent have some degree of organisation, albeit inconsistent. The marginally negligent family still operates as a family unit.

Marginally neglected children may be dirty but they are not disadvantaged by the foul smell that usually lingers around their seriously neglected peers. Receiving some affection and attention at home, they are less hostile to the outside world. They can be responsive and enjoy good relationships with teachers and classmates.

Marginally negligent parents are more indifferent than hostile to schools and teachers. They may recognise that education holds the key to success. They would like their children to 'be clever' and 'do well'. Unfortunately, they associate academic success more with having a 'good teacher' than having a supportive home background. Many of these parents want to help their children but they lack the knowledge and the confidence to become involved. If they experienced school failure, they may avoid school events. However, they are often less afraid of other teachers than of being in the company of more affluent, more successful, more insensitive parents. They feel hopelessly inadequate in their company and are afraid of saying or doing something that will cause embarrassment.

Parents who made the effort and accepted invitations to participate in school events in the early years become less confident as they begin to perceive their children as failures. By the time marginally neglected children reach the age of ten or eleven, all parent–teacher communications are likely to have ceased unless the school makes a special effort to develop rewarding relationships.

CHARACTERISTICS OF SERIOUSLY NEGLIGENT PARENTS

The most common characteristic of seriously negligent families is that the parents have chaotic lives. They tend to exist from day to day, unable to plan ahead or manage the household. Their children are often absent from school: if they 'sleep in', it is easier to let them have the day off than make the effort to take them. Depressed parents often ignore or fail to read letters from teachers. As a consequence, their children are likely to be the ones sent to school when school is closed.

The sympathy of professionals is often alienated by the parents' priorities. Typically they are in receipt of social security benefits. Without guidance, they often give priority to brightening their own lives. They fail to plan for future commitments, such as hire purchase, rent, gas or electricity, telephone bills, insurance, medicines and essential food. While their debts accumulate, they often rent the largest and latest television and the most sophisticated VCR which, until they are repossessed, provide an escape from reality.

'Why don't they buy cheap nutritious food? Why don't they grow their own vegetables?' are the questions often asked as these parents emerge from supermarkets with cans of expensive pet food and bottles of Coke. Because canned food is easy to serve, their cats and dogs are often better fed than the children.

It is difficult for the more affluent outsider to understand that sufferers from depression, low self-esteem and physical ill health do not have the energy to shop for bargains. With a limited budget and probably no transport, it is hard work searching for the cheapest cut of meat and the cheapest loaf of bread. Furthermore, it requires effort as well as know-how to turn bones into nutritious soup and create half a dozen tasty dishes from a kilo of minced beef or cheese. Most negligent parents were early school leavers who were not taught to cook, budget, plan meals or manage a household either by their teachers or by the example of their own parents. As a result, food tends to be available only spasmodically with 'Dial a Pizza' on cheque days and bread and jam thereafter.

Severely neglected children come to the notice of teachers when they steal food from shops, other children, or waste bins outside supermarkets. These children usually live in substandard housing and a home visit confirms the pervasive chaos. Ashtrays are often piled high with cigarette butts in every room. Dirty dishes fill the sink and draining board. Scraps of dehydrated and decaying food litter the kitchen and floor. The toilet and bath are sometimes filthy, stinking and blocked. In rare, extreme cases, garbage is piled high and buckets full of urine and faeces litter the floor. Such conditions horrify professionals who make home visits. 'How could human beings live like that? Animals wouldn't live in such squalor!'

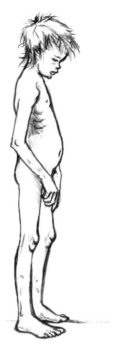

Severe neglect

In general, the poorer the family, the larger the hire purchase commitments and debts. Contracts are often made without reading the small print. These families are highly vulnerable to department stores which advertise, 'Want it? Charge it!' When they are no longer credit-worthy, they become vulnerable to loans from pawn-brokers and tricksters who advertise 'No deposit loans' but forget to mention that they charge exorbitant interest rates. Interest rates on loans through Australian pawnbrokers are up to 300 per cent, compared with commercial banking rates for credit cards of around 16–17 per cent, or personal loan rates of 10–14 per cent a year. Not surprisingly, many families find themselves owing far more than they initially borrowed.

Seriously negligent families are often large and the mother is likely to be in poor health. Her life is out of control and she will tell you that she 'takes what comes' (and that includes pregnan-cies). As a result, she is often malnourished, anaemic, tired and energyless. Her husband or de facto spouse is likely to be unemployed or unemployable due to chronic ill health or injury received in an accident while employed in an unskilled job. Most negligent families are afraid of revealing their plight for fear that their children will be removed and placed in foster care. Social workers are often perceived as punitive and authoritarian rather than helpful.

Some families are difficult to help; some receive assistance from every available agency to no effect. Mark, aged six, wore the same vest and pants every day. The putrid smell and darkening yellow stains suggested that he slept in the same clothes and suffered from enuresis. His brothers, aged four and seven, were in a similar condition. When the school nurse visited the home she found that the boys slept on a pile of urine-soaked newspapers which were infested by maggots. A charity provided beds and bedding but, a week later, the father had sold the gifts and the boys were, once again, sleeping on newspapers.

In trying to understand how this kind of situation can occur, we have to remember that successive generations of family members may have lived in similar circumstances, each generation of children experiencing the same kinds of degradation. In these circumstances, they fail to learn sound parenting and household management skills from their own parents and, when they marry, they tend to choose partners from similar backgrounds. They do not know how to conduct their lives differently; they have sexual relationships or marry at an early age to escape from their own oppressive home environments but, without early intervention, they continue the cycle of deprivation and disadvantage. Without intervention, the pattern is repeated again and again. They tend to view themselves as victims of authority and victims of circumstance to such an extent that the outside world is perceived as the enemy. As parents they are often immature. They can neglect their children because no-one visits them. The greater the degeneration of the family home and parents, the greater the isolation and the greater the health risk to the children. If there are responsible relatives, they are likely to distance themselves from a family living in filth and squalor.

THE RELATIONSHIPS BETWEEN SCHOOLS/PRE-SCHOOLS AND NEGLIGENT FAMILIES

Severely negligent parents are unlikely to view the education system as relevant to their lives. They do not accompany their

A mother and her three sons (aged 12, 14 and 16), many cats and several dogs lived in this rented house. Rubbish was piled to the top of windows in every room. The family slept in the loft and lived in the carport. Cleaners filled a 10-tonne refuse bin from kitchen debris alone. In some places, the rubbish was piled up to a metre from the ceiling and access had to be gained through windows. Three refrigerators contained food with 'use by' dates more than four years old. Neighbours complained about the foul stench to the council 'for about ten years' before action was taken. A spokeswoman for the child protection authority said that the mother had been counselled about family problems but staff were unaware of the state of the house until they were shown photographs by the council. The three boys had spent most of the past ten years in schools where teachers are mandated to report suspicions of neglect. The smell of decayed food, animal faeces and urine and the boys' inability to use the bathroom must surely have provided indications that they needed help. (Reproduced by kind permission of the Advertiser, Adelaide, 11 February 1995, p. 1)

children to school or attend open days, sports days, school concerts or plays. They seldom read or respond to letters, either because they are illiterate or because they feel alienated from schools. If they failed in the education system, they carry negative if not bitter memories of school humiliation. It requires a sensitive and deliberate effort to change hostile attitudes.

A 33-year-old man, his 22-year-old partner and their 18-month-old child lived in these appalling conditions. The house was refurbished by the council prior to their occupancy. They failed to pay the rent and received an eviction notice. An ashtray full of cigarette ends was found in the child's pram. Neighbours confirmed that the family had lived in these chaotic conditions for six months. When police were called to the house, they assumed (mistakenly) that it had been vandalised. (Reproduced by kind permission of the Advertiser, *Adelaide, 9 February 1995, p. 3)*

In the early years of school, children are devoted to both their teachers and their parents and any division of loyalty can be damaging to their progress. Disadvantaged parents are highly sensitive to tactless behaviour and staff must take care to avoid creating opportunities for complaints.

Some teachers write to parents requesting meetings to discuss their negligence but the parents seldom respond. If they suspect that they are about to be reported, they may even transfer their children to another school. Home visits reveal something of children's circumstances but parents will be suspicious and defensive if no-one from the school has visited them before and home visits are not an accepted part of the school or preschool culture.

Should a home visit be made without warning? Defensive parents may not open the door if the unexpected visitor is spotted and recognised. At the other extreme, fearful of being 'shamed', impoverished Aboriginal parents told the authors that they took out a joint loan to buy educational toys which they passed from one family to the next when they learned that a home visit was imminent. Although home visits were undertaken routinely, they did not want the school to know that they had no educational equipment.

When home visits are made, it is important to get to know the family and the parents' health, well-being and support networks without referring to the neglected state of the children. In the ideal situation, parents reveal their difficulties and confirm the need for help; the visitor tells them what is available and helps them to contact appropriate services, ensuring that, in cases where children's health and welfare are at risk, the authorities are notified of their actions. This is often more effective than appealing to a severely negligent mother for cooperation in cleaning a child. Such an appeal may have an immediate effect but, if there are serious family problems, the improvement will only be short term. On the only occasion that one of the authors approached a father about the peer harassment experienced by his unclean son, the father responded, 'I'll give the wife hell when I get home'. The following day, the boy was neat and clean but the improvement lasted a day.

Risk factors: the child at preschool or primary school.

Child neglect can be suspected when children are often:

- inadequately dressed for prevailing weather conditions;
- dirty or accompanied by a pungent, unpleasant smell;
- hungry and/or steal or beg food from others;
- in need of medical treatment, for example, for cuts and sores which become infected for want of attention;
- out of doors (unaccompanied by adults) very late at night; often sick, especially prone to chronic ear, throat and chest infections;
- getting themselves ready and walking to school unaccompanied at an early age;
- sent to school on public holidays and non-teaching days;

- late or have many unexplained absences;
- underweight and undersize for age (bearing family traits in mind).

In addition, it may be found that neglected children are:

- consistently passive or withdrawn;
- unable to create relationships with other children;
- often tired, indicating that they go to bed very late, watch late-night movies, accompany parents to bars or are locked out of the house for other reasons;
- dull-eyed and have a sad appearance;
- uncontrolled and uncontrollable, shifting from one activity to another with very short concentration spans, and incapable of listening to or following simple instructions;
- poorly skilled at communication;
- unable to express emotions, they don't cry when you would expect them to cry and they don't appear to feel pain when it obviously hurts;
- clinging and immature.

Some risk indicators based on the observation of parents

Neglect may be suspected when several of the following are observed:

- there is a poor history of parenting or a history of psychiatric illness or intellectual disability in the family;
- family organisation is obviously chaotic and the home is neglected;
- the parents are young, immature and put their own needs first;
- the mother is unwell, unkempt, depressed and angry;
- the mother has frequent changes of partner;
- the child is given inappropriate responsibilities;
- the mother reveals that the neglected child was unwanted or that she wanted an abortion but was 'talked out of it';
- parents complain that they can't cope with their neglected children, referring to them in derogatory terms as difficult, unmanageable or stupid;
- the parent greets the child indifferently: there is no eye-to-eye contact and no spontaneous joy in the relationship;

- the parent grabs the child, drags or tugs when movement is desired;
- adult–child communications are usually commands or complaints: the parent does not know how to talk to or play with the child;
- the parents show no concern for the child's well-being when one could reasonably expect concern;
- parents work shifts or at night and there are no indications that childminders are used;
- the family is isolated from other families in the community and has no support network;
- the parents have drug or alcohol problems;
- the parents are overwhelmed with other problems.

TASKS FOR STUDENTS

1 Establish who has the right to enter a house to remove a young distressed child who has been left alone for a considerable amount of time.
2 What criteria would you use for deciding whether a suspected case of neglect should be reported?

CASE STUDY

Mushtaq Ahmed (aged five) comes to school dirty, dishevelled and smelling. Other children ostracise him and do not want to sit next to him. Bearing in mind that the child's self-esteem must not be damaged nor should the parents be alienated, what if anything would you do to help the child to be accepted by his peers?

6

PHYSICAL ABUSE OF CHILDREN

The physical abuse of children commonly includes non-accidental injuries incurred by biting, burning, scalding, hitting with fists, hands, canes, belts, electrical cords and other hard objects. Young children are often injured when they are shaken or thrown against walls and other hard surfaces.

PHYSICAL SIGNS

The signs of physical abuse are numerous. They include the following.

Bruises

Physical abuse often leaves bruises. When they are of varying colours, this indicates that there have been several incidents of inappropriately rough handling. Thumb and hand prints can sometimes be recognised when the child has been firmly grasped or limbs have been pulled or twisted. Abuse may be indicated by bruises on the face, particularly when compatible with the shape of the palm of an adult's hand or fingers. Multiple linear bruises or welts may indicate the use of a strap, cane or electrical cord. Multiple bruises should be treated with suspicion in infants because they rarely suffer accidental multiple bruising.

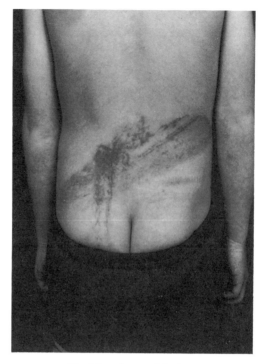

Bruising from whipping

Bilateral injuries

The presence of two black eyes should be regarded with suspicion, especially if there is no logical explanation for their presence. It is important to note that when children fall accidentally, they usually cut the protruding areas of the face, such as the chin or eyebrow. One black eye may occur if the child is hit directly with a cricket ball but the chances of being hit in both eyes by two cricket balls is very remote. Black eyes sometimes occur along with other facial or head injuries as a result of a road traffic accident.

Injuries to the body surface

When children are hit across the face, they sometimes suffer injuries to the mouth or gums (including the loss of teeth). A new bald patch on the head may indicate that a child has been dragged by the hair. Children pulled by the ears may suffer tears where the ear joins the head. Boys are sometimes injured in the genital area when they have been punched or kicked.

Burns and scalds

Cigarette burns are commonly found on young victims of physical abuse. These occur when, in a moment of rage, the adult holds the child down and presses a burning cigarette against accessible skin. These burns are found on arms, thighs and trunk. Cigarette burns darken with age and can be mistaken for chickenpox scabs.

Burns from radiators, electric fires and hot pokers are quite distinctive in that they show the shape of the hot object; for example, you can often identify the pointed end of a steam iron and the holes where steam was released. Rope burns to the arms, wrists or ankles suggest that the child could have been tied down for a prolonged period of time.

Some scalds are deliberately inflicted by the adult pouring hot water over a child's body. If perpetrators provide an explanation, it is usually that the children pulled a pan from a stove or a teapot from a table. When such accidents occur, the scalds are usually down the front of the body. When hot liquid is poured from an adult's height, the scald is more likely to include the child's head and back.

Adults sometimes punish children by holding them down in a bath of hot water. They give the explanation that the child stepped into the bath without first checking the temperature of the water. Apart from the fact that young children cannot usually climb into a bath without adult assistance, when we accidentally place one foot in very hot water, we never put the second foot into it. We remove the first foot as quickly as possible. If there is a scald mark, it is unevenly distributed across the foot and ankle. When children are held in hot water in anger or as a form of punishment, both feet are likely to be affected and the scald covers the feet evenly with a sock-like effect. If children accidentally step into a hot bath, the sole of the foot is involved; when water is deliberately poured over a foot, the sole may be undamaged.

Abrasions

Long slim abrasions appear when children are whipped with electrical cords. Sometimes the marks of the plug may be identified on the child's skin. Wider abrasions result from being abused with a belt. Sometimes the shape of the buckle is revealed.

A contact burn from an iron

Sock scalds from forced immersion

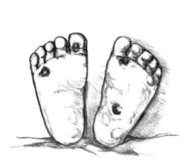

Cigarette burns

Doughnut scalds from immersion

Adult bite marks may be found on the child's body or face (crescent shaped, possibly with the indentation of teeth).

Fractures

Any fractures in a child under six months of age must be regarded with suspicion. Suspicion should increase when there are two or more fractures at different stages of resolution or the injury appears to be inconsistent with the explanation given or where a skeletal lesion is noted.

Haemorrhages

Haemorrhages may occur when a child has been severely shaken or beaten across the head. One of the first cases involving death by shaking was heard at Leeds Crown Court, England, in September 1986. Dean Clark, aged three, was shaken so violently that he lost consciousness and died. The offender, said to be engaged to the child's mother, claimed that a clock fell off the wall and struck the child while he lay in bed. Although a 'catalogue of injuries' included spinal and internal injuries, the pathologist confirmed that the death was the result of excessive shaking.

BEHAVIOURAL AND PHYSICAL INDICATORS OF PHYSICAL ABUSE

In an infant under two years indicators may include:

- brain damage from being shaken or having the head banged against a wall;
- frequent fractures;
- delays in motor development;
- unhappy appearance or frozen watchfulness as if expecting something bad to happen;
- deafness or impaired vision;
- flinching when approached by adults;
- poor sleeping patterns;
- fretfulness;
- delays in language development and communications.

In a child aged between two and six years, all of the indicators above may be present, and any of the following:

- lack of bowel or bladder control;

- aggression to get what he/she wants;
- withdrawal;
- self-destructive behaviour;
- destructiveness with pets and toys;
- poor self-image.

In a child of over six years, any of the above may be noted plus any of the following:

- poor school performance;
- truancy;
- running away from home;
- anorexia or bulimia;
- poor peer relations;
- experiments with substance abuse, such as drugs and alcohol, adhesive or petrol sniffing;
- blatant shoplifting and other forms of stealing;
- arrives at school early and postpones returning home for as long as possible;
- clings to a safe person, especially in the playground;
- flinches when there is a sudden movement.

PREDICTORS OF CHILD PHYSICAL ABUSE

There is a *high risk of abuse* when the mother has a violent partner or the partner is not the father of the child. The risks increase if the mother is a single parent or she and/or her partner are indifferent to the child. A child living in these circumstances is twenty-one times more likely to be physically abused than those in the medium risk group (Browne 1993).

There is a *medium risk of abuse* when the child lives in a disadvantaged family with many problems, such as a history of psychiatric illness and/or drug or alcohol dependency. The risk increases if the parents were abused in childhood or the baby was premature with a low birth-weight, separated from the mother at birth and bonding was severed or disrupted.

There is a *low risk of abuse* when the child and mother were separated at birth or the mother is immature or the child is living with a father replacement figure. There is also a risk for children with disabilities and those born in rapid succession with gaps between births of eighteen months or less.

In 82 per cent of British cases, it was found that there were insecure attachments between parent and child (Browne 1993).

It is important to note that two-thirds of potentially abusive parents can be helped by early intervention.

OTHER RISK INDICATORS: PARENT'S BEHAVIOUR

The parent reveals low tolerance thresholds

The parent shows impatience, a quick temper, aggression or uses verbal abuse to the child, the staff, other parents or other children when there is little or no provocation. Such parents are often overly dependent on physical punishment and use it or threaten to use it whenever children displease them. They may even authorise and expect teachers to whack their children when they misbehave.

The parents are ignorant of or disregard children's needs

Abusive parents are often immature, childlike individuals who expect children to love them and meet their own emotional needs (in other words, there is role reversal). Some abusive parents seem to be incapable of empathising with their children. They are apathetic and unresponsive when professionals express serious concerns about children's health or well-being.

Abusive parents may avoid seeking medical help when help is clearly needed. Alternatively, they move from one hospital casualty unit to another in the hope of avoiding detection. They show no concern for children's discomfort when concern would normally be expected. They show indifference to victims' achievements at school or preschool. They show irritability when children seek attention.

High-risk parents may complain that infants scream continually and cannot be satisfied. Some completely ignore children's needs for food, attention and cleanliness.

Abusive parents often give hints that they dislike their victims; for example, they complain that the children are abnormal or 'stupid'. They accuse them of being bad, deliberately difficult ('just to annoy me'), unmanageable, different from the others, unwanted, defiant, a nuisance, miserable, fretful and clumsy kids who are incapable of doing anything right.

The parents offer no explanation for obvious injuries or, when questioned, they provide vague, bizarre or implausible explanations

Most abusive parents avoid school and preschool when children are showing signs of injury. If a professional expresses concern about abrasions, bruises or burns, the abusive parent often provides an implausible response; for example, that a young baby 'fell from her cot' or 'fell down the steps' when the child is developmentally immobile.

There is a history of family dysfunction and/or child maltreatment

The family often has a long history of maltreating children and it is likely that the offending parent was abused in childhood. In serious cases, there is often a history of unexplained child deaths or injuries in previous generations. There may also be a history of children being removed from their homes and placed in the care of the state.

The parent is suffering from severe stress

Abusive parents are often highly stressed and have problems with physical and/or mental health, employment (or chronic unemployment), drug and/or alcohol abuse, substandard housing stress, financial problems, too many pregnancies or unsatisfactory sexual relationships.

In recent years, hospitals have become aware of parents who injure their children or take obviously healthy children for medical treatment to gain attention for themselves. This condition is known as Munchausen's Syndrome by Proxy (James 1994).

SOCIAL ISOLATION

Geographic or social isolation are common features of abusive families. Social isolation may involve parents spending a lot of time alone with their victims ensuring that the children have no support from friends or relatives. If children try to create friendships, the friends are belittled and derided and actively discouraged from visiting each others' homes.

Frequent home moves add to the sense of isolation. Mobility is especially likely when parents are in temporary accommodation or caravan parks and they suspect that the school or preschool staff are concerned about their behaviour.

WHO HURTS CHILDREN?

Most acts of physical abuse are committed by mothers. This is not because women are more violent than men; it is an indication of the amount of time that children spend in their mother's company. The serious injuries that feature in court cases are usually committed by men, often the mother's violent, immature partner who has been placed in a parenting role with children from a previous relationship. In many cases, the mother is aware of the violence and either ignores it, condones it or is a party to it.

Strang's analysis of non-accidental Australian child deaths showed that of the 86 children killed between 1989 and 1992, there were 60 killed by their parents or parent figures, 3 by other relatives, 12 by acquaintances, 3 by strangers and 8 unknown (Strang 1996).

THE RISKS FOR DIFFICULT INFANTS

One of the most common explanations given for physical abuse of babies is that 'he (or she) wouldn't stop crying'. The baby is fretful and colicky and cries continuously for hours at a time. The parents become desperate in the desire to locate the cause of the problem and pacify the child. The baby is fed, burped and changed. Gripe water is given and the parent rocks the baby, sings and paces the room holding the child. When the baby eventually falls asleep and is returned to the cot, the crying starts again. Anyone who has cared for a continuously screaming infant knows the sense of inadequacy, helplessness and frustration that results. Parents who started out with high expectations of parenthood feel despondent when the child cannot be placated. When they have made every possible effort to comfort the child and failed, they gain no pleasure from being parents. Lacking sleep, disillusioned and overwrought, there is then a risk that the child will be hurt.

Caregivers need help when they find themselves screaming at infants or throwing them angrily into their cots. Those who recognise that they are reaching the limits of their endurance close the door, turn on the radio to drown the sound and call a 24-hour crisis line. The caregiver who has other stresses, a short temper and does not know that crisis lines exist is likely to hurt the child because 'I couldn't stand the crying and I wanted it to stop'. Paradoxically, hitting is only likely to silence a distressed baby or toddler when the child becomes unconscious.

UNREALISTIC EXPECTATIONS OF CHILDREN

When adult caregivers have low tolerance levels and are ignorant of developmental norms, they are highly likely to punish children inappropriately for their normal childish behaviour. The most vulnerable times are those involving feeding and toilet training.

When we prepare a meal for someone, we become emotionally involved in the preparation. If the recipient rejects the food, we may feel rejected. The parent who has unrealistic expectations of children thinks, 'I prepared that just for you. You don't care about my feelings.' The child is then perceived as provocative and malicious, that is, the act of refusal was deliberately calculated to annoy the adult. If the caregiver is unsupported and unrestricted, believes in physical punishment as a legitimate option and is experiencing other frustrations in life, food refusal may trigger an excessive, violent reaction.

Similarly, violence against children often relates to inappropriate expectations during toilet training. Following his death, the mother of Melbourne toddler, Sean Dobson, told television viewers that her husband had only used excessive violence when Sean refused to use the toilet. She said that violence was appropriate in these circumstances although the child was little more than a year old at the time.

Adults who do not understand the norms of development assume that young children are capable of controlling their bowel and bladder functions. When babies soil their nappies soon after being changed, the adults think that the soiling is deliberate 'to make more work for me', attributing malice to normal behaviour.

Bed-time commonly presents problems for parents of young children who lack consistent routines. The parent tells the child to go to bed. The television watcher and the video game player demand extra time. They wheedle, coax, bargain, entreat, plead, cry and throw tantrums until eventually the adult's patience snaps and violence is used.

When there are several children in a family, their home-coming from school can also be a stressful time. Tired children seeking their mother's undivided attention are apt to whine, tease, compete, torment, bully or fight each other leading to heavy-handed parental intervention.

Stress and frustration are closely associated with the physical maltreatment of children. The frustration may not relate to the child in question; for example, there may have been an argument between the parent and another adult and the child just happens to appear and cause a minor irritation at the wrong moment. The parent's response is unpredictable and inappropriate. The insecure child may exhibit emotionally disturbed, attention-seeking behaviours which irritate the parent further.

Accidents also trigger the wrath of irritable parents; for example, the child who accidentally wipes off dad's video of the football final is likely to be smacked heavily by an enthusiastic football fan who believes in corporal punishment. Similarly, the child who disobeys an instruction (such as, 'Don't touch that can of paint') and has an accident is vulnerable to physical abuse resulting from anger and frustration.

The combination of physical punishment and rage can be deadly if the abuser does not know when to stop. Afterwards, the adult may feel badly about the loss of control and the injury inflicted on the child but if the conditioning is deeply ingrained, professional intervention is needed to teach positive child management techniques and stress management strategies.

Most abusive parents dislike what they do to children. The violence is an indication that they are gaining no pleasure from their parenting role. Most are concerned about their behaviour and fearful of the consequences. As stress increases, the adults place more and more reliance on coercion and violence to control the irritating daily events (Wolfe 1991).

Most child abusers can be helped. Only a small minority of offenders take a perverse delight in being cruel to weak, defenceless children. They are often women suffering from psychiatric illness and violent, immature men placed unwillingly in a childminding role.

FATAL ABUSE

In the United States, 'homicide and suicide are the second and third leading cause of death among children and youth under the age of 21. Sixteen to 19 year olds now have the highest rate of handgun victimisation among all age groups' (O'Donnell 1995, p. 771).

Fortunately, child homicide rates are not as high in Australia, New Zealand and Great Britain; yet as Heather Strang shows, child homicides do occur and some patterns can be identified from police data collected between 1989 and 1993. In Australia, 'the homicide rate for children under one year of age was almost half as great again as for the population as a whole' (Strang 1996, p. 4). Infants were the victims of physical assault, such as being shaken, kicked, dropped, thrown or beaten with fists, whereas older children were more often the victims of firearms and knives.

The greatest risk of homicide to Australian children is from their own parents. Fathers were the most frequent offenders, then mothers, then de facto fathers. Deaths most commonly occurred following family disputes which often led to a male becoming enraged or depressed and subsequently using a firearm to kill his estranged wife and children (often followed immediately by his suicide). The clearest risk factor of all was the child's age. Where victims were less than six months old, mothers were the most frequent offenders and where the victims were older than six months the mothers' new partners were the most frequent offenders.

Strang noted in particular that offenders were young (mostly under 21). Non-biological fathers were frequently involved and instability and poverty were very common background factors.

EFFECTS OF NON-FATAL PHYSICAL ABUSE

When children experience physical abuse on a frequent basis, they are unlikely to develop coping skills and enjoy sound emotional health (Farber & Egeland 1987). Some of the common effects of physical abuse are brain damage, intellectual retardation, deafness, internal injuries, psychiatric illness and emotional scars, low self-esteem, loneliness, self-destructiveness (drug and alcohol addiction) and suicide (Kosky 1987) and the inability to create long-term trusting relationships with others. There may be an outward manifestation of the abuse with the victim becoming the victimiser.

In school or preschool, the victim may be withdrawn or, at the opposite extreme, one who constantly seeks attention and approval. Attendance may be sporadic due to chronic illness, allergies and frequent injuries.

Children who do not receive nurturing from caregivers do not learn to trust. If they grow up to be angry people, they have a future in juvenile delinquency and adult criminality. Abused children are 40 per cent more likely than non-abused to be arrested for violent crimes (Widom 1992).

Excessive corporal punishment teaches children to resolve conflict violently. To tolerate the violence, some children 'switch off' so that they do not feel the pain. This tends to make them insensitive to other people's hurt. They then show no conscience when conscience might be expected and the abuse cycle is repeated.

APPROACHING THE PARENT SUSPECTED OF MARGINAL PHYSICAL ABUSE

When mothers are in danger of hurting their children, they often give hints that they are reaching a crisis point; for example, they may indicate that their children are unmanageable and unlovable and make statements such as, 'The kids are driving me mad . . . One of these days, I'll kill them.'

When physical abuse is suspected, it is obviously helpful if a member of staff is sufficiently at ease with the mother to receive information and empathise with her problems. Ask the parent what triggers the child's misbehaviour, when does it happen, how frequently does it happen and how does the parent respond. If she is signalling that help is needed, it is appropriate to enquire whether she is already hurting the child.

In most communities, there are services to help parents to improve their child management skills. Some services provide respite care. Others offer telephone help lines such as Crisis Care, Lifeline and Parents Anonymous. Professionals working with children should familiarise themselves with the range of services available to families in their towns or cities. Leaflets relating to services should be displayed on parents' noticeboards.

Early childhood professionals find it relatively easy to maintain a rapport with parents who bring their children or collect them from school or preschool at the end of the day. Open communications are especially likely when the school or centre practises an 'open door' policy and parent–staff contact is not limited to a few minutes at the beginning and end of the school day. When home visits are made routinely, staff can identify problems in the early stages and help to prevent abuse from occurring or becoming serious.

If the child is new to the school, it would be useful to make contact with the previous school or early childhood centre to enquire whether staff had any concerns or could throw light on the home circumstances. Teachers in Adelaide, South Australia, were concerned about the well-being of a newly enrolled child who was timid, undersized and had a large scar on her head. When they contacted her former school in a Sydney suburb, they found that the child had suffered a fractured skull as the result of a blow from her mother's lover. The couple had kidnapped her from foster parents.

It is not appropriate for members of staff to interrogate children about how they received their injuries because those who were abused will recite whatever their abusers told them to say. Sometimes children inadvertently reveal what triggered the attack when asked, 'What did you do to deserve that black eye?' However, there is a risk that victims will suffer further abuse if offenders find out that they disclosed what happened.

Despite directions to the contrary, some members of staff make the mistake of confronting parents directly with their concerns about bruises, abrasions and cigarette burns. This is unproductive because parents become defensive, fearful and feel obliged to lie about what happened. However ludicrous the story, the teacher is unlikely to say, 'I don't believe you'.

When an injury is caused by an accident, parents usually tell staff all about it when they bring the children to the centre or school. They explain what occurred with a sense of guilt and embarrassment, drawing attention to the child's injuries. By contrast, most abusive parents avoid members of staff and they make no confessions. They may appear to be indifferent to the victim's discomfort and there is rarely any sign of remorse.

Contact with parents should be made when concerns first arise. Contact must, of necessity, be personal, uncritical and non-threatening. The art of developing a helpful relationship with parents depends less on the ability to talk to them than the ability to listen and make them feel comfortable. If parents can talk freely about the stresses that engulf them, their loneliness or lack of family support, staff will be in a much better position to help the family. When they have a comfortable relationship with parents, confrontation is unnecessary. They start out from concern about the parent, *not* the child.

'How are you? I haven't seen you for ages. I was wondering about you! Can you spare a few minutes . . . I'm ready for a cup of tea' is likely to be more productive than, 'I am concerned about your son's bruises. How did he get them?'

Gentle questioning may reveal that parents are under a lot of strain. If parents sense that the questioner is genuinely concerned about the family, it becomes easier for them to be honest about their problems.

Physical abuse and neglect should be regarded as indications that a family needs help. We are all capable of hurting children in circumstances which stress us beyond the point of endurance. When parents care for their children, they can be persuaded to accept help simply because they care. This should be put forward as a positive, responsible step, not a sign of failure or weakness. Mothers tend to be much more responsive than fathers because of the social conditioning which tells men that they have to resolve their own problems.

Schools and early childhood centres that maintain contact with their local child protection officers and support agencies can assist physically abusive parents in a practical way along the lines of, 'I can see that you need help. I know someone who can help you. His/her name is (name). He/she works with (organisation). Is it okay if we give him/her a call?'

Referring parents to agencies is seldom effective. They are too embarrassed to telephone strangers and say, 'I've got a problem'. The most effective method is to phone the agency while the parent is present and, if possible, ask to speak to a social worker you know by name. Introduce yourself and the parent, informing the social worker that the parent is 'very concerned about the safety of her child (name) who is (age) years old and attends this school/centre'. Add important information, for example, that the parent is unsupported, has other children under school age and is under a great deal of stress. Conclude with, 'I'm putting Mrs (name) on the line. Here she is now.'

If staff are required by law to report suspicions of abuse, they are fulfilling their legal obligations when they use this approach. The advantage is that the parents are presented as responsible, concerned people. They retain their dignity and the staff–parent relationship remains intact. Using the formal reporting method, that relationship is likely to be strained, the child may be blamed, re-abused and moved elsewhere.

91

When staff adopt a caring approach, parents are more likely to be honest and, when further problems occur, they are in a better position to help the child.

However, it should be made clear that not all abusive parents want help or respond to genuine concerns about their families. Some parents will deny that they have a problem. Some will tell you to mind your own business. Others will provide implausible explanations for the succession of injuries. In all of these situations the abuse *must* be formally reported to child protection authorities.

In most cases, parents who use physical violence are ordinary people who love their children, suffer tremendous personal problems, lack skills in child management and are not coping with their lives. They can be helped within their own communities with the provision of services such as respite care, day care, better housing, parent education and the acquisition of child management skills (O'Neill 1994).

TASKS FOR STUDENTS

1 a Establish which professionals have the right to take injured children to hospital for the treatment of injuries which were not received on your premises.

   b When parents enrol children in schools and preschools, they are often required to give written consent for their children to receive medical treatment for injuries. Check the wording of these agreements very carefully to establish whether your parent-clients have authorised you to seek treatment for injuries not received on your premises.

2 A nine-year-old boy has several welts across the backs of both legs. He says that his dad instructed him not to ride his bike on the driveway. He ignored his father and accidentally crashed into and damaged his new Jaguar car. His dad 'whacked' him. Would you report the abuse? Discuss.

3 Sophie, aged fifteen, has two black eyes. She explains that she returned home at 3 am, gave her father a 'mouthful' and he hit her. Would you report the abuse? Discuss.

4 What help could be offered to parents who admit to having difficulty in managing their children?

7

CHILDREN LIVING WITH DOMESTIC VIOLENCE

Human society has a long history of regarding women and children as the property of men. In some cultures, marriage still gives husbands the right to control their wives and children in every social and financial aspect of their lives. Until comparatively recently, Western governments permitted husbands to beat their wives whenever it suited them. Women tolerated abuse because there was no support for those who tried to escape; without a welfare state, they were trapped by financial dependence. Unfortunately, domestic violence is still a very common problem.

There are clear links between domestic violence and all forms of child abuse. Goddard and Hiller (1993) found that 55 per cent of child physical abuse cases and 40 per cent of child sexual abuse cases occurred in families where domestic violence also occurred.

Children become indirect victims, either through witnessing violence or sharing their mothers' fears, frustration and stress. Children are often directly implicated in family violence, a factor rarely reported in academic studies.

Children's reactions to parental violence vary according to their development and gender, and position and role in the family. Other factors include the frequency and extent of the violence, the level of insecurity caused by separations and moves, economic and social disadvantage and the violence itself.

THE NATURE OF DOMESTIC VIOLENCE

Theories link domestic violence with stress and social problems such as unemployment, alcohol abuse, having large numbers of children and living in poverty (Straus et al. 1980).

Some theories explain domestic violence as learned behaviour. Retrospective accounts of men who battered their wives indicate that the vast majority witnessed similar violence in their families of origin (Herman 1986). Based on a nationwide study, Straus et al. (1980) estimated that sons who witness their fathers abusing their mothers are ten times more likely than others to perpetuate the abuse cycle. Similarly, women reared in violent homes are likely to be attracted to men like their fathers; they then adopt the victim role learned from their mothers and the cycle of violence continues from one generation to the next (Price & Armstrong 1978).

Feminist theorists perceive domestic violence as a control issue relating to structural inequalities in male and female roles. It occurs irrespective of the level of family income. Its widespread nature was only determined in the 1970s and substantiated in more recent times (Ammerman & Hersen 1990; Browne & Herbert 1993).

Browne (1993) found similarities between the personalities of men who abuse their wives and men who abuse their children. He shows that the offences are interrelated. The commonalities include a misperception of the victim, low self-esteem, a sense of incompetence, social isolation, a lack of support, lack of empathy, marital difficulties, depression, poor self-control and a history of abuse and neglect in childhood.

Although some women abuse their partners and domestic violence is not uncommon among homosexual couples, when we talk about domestic violence we are usually referring to a relationship where the woman experiences persistent or serious physical, psychological, economic and/or social abuse from her male partner and suffers sustained harmful psychological effects. Male to female violence accounts for between 90 and 95 per cent of reported domestic violence throughout the English-speaking world. Here, we are referring to a major imbalance of power, not heated arguments in which the woman 'gives as good as she gets'.

Domestic violence takes many forms: physical violence, psychological abuse, and social, sexual and economic abuse. Sexual and physical abuse are usually preceded and accompanied by psychological and emotional abuse (Browne 1993).

THE PREVALENCE OF DOMESTIC VIOLENCE

It is difficult to establish how widespread domestic violence is because the problem is well hidden, especially among middle-class families and those where separation and divorce are considered to be shameful.

In the United States, Straus et al. (1980) found that a third of all women were physically abused by their partners at some time during their relationship. In Canada, MacLeod (1980) estimated that 10 per cent of all women are victims of physical violence each year. Figures are remarkably similar in the United States, Canada and the United Kingdom (Jaffe et al. 1990; MacLeod 1987; Dobash & Dobash 1979). Some studies have shown that there are 30 to 40 violent episodes before the police are called (Daw & Male 1992).

Roy (1977) noted that 95 per cent of American victims did not report the violence, not even when the children were victimised. Managers of women's refuges claim that even fewer reports (i.e. 1–2 per cent) are made by Australian victims (James 1994).

Interviews with 258 New Zealand children showed that one-third of five-year-olds and a quarter of all six-year-olds lived in homes where fathers or father figures abused their mothers. Many of the Pacific Island children reported witnessing their fathers and uncles use traditional fishing knives to instil fear and inflict injury on their mothers and other relatives (Briggs 1990, 1991a & b, 1994). New Zealand mothers told the authors that they instructed their children to remain silent because 'what goes on in our house is nobody else's business' (Briggs & Hawkins 1996a). The reluctance to report relates to fears of reprisal, feelings of guilt and shame, exacerbated by the history of unsupportive responses from police and criminal courts.

THE PSYCHOLOGICAL (INCLUDING VERBAL) ABUSE OF WOMEN

Psychological abuse is involved in all forms of domestic violence. It includes threats, harassment, denigration of the woman's personality, her appearance, and her capacity as a household manager, cook, wife, mother and sexual partner. It consists of persistent 'putting down' to demean and destabilise, thereby increasing the power of the male abuser.

At the bottom end of the continuum, psychological abuse starts with constant carping about her appearance or body image ('you're gross . . . have you looked at yourself lately?'), her sexual attractiveness . . . ('there's no need to look at yourself in the mirror . . . you're just a slut'), her inadequacies in the performance of minor household tasks and her inability to cope alone ('I don't know what you'd do if I wasn't around; you wouldn't cope for five minutes on your own'). The abuse is neither obvious nor measurable but it can be devastating in its effects. 'Many women endure such abuse for decades. They come to believe what is said; they become certain of their own incapacity to cope; and feel guilty about this state of affairs' (Mugford 1989, p. 2).

Verbal abuse escalates to frightening, constant harassment: 'You're a bitch, a whore, a slag. Why don't you take your ugly face out of here. I wish I'd never set eyes on you.' The aim of the abuser is to humiliate, degrade, demean, intimidate and subjugate, and increase his own control.

Threats constitute a form of psychological abuse. They can be direct, such as 'I'll kill you and the kids', or indirect, such as 'If you won't be mine, I'll make sure you're no-one else's'.

THE SOCIAL ABUSE OF WOMEN

There are three main manifestations of social abuse. First, there is the persistent denigration and verbal abuse of the female partner in the company of others. He makes snide remarks about her appearance, personality and capabilities and uses her as the butt for his jokes to destroy her self-esteem.

Second, it is social abuse when women are prevented by their partners (for example, by geographical isolation, lack of access to transport and telecommunications) from making social contacts. This can also happen in cities. An Asian 'mail-order bride' with no knowledge of English was virtually incarcerated in her home. Her husband intercepted her phone calls and mail from relatives. She was not allowed to sit in the living room or watch television. Although a university graduate, she was constantly told by her uneducated spouse that she was a stupid, 'no good' wife who would be deported in disgrace if she attempted to leave him. Women's shelters confirm that it is not unusual for 'correspondence brides' to be subjected to this kind of treatment. They may lose their confidence and in time perceive themselves exactly as they have been described.

The third type of social abuse involves 'smothering' the female partner. Initially, she feels flattered and cherished. He takes her to work, brings her home and phones several times during the day. Gradually, his attention becomes oppressive. He constantly checks her whereabouts and demands explanations for momentary absences. He accuses her of unfaithfulness if she is not instantly available. In mixed company, she dare not talk to males because she knows that she will be accused of 'flirting'. He likes her to look attractive to benefit his own ego but, if anyone else pays attention to her, he accuses her of behaving like a 'slut'. By his use of various ruses, she is gradually prevented from seeing former friends. Her supportive relatives are banned and branded as 'trouble'. She is made to feel guilty and disloyal if she seeks anyone's company other than his. If there is no intervention, she loses her support network and her social and survival skills. The social abuser acquires total control over her life and becomes her only reference point.

PHYSICAL VIOLENCE

The most obvious form of domestic violence is physical abuse. On a continuum, this begins with a lack of consideration for the partner's needs, escalating to actions such as shaking, pushing, kicking, shoving, twisting limbs and immobilising her by putting pressure on parts of the body. At the extreme, physical violence results in physical injury or, in some cases, death.

A New Zealand study by Church (1994) of 101 abused women found that 100 of the women had been physically abused and 67 per cent were subjected to one or more beatings which were so serious that, at the time, the women doubted whether they would survive. Sixty-two per cent of the women said that their husbands had threatened to kill them on more than one occasion and 20 per cent had been threatened with a gun.

SEXUAL ABUSE AS DOMESTIC VIOLENCE

Sexual abuse is also associated with physical abuse. This may start with the sexual objectification of the partner through sexual jokes and humiliating, derisive comments in the company of other men. It escalates to rape, non-consensual anal intercourse and sadistic, degrading or violent acts involving animals, the use of penetrating household objects and injury to the reproductive organs, for example. Women who live with domestic violence are often expected to provide sex immediately after a beating. They endure this form of abuse when they have been conditioned to believe that they are helpless and incapable of managing their lives without their abusers. Some cultures and religions also inhibit women from leaving their marriages, whatever the circumstances. It is especially difficult to leave an arranged marriage where the bridegroom's family paid for the bride.

ECONOMIC ABUSE

Two forms of economic abuse are commonly encountered. One is when the man provides the woman with an inadequately small housekeeping allowance and demands that she does the impossible with it while he spends the remainder of his income on his own pleasures. When she fails, this results in verbal and/or physical abuse.

The second form is when the woman is prevented from gaining access to money which is rightfully her own, such as her wages or an inheritance. The lack of financial independence traps her in the relationship.

Women are least likely to leave violent relationships when their husbands hold high status positions, the women are financially dependent and they live in comfortable homes.

THE CYCLE OF PHYSICAL VIOLENCE

Most domestic violence follows a cyclical pattern. There are three obvious phases: the *build-up* period, the *explosion* and the period of *remorse* which incorporates the *buy back* or *honeymoon* phase. The capacity to identify these phases is useful to both partners in that it helps them to have a better understanding of the problem and helps the victim to understand that she is not responsible for his outbursts. This sequence of events happens so frequently that it is referred to as a pattern.

In the *build-up* period he insults, provokes, complains and verbally abuses. This period may last for several days or several minutes. The anger grows more intense and there is nothing that the victim can do to quell it. He cannot express himself coherently. He brings up trivial grievances from the distant past and tells her that she has no genuine friends and is disliked by everyone. He may raise issues of independence ('For God's sake leave me alone') or dependence ('You don't care about me. You only care about yourself').

The *explosion* is the most dangerous phase because he appears to be out of control and lashes out with physical and verbal violence, sometimes smashing treasured possessions and using whatever weapons come to hand. Abusers are usually not truly 'out of control' because they often restrict their violence to the privacy of the home, rarely assault their partners in the presence of adult witnesses and sometimes deliberately aim blows at areas where bruises cannot be seen. They abuse when they have been drinking alcohol but this should be regarded as an excuse for, not the cause of violence.

The *remorse* phase is characterised by feelings of guilt and sadness. He says that he is sorry and promises faithfully (and truly believes) that it will never happen again. He does not accept responsibility for his actions but seeks explanations outside himself. He is most likely to respond to help at this stage because he is in touch with his own pain. If nothing happens to change his pattern of behaviour, old conflicts reappear, tensions rise, old habits and attitudes return and the build-up begins once again. Without professional intervention, the periods between explosions become shorter and shorter. The assaults increase in severity and/or frequency.

The point is reached where the victim realises that there is a problem but they both believe that she provokes the attacks or that the cause is some outside factor such as alcohol, fatigue, work-related stress or exhausting children. She considers seeking advice but believes that she will be blamed or no-one will believe her (because he is charming to friends and relatives). She doubts her own judgement about the seriousness of the situation because he tells her (and she accepts) that she is a stupid, neurotic, over-sensitive bitch if not a psychiatric case.

When she threatens to leave, he increases the level of control; he tells her that she will lose everything—home, family and what little money she has. She tries harder to please him. She urges the children to remain silent when daddy is around because 'we don't want to upset him'. The abuse continues until something happens which makes her realise that she has to leave for her own or her children's safety. The breaking point may be when she finds that he has sexually abused the children. It may happen when she is seriously injured and is counselled to leave.

She leaves but feels guilty because she is still convinced that she is at fault. She loses the home that she created and she probably has no money. She perceives herself as depriving her children of their father, home, possessions, friends and financial support. She senses that she is a failure as a wife, mother and human being. Disempowered by her former partner and devoid of confidence, she is afraid of having to cope alone. She feels isolated but knows that relatives will neither believe nor support her.

Women in refuges are advised not to inform their mothers of their whereabouts because their mothers tell their fathers who, in turn, contact the abusers and tell them where to find their wives and children. Grandfathers often assume that offenders used their children for sex because their wives rejected them. Misunderstanding the nature and severity of the crime, they tell the abusers to 'get round there, take her home and make her behave like a proper wife'.

The abuser pursues her, tells her that he needs her and seeks her sympathy. In the *helpless* mode he makes her feel guilty when he complains that he isn't well, can't sleep, can't cook, hasn't any clean shirts and has lost his appetite. He neglects himself and the house. He says that he is lonely, misses her and can't manage without her and the children. He may threaten to commit suicide if she will not return. She capitulates because she feels needed and responsible for his depressed state of mind.

Alternatively, he resorts to the *buy back* mode, also known as the *honeymoon* phase. This is the time when he tries to show his sincerity by showering her with gifts, chocolates, flowers, promises of holidays and outings. She feels loved, attractive and valued again. He apologises profusely for past behaviour and swears that he has changed. There are strong pressures to return home because, at this stage, she is likely to have housing and financial problems, no home comforts and no support. He promises that the violence will never happen again. She wants to believe him.

His third option involves reliance on *terror* to achieve his goals. If she goes home, the pattern of abuse builds up again. If she escapes, he may dedicate his entire life and his resources to pursuing and stalking her and she may have to abandon her friends and relatives, to leave the area and change her and the children's names and identities.

He drives slowly past her new home many times a day, loitering near the school or her place of work. He threatens to destroy the home and everyone inside it. He persuades her to let him in to 'talk things over' but this provides just another opportunity for abuse. He makes threatening telephone calls at all times of the day and night. If she refuses to return, he escalates the pursuit in his desire to control her. He says that he will abduct the children and they also live in a state of terror, waiting for him to carry out his threat. He laughs at restraining orders which, more often than not, are never enforced. He thumbs his nose at the law and gets away with it.

The deaths of a large number of women who were 'protected' by restraining orders has led to the introduction of stalking legislation in most Western states and countries. If the victim remains strong and survives, the violent male finds another partner and the pattern begins all over again.

WHY DO WOMEN REMAIN WITH VIOLENT PARTNERS?

That question is often asked. The factors that prevent them from leaving vary from individual to individual but the commonly given reasons are that they:

- fear staying at home slightly less than they fear leaving;
- many women are threatened that, if they leave, the men will pursue them and kill them and the children (and some do);
- lack knowledge about support services;
- have neither access to transport nor money;
- have no support from family members;
- are restrained by shame relating to cultural, religious and traditional factors and/or the need to protect the family name;
- have 'nowhere to go', because there are no women's refuges in many rural areas;
- are reluctant to give up hard-earned financial security (women living in beautiful homes with high status men are the ones least likely to be believed and the least likely to leave, especially if they have children and no career);
- have limited opportunities for employment; and
- believe what their menfolk have told them over the years, that is, that they are helpless, stupid and will never cope without their abusers.

COMMUNITY ATTITUDES TO DOMESTIC VIOLENCE

In 1988, the Office of the Status of Women in the Department of the Prime Minister and Cabinet (Australia) commissioned two projects to survey community attitudes towards domestic violence. The second of these was an in-depth study which included rural, Aboriginal and non-English-speaking migrants. The nation was shocked to learn that one-third of the 1504 subjects believed that domestic violence was a 'private matter' that should be handled within the family. One in five respondents condoned the use of force by men against women and, surprisingly, there was no significant difference between male and female attitudes (17 per cent female: 22 per cent male). The survey also found that people with sexist attitudes were the ones most likely to have pro-violence attitudes, such as the belief that women who are beaten must have done something to deserve it. In other words, there was a strong feeling in the community that, in some circumstances, it was acceptable for a man to beat a wife (Office of the Status of Women 1988).

Edgar (1988) argues that the cultural toleration of violence is derived from our child-rearing values and practices and he suggests that we need to question and challenge the means by which we socialise boys to be aggressive and girls to be passive. We need to ask ourselves why we perpetuate a socialisation process which turns male victims into victimisers and predisposes female victims to choose relationships which replicate those of their parents.

RISKS TO CHILDREN IN VIOLENT HOMES

In most cases of domestic violence, children are present while an adult is abused. In the Queensland Domestic Task Force Phone-In (1988), 88 per cent of the 856 respondents reported that dependent children were present while they were abused and 68 per cent of these children were also abused by the same perpetrator (physical abuse, 68 per cent; psychological abuse, 70 per cent; sexual abuse, 8 per cent). Physical or sexual abuse of children was also identified in one-third of violent families studied by Hilberman and Munson in 1977–8.

Other international studies show similar results. Carlson (1984) estimated that 3.3 million American children lived with domestic violence and in 68 per cent of female-partner assault cases, children were present (Leighton 1989). Gayford (1975) found that four-fifths of battered women in British refuges could recall witnessing their mother being assaulted by their father in their early years. Pahl (1985) found that in 90 per cent of partnerships there was a child under five years present when the violence was taking place.

In the New Zealand study by Church (1994), 101 abused women reported that 29 per cent of their children had been severely beaten and 8 per cent had been sexually molested by the same male offender. In the United States, Straus et al. (1980) also found that parents in violent relationships were the ones most likely to abuse their children.

DOMESTIC VIOLENCE AS A LEARNED BEHAVIOUR

Social learning theory suggests that the experience of growing up in a violent family teaches children that violence is an integral part of family life, child management and partner behaviour. The role models most frequently learned from domestic violence are based on male aggression and female victimisation. Child witnesses may learn that:

- it is acceptable to show disrespect for their mothers, women in general and their adult female partners in particular;
- the way to cope with stress is by using violence;
- it is possible to love and physically hurt someone at the same time;
- violence is an acceptable and effective tool for conflict resolution;
- it is legitimate to use force and violence to accomplish personal goals.

In Church's (1994) New Zealand study, three-quarters of abused mothers had concerns about the emotional and social development of their children. Boys reproduced the male abuser's behaviour, physically and verbally abusing their mothers. Girls were so terrified of their fathers that they avoided them. Almost a quarter of all children were excessively aggressive and 18 per cent were withdrawn, 19 per cent were over-fearful and 19 per cent were clinging and insecure.

In a classic study undertaken by Bandura, it was shown that preschool children imitate the aggressive behaviours of an adult model when playing with dolls (Hetherington & Parke 1986) and the basis of transgenerational repetition of abuse seems to be linked with observational learning.

EFFECTS OF DOMESTIC VIOLENCE ON INFANTS AND PRESCHOOL CHILDREN

Infants are reactive to their environments. When they are distressed, they cry, scream, refuse food, become colicky and/or withdraw. The screaming increases their vulnerability to abuse. These children are highly susceptible to inconsistencies in handling and maternal deprivation, both of which are common features in violent homes (Jaffe et al. 1990).

Developmental evidence suggests that children begin to learn the importance of emotions for communication and regulation early in life. They turn to their primary caregivers for cues and, in violent homes, adopt their mothers' negative emotions (James 1994).

Toddlers and preschool children living with violence suffer frequent illness, increased anxiety, difficulty with attachment bonding, sleep problems, conduct disorders and psychosomatic difficulties, severe shyness and low self-esteem (Butterworth & Fulmer 1990). They exhibit behaviour problems such as hitting, biting, pinching, kicking and being argumentative with peers and younger siblings. Their mothers frequently find them 'demanding and unmanageable' which increases the risks to the children (Church 1994).

Cummings et al. (1981) found that expressions of anger cause distress in toddlers and this distress increases when verbal abuse is accompanied by physical violence. The more children are exposed to parents' rows, the greater the stress reactions. In other words, exposure to a harsh environment makes children feel insecure.

Gender differences often emerge in preschool years. Boys show more aggression, especially with their peers. They externalise their distress and get into trouble in early childhood centres for using violence to achieve their goals. Girls tend to be more introverted, passive, withdrawn, anxious and fretful. They cling to the early childhood staff with whom they feel safe (Blanchard et al. 1992; Blanchard, 1993).

EFFECTS OF DOMESTIC VIOLENCE ON CHILDREN AGED 5+

Osofsky (1995) has reviewed the effects of exposure to violence on young children. First she reported levels of violence which fortunately have not yet been matched in developed countries outside the United States. For example, Osofsky reported the study of Bell and Jenkins (1991) which showed that in a particular Chicago neighbourhood, 'one-third of all school age children had witnessed a homicide' (Osofsky 1995, p. 783). Osofsky also reported one of her own studies which showed that when children were asked to draw what happens in their neighbourhoods, they 'drew in graphic detail pictures of shootings, drug deals, stabbings, fighting, funerals and reported being scared of violence and of something happening to them' (Osofsky 1995, p. 783).

Osofsky's review noted:

- reactions to observing violence and aggression are likely to be generally similar to those following actual abuse and neglect;
- there are sex differences, with boys exhibiting more externalising responses and girls demonstrating more internalising responses;
- a dosage effect seems to occur (more negative outcomes are associated with greater exposure to anger);
- having a supportive person available and having a safe place in the neighbourhood are important factors for helping children cope with violence.

At this stage of their development, children look to their parents as role models. In violent homes they learn that violence is an effective way of resolving conflict and controlling others to achieve goals. At this stage, sex role stereotyping becomes evident, with boys using aggressive and disruptive behaviours and girls becoming passive, withdrawn, clinging and anxious (Butterworth & Fulmer 1990; James 1994). Church (1994) found that differences between boys and girls intensified at the 9–12 year age level.

At this age level, children in violent homes are able to talk to trusted adults about their anxieties, fears and dislike of their parents' behaviour but they may continue to blame themselves for what happens (Jaffe et al. 1990).

Other effects on children of 5–12 years from violent homes include:

- difficulties with school work, poor concentration, poor academic performance and school avoidance (Hughes 1986);
- psychosomatic illness, headaches, abdominal pains, asthma, stuttering and enuresis, depression and aggression;
- a high incidence of male to female peer violence in schools, ignoring antiharassment and antiviolence rules;
- poor social skills, fewer social activities, constant fights with peers, ignoring instructions and defying adult authority (Jaffe et al. 1990);
- decreased interpersonal sensitivity, that is, a reduction in ability to understand social situations including the thoughts and feelings of others directly involved (Family Violence Professional Education Taskforce 1991);
- more behaviour problems and lower social competence than those from non-violent homes (James 1994);
- 40 per cent had reading ages more than a year below their chronological ages (Mathias et al. 1995).

Through an attempt to rationalise their parents' violence, adolescents reared in violent homes form a negative self-image resulting in aggressive behaviour, poor sexual image, depression, helplessness and poor peer relationships (Butterworth & Fulmer 1990). Through the process of imitation, they can become socially deviant, often resulting in substance abuse, criminal activity and delinquency.

Teenage sons are more likely than others to accept and use violence as 'normal' behaviour in their relationships. They view females as appropriate targets for violence and violent sex. They are the ones most likely to exhibit conduct and personality disorders and experience profound, negative effects on social relationships (Butterworth & Fulmer 1990; Jouriles et al. 1989). Both boys and girls find it difficult to create long-term, trusting sexual relationships and this incapacity usually accompanies them into adulthood.

IMPLICATIONS FOR TEACHERS AND EARLY CHILDHOOD PROFESSIONALS

Schools and early childhood centres play an important role in providing community education for parents on the subject of domestic violence. Most domestic violence services are happy to provide talks to local groups.

Professionals working with children also need to understand that women who are frequently beaten by their partners are often looking for a way to escape from the violent relationship. They usually lack opportunities (and confidence) to investigate what services are available to help them.

The need for professional intervention

Early childhood professionals are often the first to know that a mother is being battered by her partner. They see the new bruises and black eyes when she brings her children to the centre. She may even confide to staff that her life has become intolerable and she must leave 'for the sake of the kids'. Professionals working with families should always know the whereabouts of domestic violence services and women's refuges so that they can talk knowledgeably about what is available and refer victims to appropriate support services. They should know the procedures for gaining access to shelters by night as well as by day.

Once the women are safe, counsellors work towards the development of their self-confidence, self-esteem and capacity to manage their lives. They provide opportunities for independence, assertiveness training and decision making, irrespective of whether they return to their partners.

Many men accept counselling when they realise there are more rewarding alternatives to abusive behaviour. Domestic violence services involve men's groups and individual, couple and family counselling. The evaluation of South Australian services suggests that in 80 per cent of cases, the violence ceases when men complete a programme.

The children and parents least able to obtain help are those in rural areas where no services exist.

Teach alternatives to violent behaviour

It is clear that young children from violent homes exhibit more problem behaviours than children from non-violent homes. These children need extra love and understanding and it is important that they are taught how to cope with the frustrations of their everyday lives so that they do not perpetuate the family violence as a perpetrator or as a victim.

Given that between one in three to five children come from violent homes and that 20 per cent of the population condones the resolution of domestic conflict by violent means, it is important for schools and early childhood centres to teach non-violent conflict resolution skills to all young children. They need to understand that violent behaviour is unnecessary and unacceptable. This means that educators and child care personnel must respond firmly to coercive and aggressive behaviours in children rather than attempt to compensate for a harsh home life by being more tolerant and lenient (Church 1994). Adults should be firm and not give in to temper tantrums or violence from conduct-disordered children because 'unless this lesson is learned at school, the chances are that the children from violent families will grow up to repeat the behaviour patterns of their parents' (Church 1994, p. 4).

Conflict resolution strategies should have the long-term aim of developing self-discipline, trust and helping children to feel more competent and in control of themselves. Adults show respect for children when they help them to see the possible consequences of their actions and give them the option of controlling their behaviour. This can be on the lines of, 'This is what you are doing right now. What do you think will happen if you continue? Is that what you really want? What can you do instead?' This approach indicates that we regard children as sufficiently sensible and reasonable to control themselves. Most will respond to this approach most of the time.

Butterworth and Fulmer (1990) wrote a curriculum for use in early childhood centres to empower all children and victims of violence in particular. It contains activities to assist children to:

- identify, label and express their feelings in socially acceptable ways;
- learn listening skills. Good communications are essential for negotiation during disputes;
- develop and practise problem-solving skills. This is important given that children from violent homes lack appropriate problem-solving strategies;
- develop self-esteem;
- learn gender equity.

The penultimate section of the curriculum provides a story, 'Sometimes mummy and daddy fight', and a bibliography of books for teaching children about using peaceful conflict resolution methods.

Teach children about domestic violence

Given that domestic violence is such a widespread problem, many schools now include the topic in studies relating to health or human relationships. It is, for example, part of the Kindergarten to Year 10 Prevention Education Supplement to the Health syllabus in schools in the state of Western Australia. The focus is on understanding the nature of domestic violence. The syllabus emphasises that healthy relationships are dependent on equal sharing, open communications and sensitivity to the needs of others without being victimised.

Teachers should provide information about services for children in violent homes. Children in primary and secondary schools should also be made aware of crisis and help telephone lines.

Watch out for child abuse

Teachers and child care personnel need to be aware that, in families where one parent is abused by another, there is a high risk of child abuse of all kinds. Teachers should remain alert to the signs and symptoms of emotional (psychological), sexual and physical abuse.

STATEMENTS TO THE FAMILY COURT

Increasing numbers of separated fathers are seeking the day-to-day care of their children through the Family Court.

Because teachers and early childhood personnel see children more frequently than social workers or anyone else outside the family and they witness the distress of children caught up in matrimonial disputes, they are in the best position to contribute to court decisions in relation to children. They may be asked questions about children by court counsellors and solicitors acting for abused mothers. Most people (understandably) want to avoid involvement with courts and family disputes and some pretend that they have no useful knowledge about the children in question. Although teachers and early childhood professionals often resent the many social expectations that are placed on their shoulders (Butterworth & Fulmer 1990), their evidence is important if, for example, there has been an improvement in the child's behaviour, confidence or sociability since the parents separated.

If the teacher has evidence that a parent is abusing the child, details of that should also be given to the legal representative acting for the child. If there is evidence to show that the child dreads visiting either parent or that parents fail to carry out their promises or obligations, this needs to be taken into account by the court making the decision about visiting rights and who has care of the child.

CONCLUSION

Children are the victims of adult violence. They are also the pivot on which this institutionalised cultural problem can be turned around. The widespread availability of counselling for perpetrators and female victims is obviously essential for the control of the problem but there must also be enforceable laws and harsher penalties to deter violent people from stalking, harassing and abusing their former partners. Community education is essential to raise awareness of the problem. More importantly, however, we must focus attention on the current generation of victims who will, without intervention, become the next generation of perpetrators. Walker (1979) and Wolfe et al. (1986) suggest that children can recover from trauma if they receive ample parent support and professional counselling and are removed from the violence. If education, socialisation and intervention policies are adopted, child victims could break the transmission of intergenerational violence.

TASKS FOR STUDENTS

1 Locate and contact the domestic violence services in your nearest town or city and obtain information about the availability of counselling for:
   a women abused by men;
   b men abused by men;
   c domestic violence in homosexual relationships;
   d children in violent homes.
2 Collect leaflets and booklets on domestic violence to have available for parents.
3 Locate the women's shelters in your area and inquire about procedures for referring clients (night and day).

4   If possible, visit two shelters to meet staff and find out more about the admission of clients and what happens next.
    a   How long do clients stay in shelters?
    b   What help do they receive?
    c   What kinds of services do they need?
    d   What happens to the children?

5   Obtain and (if you are a professional) publicise information about crisis and help lines for mothers and children in violent households.

6   You receive a call from a lawyer acting for a child in your group. She asks you to make a statement relating to the emotional well-being of a child in your care whose parents are about to divorce because of domestic violence. You have been concerned about the child's nervous state for some time. Would you be willing to make a statement? If not, why not?

7   If possible, arrange to visit a Family Court to observe cases involving disputes relating to the care of children and/or visitation rights.

8   Find out what the procedures are if:
    a   a violent father snatched his children while they were in your care;
    b   a separated father came to collect his children saying that their mother has asked him to do this because her aunt was ill. When you try to telephone the mother for confirmation, there is no response;
    c   a mother said that she had separated from her violent partner and he must not be given any opportunities for contacting his children.

9   Obtain copies of leaflets available from the Family Court to guide separating or divorcing parents on their rights and responsibilities relating to children.

10 If you are a student, ask a Family Court counsellor to show you a copy of a court order relating to the care of a child and visitation rights.

11 Do you know what procedures to take if a parent who has lost access rights to his or her children comes to talk to them in the playground?

CASE STUDY

You have long been concerned about the behaviour and well-being of Dominic, aged five. He has frequent, unexplained absences, is often bruised and uses violence to achieve his needs.

When you ask Dominic's mother about her own health, she bursts into tears. A cup of coffee and several tissues later, she discloses that her husband drinks heavily, is unemployed and abuses her and the children. She describes several beatings which caused injuries. The mother seeks your assurance that you 'won't repeat this to anyone'. She explains that she is terrified of what her husband will do if he finds out she has shared her problems with someone else.

a   How would you respond to this request?

b   What might be the consequences if you keep her secret?

c   What might be the consequences if you report the abuse of the child?

d   Breaching confidence is always difficult. We must not just take account of the present circumstances but must consider the likely consequences if no report is made. Discuss.

8

CHILD SEXUAL ABUSE

Definitions of what constitutes child sexual abuse vary considerably from country to country. Most current definitions emphasise the fact that children, by virtue of their incomplete cognitive development, are unable to give informed consent to sexual activity.

All definitions include the use of children's bodies for sexual gratification using force or by gaining the victims' uninformed consent. Child sexual abuse:

> may involve activities ranging from exposing the child to sexually explicit materials or behaviours, taking visual images of the child for pornographic purposes, touching, fondling and/or masturbation of the child, having the child touch, fondle or masturbate the abuser, oral sex performed by the child or on the child by the abuser, and anal or vaginal penetration of the child (Tomison 1995a, p. 2).

In spite of any impression gained from newspaper reports of traumatic sex crimes, child sexual abuse is not always violent. It often involves a process of seduction or contrived compliance based on trickery, deceit and secrecy. Because of the secrecy involved, the prevalence of child sexual abuse is hard to determine.

Historical views that children are at risk of sexual abuse predominantly from strangers have given way to the knowledge that most sexual abuse of children occurs at the hands of people the victim knows. These people most commonly include family members and family friends.

Abusers do not conform to an easily identifiable subgroup of the population. The 'dirty old man' stereotype is not helpful, since abusers can come from all walks of life and from all age groups. There is no reliable psychological profile of a typical abuser. While it is true that most child sexual abuse is perpetrated by men, in recent years there has been widespread recognition that children are also sexually abused by other older children and adolescents as well as by female adults.

Finkelhor (1984) has provided a description of the abuse process. This model does not really let us understand why abuse occurs but it is useful to help understand *how* it occurs. In Finkelhor's model, four conditions must be met for abuse to occur.

1 A potential offender needs to have some desire to abuse a child.
2 A perpetrator must overcome internal inhibitions that block acting on the motivation to abuse.
3 External impediments to carrying out acts of abuse must be overcome; typically this means that an opportunity to be alone with the child must be found.
4 Any resistance offered by the child must be overcome.

WHY ALL CHILDREN ARE VULNERABLE TO SEXUAL ABUSE

All children are vulnerable to sexual abuse regardless of their age, gender or where and with whom they live. There are many reasons for their vulnerability.

Children are powerless

Sexual abuse involves adults and more powerful or better informed children and adolescents using weaker and/or less informed children for their own sexual gratification. Children are powerless because they depend on adults to meet their basic needs. They are particularly powerless when they are deprived of developmentally appropriate sexuality education, information about their rights and opportunities to develop and practise personal safety skills.

Uninformed children trust all adults

Five-year-olds are noted for their fearlessness. Six- and seven-year-olds worry about monsters, ghosts, witches, night-time shadows and being at home alone, but without education for child protection, they trust all adults who look kind or seem kind. They view their parents as totally safe, even when they are in jail for serious acts of domestic violence (Briggs 1991a, 1991b; Briggs & Hawkins 1993a).

Young children are incapable of assessing adults' motives

Piaget's theory of moral development (1965) told us that children operating below the eight-year level are incapable of judging adults' motives. They assess people as good or bad by their appearance, manner and the outcome of their actions. Paedophiles are often perceived as kind and good people because they present gifts to their victims, flatter their egos, show affection and encourage confidences. Children tolerate painful abuse for emotionally beneficial outcomes.

Children are taught to obey adults

Unless taught to be more discriminating by involvement in a child protection programme, parents routinely teach children to obey adults. They tell them to 'Be good and do as you're told' when they leave them at early childhood centres and with childminders. Australian and New Zealand children disclosed that they would keep this rule even when the adults asked them to do something that they knew to be wrong (Briggs 1991a, 1991b). Children are afraid that, if they disobey adults, their parents will reprimand them, punish them and withdraw affection. This fear enables deviant adults to manipulate and abuse children with little fear of rejection.

Children are naturally curious about their own bodies

Young children are known to be especially curious about their bodies. Boys acquire a sexual language before girls and, because their genitals are conspicuous, they handle them frequently. Boys are sexually aroused by the sight of other boys' erections and sexual interaction may result. Sexualised peer groups have the attractive qualities of secret societies which boys enjoy. Membership increases opportunities for sexual encounters with victims of abuse as well as juvenile and adult offenders (Cook & Howells 1981; Briggs & Hawkins 1994).

Children are deprived of information about their own sexuality

Parents commonly regard children as asexual. That absolves them of responsibility for providing sexuality education. They argue that they don't want children to be taught safety skills because it might 'spoil their innocence'. They ignore the fact that, in the English-speaking world, children frequently hear sexual words, watch simulated sexual intercourse on television and have access to pornographic videos. Children hear of rape and sexual abuse on news reports and documentaries. They are shown pornographic magazines by their peers in school yards and some children have access to horrendous forms of pornography through the Internet. Despite all of this, some adults continue to delude themselves that children are deaf and blind where sexual matters are concerned.

Parents often create a taboo around the human body. Few parents give children a vocabulary for their genitals. Hindman referred to the contradictory situation where 'by avoiding references to genitalia, we demonstrate our inability to talk about even the simplest aspects of sexuality to children. The message is that we can't say these words but they should be sure to come and tell us if someone touches these "parts", "stuff" and things "down there"' (Mayes et al. 1992, p. 45).

Boys and girls want and need information about the functioning of their own bodies. Puberty is much too late to introduce sexuality education to boys because they learn about masturbation, erections and ejaculation much earlier from their friends, older brothers and abused boys. The onset of menstruation is also far too late to begin to provide information to girls.

Paedophiles take advantage of parents' avoidance of sexuality education. They incite victims' curiosity by introducing 'dirty' talk and pornography. They claim to be providing important education neglected by their uncaring parents (Briggs 1995b; Briggs, Hawkins & Williams 1994; Briggs & Hawkins 1996b).

Unfortunately, parent–child communications do not improve as children reach adolescence. In an Australian study of parents and their sixteen-year-old children, the adults claimed to have discussed sexual matters such as AIDS, safe sex and homosexuality, all of which were of concern to these adolescents. When questioned separately, the children denied their parents' claims, insisting that there had been no conversations about any of the topics. Professor Rosenthal of Melbourne's La Trobe University said that present-day parents have a 'rosy glow' about their role as sex educators but they are 'deluding themselves' about their contributions to children's knowledge (Weekes & Westwood 1993).

HOW COMMON IS CHILD SEXUAL ABUSE?

Prevalence statistics are widely discrepant. Reports are unreliable because different studies use different definitions of abuse and are often not based on true random population samples. Since it is very difficult to substantiate many cases of alleged abuse, prevalence figures differ when claimed versus substantiated cases are discussed. Reports have given an upper limit as high as 62 per cent for all females (Wurtele & Miller-Perrin 1992) and 31 per cent for all males (Kolko 1988). The Australian figure for cases not only reported to authorities, but also investigated and substantiated, is approximately one case per 1000 children (Angus & Woodward 1995). Clearly the difficulties involved in investigation and substantiation mean that this figure is likely to be an underestimate of the underlying true prevalence rate. While attempts to be precise about the incidence of child sexual abuse have been unrewarding, the median rate across abuse reports is 15 per cent for females and 6 per cent for males (Berrick & Gilbert 1991, in Perniskie 1995).

Attempts to quantify abuse are typically made by analysis of reports from victims, reports from abusers, or from surveys of the general population (Dougherty 1986). The problems in obtaining valid data from any of these sources are considerable: victims are often reluctant or even afraid to report offences; perpetrators would be acting against self-interest to report their own offences; the need to cope with their abuse leads some victims (boys and girls) to deny that it occurred; and the general cloak of society-level denial and secrecy effectively conceals many cases. An additional factor is that few male victims identify sexual misbehaviour as abusive when it happens to them.

In terms of persuading governments and funding sources to provide resources for prevention and treatment programmes, documentation of the quantitative size of the problem is important. However, at the day-to-day level, although we cannot be sure of precise numbers, we certainly know that the size of the problem is significant and that official statistics underestimate its extent.

THE EFFECTS OF SEXUAL ABUSE ON CHILD VICTIMS

The effects of child sexual abuse can vary enormously from case to case. Several significant reviews of effects have been published, notably those of Browne and Finkelhor (1986) and Beitchman et al. (1991, 1992). Most reviews have commented on the difficulty of attributing effects to sexual abuse per se, since it so often occurs in a context of other forms of abuse. It is also difficult to separate out the effects of family dysfunction, the stress of reporting and investigation and any pre-existing psychopathology in the child. Some findings though, are very clear. For example, it is known that 'The most negative consequences result when the abuse occurs at the hands of the victim's father and involves genital contact with the use of force' (Wyatt & Powell 1988, in Perniskie 1995, p. 7).

Following child sexual abuse, people vary in the rate and extent to which they recover. The quality of maternal warmth has been found to effect recovery substantially in terms of psycholog-ical difficulties in adulthood (Peters 1988). In general, 'marital conflict and parental psychopathology are thought to have a pivotal impact on the child's response to the abuse and on the long-term outcome' (Beitchman 1992, p. 115).

Browne and Finkelhor (1986) described responses to sexual abuse under four headings.

Traumatic sexualisation: Since abuse can reward or reinforce inappropriate sexual behaviour, especially when it is presented as 'love', it can lead to the sexualisation of emotions or power which contributes to problematic interpersonal relationships. Alternatively, victims avoid situations which remind them of the abuse and this leads to difficulties with sexual relationships. Victims often have flashbacks of abusive acts and the fears associated with them. They become preoccupied with sexual thoughts. This affects their concentration and progress in school and may lead to inappropri-ate sexual behaviour, the abuse of other children or their own re-abuse.

Powerlessness: Invasion of the body by the abuser results in feelings of powerlessness in the victim. Victims become excessively anxious and fearful, sensing that they have no control over what happens to them. The consequent psychological state leads to widespread difficulties in living, sometimes resulting in compen-satory aggressive behaviour and the need to control or dominate others.

Betrayal: Betrayal occurs when the abuser is a trusted person or the abuse occurred when parents placed the victim in the control of someone they trusted. Victims feel confused and unable to trust anyone. Distrust can be lifelong. Adolescent and adult survivors often go from one intense, short-lasting relationship to the next, resulting in feelings of disappointment, inadequacy and loneliness. These feelings can, in turn, lead to hostility and a desire for revenge which can result in antisocial behaviour.

Stigmatisation: Stigmatisation occurs when the victim feels responsible for the abuse and subsequent outcomes, such as removal to foster care ('He said they'd take me away if I told'), the acquittal of the offender ('Nobody believed me'), family separation or imprisonment of the offender ('It's all my fault'). When victims accept the blame, they isolate themselves, believing that they are worthless. This often leads to self-destructive behaviour including suicide and sexualised behaviour which teachers may label as 'promiscuous'.

Beitchman et al's papers (1991, 1992) separated effects into short-term and long-term effects, noting that some effects are age specific (guilt, for example, is less likely to be observed in preschoolers than it is in adolescents).

Short-term effects

Beitchman et al. (1991) found the short-term effects of child sexual abuse to be too varied to postulate an easily identified 'sexual abuse syndrome'. Nonetheless they noted a range of common symptoms.

- There were age-related patterns. Younger children often demonstrated inappropriate sexual behaviour including 'sexual play with dolls, putting objects into the vagina or anus, masturbation, seductive behaviour, requesting sexual stimulation and age-inappropriate or precocious sexual knowledge' (Beitchman et al. 1991, p. 539).
- Preschoolers tended to show increased withdrawn behaviour as opposed to acting-out behaviour which was a feature of older children.
- Depression was a common feature of older sexually abused children and adolescents engaged in more acting-out behaviours including running away, truanting, alcohol/drug abuse, promiscuity, prostitution and delinquent or criminal behaviour.
- A poor self-concept was common and this factor, when coupled with depression, shows the reason for the increased incidence of suicide and suicidal ideation.
- Several authors (for example, Johnson & Shrier 1985) found a significantly higher prevalence of homosexuality (48 per cent

vs 8 per cent) and bisexuality (10 per cent vs 3 per cent) among young adult males who had been sexually abused in childhood, than in non-abused controls.

- Sexually aggressive behaviour was noted particularly in the behaviour of children who had received more severe forms of abuse (performed fellatio or experienced anal or vaginal intercourse).
- Sexual abuse by more than one perpetrator was associated with more severe outcomes as were sexual experiences which involved force and penetration.
- The majority of children who were sexually abused came from single or reconstituted families and family pathology (including alcoholism and depression) was common, as was a history of sexual abuse in mothers.

Long-term effects

Some effects are not apparent immediately after sexual abuse. Beitchman et al. (1992) point out, for example, that sexual dysfunction cannot be evident in a prepubertal child although it may emerge as a symptom as the child develops into adolescence. Sexual dysfunction is a common long-term symptom of child sexual abuse.

As with short-term symptoms, the most severe long-term consequences followed father–daughter incest and abuse involving penetration.

Sexual preference seems to be affected by abuse since the incidence of homosexuality was again found to be higher in abused than in non-abused women and men (Briere & Runtz 1986).

The anxiety, fear and depression previously noted as short-term symptoms tended to become chronic and remain as long-term symptoms. Suicide was also a long-term risk (Briere & Runtz 1986).

Another long-term consequence was revictimisation, with battering in an adult relationship or rape occurring more frequently in individuals who were sexually abused as children than in other individuals.

While Briere (1984) argued that a postsexual abuse syndrome exists which includes long-term symptoms of fear and withdrawal, Beitchman et al. (1992) found that the evidence was too fragmented as yet to justify the existence of such a syndrome.

THE RISKS TO GIRLS

Historically, the sexual abuse of girls has been better investigated and documented than the abuse of boys. It was the growing awareness of the extent of sexual abuse of girls which led to the now common child protection programmes in schools.

Report statistics show that girls are at greater risk than boys within the family home, with offences perpetrated predominantly by father replacement figures (stepfathers or mother's new partners) and by fathers. It is very clear that the incest taboo is more frequently broken by father replacement figures than by biological fathers. Russell (1984) found that the rate of abuse of stepdaughters (17 per cent) was far higher than the abuse of daughters (2 per cent).

Various theoretical models have attempted to explain why the sexual abuse of girls occurs. The feminist perspective sees the abuse of girls as symptomatic of a broader male-dominated society. The family systems approach doesn't blame men so much but sees the abuse as symptomatic of broader deficient family dynamics. Psychoanalytic approaches point to personality and relationship deficits, and sociological approaches see the abuse as a consequence of oppressive societal conditions including poverty and isolation. None of these theoretical models is particularly helpful. Each may contribute a small insight, but even after exhaustive study, a reader is left with the feeling that the problem is poorly understood.

Some theorists have pointed to a breakdown in the husband–wife and wife–daughter relationship as contributing to incest:

> . . . the mother emotionally and physically withdraws from the family, usually turning over her child care and household duties to the daughter. A father–daughter coalition forms. Deprived of a partner, his sexuality perhaps in question, the father may be willing to sexualize this coalition [or] the father is seen as imperious and domineering. The mother is immature and dependent, filling the role of a child in the family rather than an adult (Brassard, Germain & Hart 1987, p. 74).

While such descriptions may apply to particular cases, the profile of offenders is too heterogeneous for these descriptions to be generally helpful.

THE RISKS TO BOYS

Prevalence statistics invariably suggest that boys are less vulnerable to sexual victimisation than girls, but the risks to boys have generally been underestimated in the past. Even today, boys may be relatively ignored, as shown in a recent child protection programme which focused entirely on girls (Kitzinger 1994).

Child sexual abuse is a highly sensitive subject and the responses of adult victims vary not only according to the way in which questions are worded but by whom and how they are asked. For example, when child abuse is referred to as 'unwanted sexual touching' or 'abuse', few male victims admit that they were victimised. When the same subjects are asked about their sexual experiences in childhood, it becomes apparent that many boys were used for sex by older people but did not classify their experiences as abusive (Briggs, Hawkins & Williams 1994; Lewis 1985).

Dube and Hebert (1988) found that earlier researchers were asking the wrong questions: male victims do not recognise sexual abuse as such because sexual experiences per se are acceptable to the male culture whereas victimisation is not. Denial of abuse and victimisation is especially necessary for boys because the male culture demands that they remain strong, self-sufficient and in control.

Boys are thus particularly loathe to report sexual abuse. In our Australian study of almost 200 adult male survivors of sexual abuse, only 14 per cent of victims reported abuse to a trusted adult. Complainants were older boys who waited at least a year before informing their mothers (50 per cent) or their teachers (17 per cent). In every case except one, their reports were ignored or disbelieved. Only one of some 1640 offenders and many thousands of offences was reported to authorities and no prosecutions took place (Briggs, Hawkins & Williams 1994).

Unfortunately, failure to identify abuse does not reduce the damage it causes to victims' lives.

Boys' failure to report abuse can be attributed to several factors.

- Boys are constrained by sex-role conditioning which, from an early age, tells them that they must be self-sufficient, brave and strong. Victimisation is the antithesis of society's definition of masculinity.
- Boys are most frequently molested by members of their own sex. When they are old enough to understand that what is

happening is wrong, they are also aware of the taboo on homosexuality. They assume that they were chosen because they are gay and anxiety about their own sexuality silences them.

- Sexual abuse by men is often presented as normal male behaviour: 'it's fun', 'it's only sex', 'it's what men do together', 'look, everybody else does it'.
- Abuse of boys by females is often not regarded as abuse. More than a third of the men in one of our studies were abused by females (Briggs, Hawkins & Williams 1994). The male culture is tolerant of sexual experimentation per se and sex with older females is viewed as a beneficial, educational experience.
- Boys often accept responsibility for what happens to them because, even when they are unwilling participants, their bodies respond sexually, that is, they have an erection.
- As well as sometimes completely denying that particular acts constituted abuse, boys may not complain or report abuse because they believe that they were in some way complicit. If, for example, they liked some aspect of the abuse (as many of the men in our study did when the sex was non-violent and occurred in a context of affection and attention), boys are unwilling to blame the perpetrator.
- Boys may believe that the abuse was insignificant and did them no harm. Again in our study, men who had been abused as boys and were now in jail for sexually molesting children themselves still saw no connection between their own abuse and their disastrous lives.

In their unique American study of unprosecuted child molesters, Abel et al. (1987) found that offenders choose boy victims far more frequently than they choose girls. Boys are about ten times more likely than girls to be abused by women and adolescent girls. Boys are at greatest risk outside their homes and risks increase as they become more independent.

In our Australian study of abused males, 34 per cent were incest victims and 19 per cent were abused by other family members. It is important to note that when boys were first abused at home, they were abused later outside their homes by unrelated male perpetrators (Briggs, Hawkins & Williams 1994). Eighty-five per cent of the boys were abused by male perpetrators and 35 per cent by females. These figures replicated those obtained by a 1993 Western Australian male survivor phone-in. The ISPCC

(1993) Irish survey also showed that 28 per cent of abused boys were victimised by women compared with only 4 per cent of females. Fifteen per cent of Australian male victims were abused by priests, 65 per cent by male neighbours and 13 per cent by strangers. More than half (52 per cent) were anally raped and 57 per cent had to provide oral sex. More than three-quarters of the boys (79 per cent) thought that the abuse constituted normal behaviour and 43 per cent reported enjoying some aspect of the experience.

Those who later became offenders were the ones most likely to have denied the abuse, reported that they enjoyed some aspects of it (69 per cent) or regarded it as 'normal' behaviour (88 per cent).

Every victim in the study (N = 200) had been abused by more than one offender. Boys who did not become offenders were abused by an average of 2.2 perpetrators while those who became offenders were abused by 14.2 (Briggs, Hawkins & Williams 1994).

BOYS ARE LESS PROTECTED THAN GIRLS

Because the risks to boys have been underestimated, child protection programmes have focused on the needs of girls and have neglected boys. Boys are disadvantaged because parents do not realise their vulnerability. They grant boys more freedom and independence than girls but deprive them of safety knowledge. Not expecting abuse, they seldom recognise the signs or respond to boys' hints and reports that abuse has occurred.

Boys are not safety conscious; they believe that sexual abuse and rape only involve girls. Boys seem to be curious about their bodies at an earlier age than girls and yet they are deprived of sound sexuality education before adolescence. Paedophiles tap into that curiosity.

Boys are not taught that their genitals are private parts which are special and should be cared for. To the contrary, their genitals are very public parts and as teachers know only too well, young boys not only compare the size and shape of their genitals in school toilets, they compete to see who can perform the greatest urinary feats. And when they happen to join a highly sexualised peer group, sexual activity becomes habitual and addictive.

When a juvenile offender gains access to a group of curious young boys, they feel flattered that an older boy is prepared to demonstrate his sexual skills and share new information. It is only when abuse becomes violent or they are forced to reciprocate unpleasant oral sex that they want to opt out. Then they find they are trapped. Afraid to share their terrible secret, they accept responsibility for their own victimisation.

Boys are especially vulnerable to sexual abuse by paedophiles when they lack physical affection from their own fathers. When their emotions have been sexualised, some children go looking for sex in lieu of love. Eventually they may accept payment for what they do. When boys are trapped in paedophile rings, payment goes to the organisers.

When abuse seems to be inevitable, victims accept it as 'normal'. There is then a high risk that victims will become offenders. It is particularly important to redress the insufficient attention to the sexual abuse of boys. Boys become men, and as we have seen, it is men who are most commonly the perpetrators of abuse. Although community education and awareness have certainly contributed to the huge annual increases in reports, researchers confirm that the crime of child sexual abuse is increasing.

Bentovim informed the 10th International Congress on Child Abuse and Neglect (1994) that his British study confirmed American findings that 20–25 per cent of male victims of sexual abuse become offenders. No similar studies have been published relating to female victims. As about a quarter of male victims become offenders, it follows that there will be an increase in the incidence of child sexual abuse from generation to generation unless parents, schools and the community take the problem seriously and act to break the cycle.

WHO ARE THE OFFENDERS?

Child molesters come from all walks of life. They cannot be identified by their appearance, their educational level or their status. Their most common characteristics are those of gender, their history of victimisation in childhood and the denial of their offences when reported. They are caregivers and teachers, diplomats and judges, police officers and youth workers. They are MPs and lawyers, priests and businessmen as well as the chronically unemployed. They are mothers and fathers, brothers and sisters, grandparents, aunts and uncles. It soon becomes clear that no-one can be trusted on the basis of their gender, professional status or their relationship to children.

MALE OFFENDERS—PAEDOPHILES AND PEDERASTS

Report statistics show that most child molesters are males. Paedophiles are men whose sexual interest focuses on children. Pederasts are men who prefer sex with boys. Paedophiles and pederasts often gain entry to professions and services for children. They are usually admired by unsuspecting parents for their 'dedication' to children's activities. It is thought that paedophiles are buying child care centres because they provide easy access to the young.

Some target unsupported mothers and become lodgers and childminders. Because they make no sexual demands on the women and they are perceived to 'get on well' with children, they gain many opportunities to commit offences. They justify their behaviour by telling themselves that the parents are negligent and they, the offenders, 'care more about the kids than anyone else'. Paedophiles can be found wherever unaccompanied children congregate. They seek out victims in public toilets, amusement arcades, shopping centres, beaches, playgrounds and sporting events. They select and 'befriend' the losers, the sad and the lonely. They listen to them, buy treats, provide physical affection and flatter them. They gain great satisfaction from planning the seduction process and they fantasise future encounters.

Perpetrators also go to enormous trouble to develop the parents' trust. This is calculated to increase opportunities for access to the children and strengthen their own safety. When perpetrators have the approval of parents, confused victims are more likely to accept that what is happening is 'normal'. Furthermore, trusting parents defend perpetrators and ignore victims' concerns when they hint that all is not well.

Some professionals are members of highly organised paedophile/pederast networks which serve several purposes:

- they are protective, provide mutual support and, by sheer weight of numbers, give a sense of legitimacy to what members do;
- they circulate information about child victims;
- they share pornography;

- they lobby parliamentarians for changes to legislation; for example, the removal or lowering of the age limit for sexual activity.

Children trapped in paedophile networks are subjected to horrendous sadistic, degrading and violent forms of abuse by large numbers of offenders. Men of high professional status protect themselves from prosecution by terrorising their victims.

American and British researchers have also confirmed that one perpetrator can damage hundreds of lives. This was well demonstrated by a study of 558 convicted incest offenders in a treatment programme at Great Ormond Street Children's Hospital, London. On admission, only 15 per cent admitted that they had committed any offence; within a year, they had confessed to an average of 522 crimes per person (Bentovim 1991). This parallels the American findings of Abel et al. (1987) in which 561 self-reported non-incarcerated sex offenders disclosed that they had completed 291 737 previously undisclosed acts involving 195 407 victims. In other words, the average offender had committed more than 520 offences and created more than 348 new victims prior to being interviewed. Given that the mean age of subjects was only 31.5 years and they were not in treatment programmes, it is reasonable to predict that the number of their victims will more than double before the end of their lives.

While homosexual offenders are not unknown, there is no evidence to suggest that gay men are more likely than heterosexual males to sexually abuse children. Clearly, an adult homosexual preference does not necessarily also mean an attraction to young children of the same sex. Studies show that more than half of all male offenders are married and give the appearance of being normal heterosexual family men.

Incestuous fathers are often perceived by teachers and caregivers as caring but overprotective, overattentive, strict or religious parents who are in control of their families. They often prevent their victims from developing peer relationships. They ban them from attending normal, harmless school social functions such as Christmas parties and excursions. Incest offenders often see themselves as owning their families. Their wives are often shadowy figures who were victimised in childhood.

Incest offenders do not confine their sexual activities to their own children. They commit a wide range of offences against their children's friends, relatives and anyone else who happens to be accessible (Abel et al. 1987). The literature shows that most male molesters:

- were sexually abused in childhood but deny that their experiences harmed them;
- are immature people with poor social skills, poor self-esteem and a lack of conscience and empathy for others;
- are attracted to children because they are trusting, easily manipulated and do not reject them;
- commit hundreds (and, in some cases, several thousands) of offences in a lifetime;
- start committing offences during childhood or adolescence;
- abuse other children as well as their own;
- come from all ethnic, religious, racial, social, professional and educational backgrounds;
- know that what they do is socially unacceptable but deny or minimise the seriousness of their offences;
- show distress if caught red-handed and swear that it will never happen again;
- re-offend very quickly unless there is punitive and specialist intervention to change attitudes and their sexual attraction to children;
- tend to abuse children of the same gender as their own abusers and use the same seduction methods.

The distorted thinking of male offenders enables them to see their victims as equal, informed partners who want, invite or even enjoy being sexually assaulted. They conveniently forget the imbalance of power and the tricks that they use to gain children's compliance. This ensures that they have few guilty feelings about what they do. Their concerns centre around themselves and their fears of being apprehended and jailed. Bouts of self-pity lead to the commission of further offences.

Offenders are very daring. They often molest children while they are in the same car or room as their parents. The more bizarre and more daring the offence, the less likely that the victim will be believed.

Proclamations of love are commonly used by child molesters to gain the compliance of victims and develop their emotional dependence. Children are highly sensitive to touch and, although genital fondling can be confusing, it can also be perceived as pleasant and fun. When victims are firmly trapped in an abusive relationship, offenders demand sexual satisfaction for themselves.

This confuses victims; why would men who claim to love them demand unpleasant and very painful activities?

Perpetrators maintain control by making victims feel bad, helpless and wholly responsible for their victimisation.

FEMALE OFFENDERS

Little is known about female offenders other than that most were victimised in childhood. Only in recent times have researchers even begun to consider what some have referred to as the last taboo, that is, the sexual abuse of children by women. The reason for our ignorance is not that offences by females are uncommon but that they are rarely reported. Furthermore, when a complaint is made, it is seldom taken seriously. As a result, female offenders have not received societal permission to admit that they have problems and few treatment services make provision for them. Reported mother–son incest was so rare that, in 1960, Wahl found only four cases of mother–son incest in the literature. More recently, studies have shown a significant amount of abuse by women and a number of specialist texts have been published on the topic.

Most readers would probably not have noticed that the definition of child sexual abuse presented at the beginning of this chapter did not include the example of vaginal penetration of an adult woman by a child. In spite of being a very current definition (1995), the example shows how common it is to ignore or minimise the sexual abuse of children by women.

The neglect of offences by females relates to many mistaken beliefs about sexual abuse, for example, that:

- the damage to victims is physical (not psychological). From that, it is assumed that female offenders are less dangerous than males because women have no penis to rape with and they are incapable of making victims pregnant. This minimisation is unfortunate because most offences by women involve incest and incest which is especially damaging when it involves the primary caregiver;
- women are innate nurturers and protectors of children;
- women would not gain any satisfaction from molesting children.

Contrary to popular belief, few intrafamilial offences by females are committed under the influence and direction of male offenders (Briggs, Hawkins & Williams 1994).

CHILD SEXUAL ABUSE IN DAY CARE CENTRES

In their studies of sexual abuse involving 270 American day care (preschool) centres, Finkelhor, Williams and Burns (1988) were most surprised to find that 73 per cent of female offenders abused children in conjunction with other female staff, occasionally in the company of a male director or owner. Females were also more likely than men to commit multiple acts involving terrorising and penetrating victims with objects. The researchers found that female group abuse was, in fact, more damaging and more prolonged than abuse by lone perpetrators of either sex.

Parents underestimate the risks and the damage to the extent that, in Australian and New Zealand cases, they continued to send their children to day care centres after others had reported child molestation. The lack of parental concern is difficult to comprehend although the following myths may be partly responsible:

- children are safe in groups;
- children are safe with female caregivers;
- preschool-aged children imagine sexual abuse;
- if sexual abuse occurs, young children soon forget about it;
- the media exaggerate the size of the problem.

In some cases, signs of abuse were overlooked because of parents' loyalty to staff. Some parents did not want the inconvenience of changing to a new centre which might incur additional travel. There was also a deep-seated but illogical suspicion that child sexual abuse victims, like rape victims, must have 'done something to deserve it', albeit at three years of age.

The American study showed that child care centre offenders were highly respectable, well-educated married women, many of whom were regarded as 'pillars' of the community. Some involved the children in sexual exploitation for money through prostitution and pornography. Some were involved in ritual abuse involving membership of satanic or religious cults. Some were economically dependent on the leading perpetrators. Others had been 'socialised by other perpetrators and were encouraged to show allegiance and friendship by participating' (Finkelhor, Williams & Burns 1988, p. 48).

Finkelhor also speculated that some of the women abused children to satisfy a desire for power and control over the smallest and most gullible members of society. Some offenders had histories of abusing other children, including their own sons. Most were victims of abuse in childhood.

JUVENILE OFFENDERS

When rapists of ten and twelve years of age are identified, expressions of disgust, disbelief, shock and horror ripple through the community. When powerful emotions are aroused, few pause to wonder where a child learned to become an offender.

Child protection services in the United States have long recognised the existence of children whose sexual behaviour is inappropriate and damaging. Therapeutic programmes have been developed to respond to preschool as well as primary school aged and adolescent offenders. The American response stimulated interest in the United Kingdom and, following concerns expressed by British welfare authorities, led to conferences such as that convened by the National Children's Bureau (Hollows & Armstrong 1992).

New Zealand parents and government welfare services are also struggling with increases in reports of serious abuse involving primary school aged children in towns and cities where, as in the United Kingdom and Australia, there is a shortage of treatment facilities.

Our Australian study of male victims showed that abuse by juveniles replicates adult abuse in its violence, frequency and duration and, for those reasons, it must be taken seriously (Briggs & Hawkins 1996b).

A quarter of all male victims interviewed were abused by older children before they reached the age of six. The perpetrators were equally likely to be male or female. The females were the boys' older sisters (33.3 per cent) and their sisters' friends (66.6 per cent). Abuse by males involved older brothers (40 per cent), their brothers' friends (40 per cent) and neighbours.

More than half of the Australian male victims (54 per cent) were sexually abused by adolescents when they were aged 6–10 years. One-third were abused by females and two-thirds by males. Anal rape was involved in 63 per cent of cases and oral rape in 45 per cent. Early sexualisation made victims vulnerable to multiple abuse by adults over a prolonged period of time.

Although all victims hated anal sex and found it excruciatingly painful, they believed the abuser's explanation that it would become more enjoyable with practice. When the enjoyment failed to materialise, they tolerated the discomfort believing that they were abnormal.

Some boys felt flattered to be invited to participate in sex with older youths. As one explained, 'It was like joining a secret club for big people'. Victimisation by older siblings was assumed to be 'normal behaviour'.

A British report (National Children's Home 1992) showed that juvenile offenders:

- have invariably been sexually abused;
- know their victims;
- without treatment repeat the offences and become habitual offenders; if they have been victims, treatment should involve dealing with their experiences as victims as well as their behaviour as perpetrators.

The British report concluded that adolescents must be made accountable for their inappropriate sexual acts. Court appearance was viewed as desirable because court orders can formalise treatment programmes.

A recent Australian investigation has similarly stressed the importance of dealing adequately with juvenile offenders. The Crime Prevention Committee in Victoria noted that 'adolescents displaying the early signs of sex offending tend to grow up and commit sex offences unless they are provided with treatment' (Tomison 1995b, p. 40).

To stop the offending behaviour pattern, it is necessary to help juvenile perpetrators to:

- understand the impact and consequences of their behaviour;
- empathise with victims;
- reorganise and modify fantasies about sex with children;
- recognise and avoid situations which have previously been antecedents of abusive behaviour; and
- implement and practise a prepared strategy when the potential for an abusive experience arises.

In addition, given the frequency with which children are abused by juvenile offenders in foster homes and other forms of residential care, the report strongly recommended that children who have been sexually abused should not be placed in residences alongside non-abused children. It also stressed the importance of providing personal safety programmes for children and training foster parents for the care of sexual abuse victims.

Unfortunately, international literature shows that teachers in secondary schools are the ones most likely to ignore evidence of juvenile offending. All too often, they dismiss the unacceptable sexual behaviour of adolescent victim/offenders as normal sexual curiosity, early sexual development or 'boys will be boys'.

Differentiating between normal curiosity and sexual abuse

In the midst of all the uncertainty surrounding the sexual abuse of children, there is growing concern that perpetrators are often juveniles. Sexually abusive behaviour is usually initiated by abuse victims who replicate their own abusive experiences. Teachers and early childhood professionals are usually the first to be alerted to the activities of young offenders when they witness or receive reports of sexual misbehaviour in toilets and play areas. It is important that professionals and parents understand the differences between normal curious behaviour and evidence of sexual abuse. Uninformed adults often confuse the two. If they reprimand offenders or deprive them of privileges, untreated offenders continue to abuse but take greater care not to be caught.

Normal curiosity involves activity that can be described as 'information gathering', visual more than tactile and of limited duration (Johnson 1988). It involves equal sharing by all participants on the lines of, 'You show me yours and I'll show you mine' (Goldman & Goldman 1988).

Abusive behaviour is usually more intense and more involved. It mirrors the sexual abuse of children by adults. There is usually disparity in the power of the parties involved. Instigators are likely to be bigger, older, stronger or better informed than their victims. Some coerce peers into abusing a younger, smaller, isolated or disabled child. Juvenile offenders often use force, bribes, tricks, blackmail, coercion, threats, violence or secrecy to achieve their objectives, replicating the methods used by their own abusers. Sometimes very young female abuse victims teach older boys 'what to do'. Uninformed teachers often assume, mistakenly, that the boys are the instigators.

Professionals and parents need to be aware that it is not 'normal sexual curiosity' when a child invites others to kiss or suck their genitals or a child offers to do so. It is not 'normal sexual curiosity' to insert objects of any kind into anal or vaginal openings and it is not normal curiosity for the instigators of these acts to enquire whether their victims like what is happening. These behaviours should always be regarded as indicators that the initiator has probably been subjected to sexual abuse. Incidents must always be investigated calmly, casually and sensitively without distributing blame. Ask the young initiator who showed him/her how to play 'that game', where it is played and who else plays. The responses may help to clarify whether the initiator is an abuse victim.

Children who report juvenile offenders should be assured that they behaved responsibly in making the reports. This is also a good time to revise or introduce personal safety education and develop children's awareness relating to their rights.

NOT ALL VICTIMS BECOME OFFENDERS

It should be clearly understood that, while most offenders were victimised in childhood, not all victims become offenders. Those who survive best are the ones who:

- have affectionate family relationships;
- experience single non-violent incidents at the hands of strangers;
- recognise that what happened is wrong and managed to escape, feeling that they are still in control of the situation;
- recognise that the offender is the one with the problem;
- feel no long-term responsibility or guilt for what happened.

Conversely, the greatest damage is done when the offender meets the victim's emotional needs and the abuse is repeated over a long period of time, or the offender is a parent and the abuse represents a particular abuse of trust.

In a search for the differences between offenders and victims who were not offenders, Briggs, Hawkins and Williams (1994) found that convicted sex offenders were:

- sexually abused by many more adults than non-offenders who had also been abused (prisoners: mean = 14.2; non-offenders: mean = 2.2);
- more likely to have accepted the abuse as normal behaviour (88%:69%) and liked some aspect of the abusive relationship (69%:17%).

When subjected to years of victimisation by multiple perpetrators,

134

those who became offenders had learned to accept sexual abuse as a way of life.

Victims who were not offenders disclosed that they were often sexually attracted to children, especially sad and lonely boys who reminded them of themselves. A small number of these men had been tempted to abuse a child 'for revenge'. It was only their understanding of the damage inflicted by sexual abuse that prevented them from responding to those urges.

It should be noted that some individuals have a capacity to survive childhood sexual abuse without major apparent consequences. Some victims do not report any of the common long-term effects of abuse. Their resilience or recovery does not diminish the seriousness of abuse, but rather gives hope to the many abuse victims who do suffer. They may, especially with the assistance of psychological therapy, rebuild damaged lives.

CASE STUDIES

1 An unsupported father asks your advice about his daughters' weekend visits to their mother. He has a 'gut feeling' that they are being abused by their mother's live-in boyfriend. They feign sickness to avoid the visits and are difficult to manage when they return home. He has tried to question them but they 'close up'. Over a period of several months you have noticed a deterioration in the behaviour of the seven-year-old who is in your group. What advice would you give the father? Why?

2 A mother tells you that her twelve-year-old daughter has accused her father of incest. The mother seeks your confirmation that the accusation is likely to be false. She has already challenged her husband who says that the girl has made up the accusation as an act of vindictiveness because he's been 'too strict' with the girl. What would you say? What, if anything, would you do? Why?

3 Paul, aged eight, gives you, as his teacher, a great deal of cause for concern. He has a sophisticated knowledge of the world which you attribute to the fact that he lives on a farm. In a casual conversation with Paul when you are on playground duty, he reveals that his stepbrother, aged 26, often comes into his bed 'in the middle of the

night', sometimes when drunk. What would you say to Paul? What, if anything, would you do?

4 Tim, aged twelve, inadvertently reveals that his father has shown him how to find hard-core pornography on the Internet and they look at it together. What would you do? Why?

5 Seven-year-old Sophie is a quiet child who is always on the fringe of group activities, looks sad and slightly neglected. While on playground duty, you find Sophie in tears. She says the big boys behind the bicycle shed were calling her 'screw rat'. The boys are about twelve years old. When you ask them what happened, they say that 'She's always wanting to teach us how to screw' (meaning sexual intercourse). What would you say? What would you do? Why?

9

CHILDREN'S REVELATIONS OF SEXUAL ABUSE

Children reveal that they've been sexually abused in a number of ways. Some victims try to describe oral sex but they lack the language to make themselves understood and resort to the terminology used by the offender, referring to his foul-tasting milk, ice-cream or magic fountain (semen).

Older children sometimes draw attention to themselves in sexual ways in the hope that their teachers will understand the problem. A twelve-year-old victim drew the teacher's attention to a crude sexual drawing on the floor beneath her desk. Initially the teacher made a typical response: 'Who drew that disgusting picture? Clean it off the floor immediately.' The girl feared a reprimand and denied involvement. The next day she called the teacher to look at a similar picture under her desk. Fortunately, the teacher had mentioned the earlier incident to another member of staff who suggested that this might be a cry for help. As a result, she invited the child to talk to her privately and her abuse was revealed.

Many children will show a deterioration in school work. However, some bright incest victims concentrate even harder on academic achievement to offset the worries at home.

Some of the indicators listed below could obviously relate to conditions other than child abuse. In deciding whether a suspicion is justified, we need to consider the behaviour and well-being of the child as a whole. However, if there is a clear disclosure of sexual misbehaviour, it must always be reported.

Indicators of sexual abuse

Sexually abused children come to the notice of staff in schools and early childhood centres when they:

- reveal sexual knowledge that is inappropriate for their age;
- use dolls or stuffed toys to simulate oral sex or anal or vaginal intercourse;
- show an unhealthy, obsessive interest in genitals and sexual matters;
- act sexually with other children or teach others to act sexually;
- tell their peers about what happened and their peers tell others;
- withdraw from former friendships previously enjoyed;
- show personality changes or unexplained emotional responses or anxiety traits; for example, a previously outgoing child may become sad, withdrawn or angry;
- cling excessively to the limbs and clothing of trusted adults to the extent that the adults may resent the loss of personal space and try to peel them off: victims fight to regain their leech-like hold;
- commit or threaten to commit acts of self-mutilation, for example jabbing their bodies with knives, needles and scissors or sniffing or drinking harmful substances. Some victims behave suicidally, such as walking on railway lines or motorways or take risks that might result in revictimisation;
- behave in a 'promiscuous', sexualised way with older people (for example, teachers or older children in the playground). This happens when children have been taught that, to please adults, they have to behave sexually: it results in multiple abuse by multiple offenders;
- draw pictures that show emotional disturbance;
- display emotionally disturbed behaviours that cannot be explained;
- reveal offences inadvertently; for example, when a boy was reprimanded for trying to masturbate another boy he replied, 'But my daddy does it to me';
- show signs of physical discomfort in the vaginal or anal areas;
- give vague verbal hints such as: 'I don't like the new babysitter. She's mean'; 'I don't like going to visit —— any

more. I don't like the games he plays' or 'I don't like the way he teases me'; 'Promise you won't tell anyone if I tell you a secret' or 'I've got a secret I can't tell. Do you always have to keep secrets?' Sadly, unsuspecting adults usually reply that secrets must always be kept.

CHILDREN'S DRAWINGS GIVE CLUES ABOUT SEXUAL ABUSE

Young children cannot verbalise their feelings about sexual abuse. As a result, some express their emotions through their artwork. Drawings can be useful for identifying children's anxieties and feelings. They can add confirmation to suspicions of abuse alongside other aspects of their behaviour.

Sexually abused children often produce drawings that are immature and increasingly bizarre. Some become nightmarish and the onlooker senses that something is wrong.

In a study of the drawings of a four-year-old (confirmed) victim, there was a marked deterioration in the child's drawings over a four-month period (Briggs & Lehmann 1989). The child was molested by a stranger when she used the toilet while attending a family barbecue. She reported the offence to her mother who believed her and telephoned the police.

Prior to this incident, the child drew pretty pictures with neat houses and flower gardens. Her self-portraits were detailed and sophisticated. The day after the abuse, she began drawing herself without arms and her self-portraits remained armless until she received therapy. By contrast, portraits of the offender had outsize arms and huge hands.

The child's behaviour deteriorated at home and at the centre. She had frequent toileting accidents, refusing to use the bathroom because of its associations with the abuse. She kicked her mother and screamed hatred at her when she left the centre. The mother denied the need for therapy, convinced that, given time, the child would 'forget'.

The deterioration in the child's behaviour was paralleled by a deterioration in her artwork. Her drawings regressed to scribble in black, red and purple colours which she explained as 'the bad man in the bathroom' surrounded by witches, monsters, spiders and snakes.

The day after being molested, a young victim began drawing self-portraits without arms. By contrast, the offender was depicted with huge arms and hands. The armless self-portraits continued until the victim visited a therapist.

After several months of emotionally disturbed behaviours, the mother was persuaded to take the child to a therapist.

The therapist found that the child viewed the offender as a snake-like monster which she drew on a large piece of card. With the aid of a 'brave puppet', the child destroyed the monster by cutting it into pieces. She repeated the activity several times and, the following day, although her body image remained less sophisticated than others, her self-portraits were no longer armless.

Child sexual abuse should always be considered as a possibility when there is concern about the behaviour of young children who also:

- choose 'angry' colours (such as purple, black and red) for 50 per cent or more of the time when they have a free choice of colours (Lewis & Green 1983);
- consistently draw armless self-portraits while their drawings of other people demonstrate that they are technically capable of drawing arms (Yates, Beutler & Crago 1985);
- consistently create faceless self-portraits while drawings of other people have mouths, eyes and noses;

Good try paul.

Take note of children who persist in creating sexually explicit drawings. A teacher expressed concern about the sexualised behaviour of Paul, aged 10 years. She had a 'gut feeling' that the boy was being abused. A glance at the boy's workbook showed that he had drawn outsize genitals on male figures throughout the term. Keen on sports, he portrayed whole teams of players with erections. The teacher failed to notice 'because I was only looking at his writing'. It was later confirmed that the boy lived in an incestuous family and had been abused by his father, grandfather and uncle.

- use phallic symbols in their artwork;
- draw an adult male (the offender) with an outsize erect penis. In the drawings of preschool aged victims, this may be mistaken for a third arm;
- show an obsession with sexual matters, for example, drawing outsize genitals on all male animals or humans and bringing them to the adult's attention;
- present sexually explicit pictures which suggest that they have seen pornography or sexual activity.

The adult should enquire, as casually as possible, who the people are in the picture, what they are doing and where this

142

happens. If young children reveal that they are viewing porno-graphic movies, the matter should be reported because they are at high risk of more serious abuse. Some adults involve children in acting out what they see in pornographic videos.

The drawings of sexually abused children often give viewers a 'sick' feeling; for example, abused children sometimes draw themselves as tiny figures inside an adult's body. When they have been used for oral sex, offenders are often depicted with exaggerated, round mouths and large, jagged teeth.

Adults may find out the cause of the problem if they invite children to draw pictures of people who make them feel happy and then people who make them feel worried or sad. The adults remain with the children and ask questions about the people featured in the drawings.

Five-year-old David confirmed the teacher's suspicion that someone was making him sad. He drew all the members of his family, assuring the teacher that none of them was responsible for his unhappiness. The teacher checked this in the following way: 'We know that someone is making you unhappy. You drew mummy and said that it wasn't her. You drew daddy and said that he hit mummy but he never hurts you. Is that right? You said that your grandpa, grandma, your brother and your sisters aren't the ones making you sad. So how about drawing me a picture of the person who is upsetting you.' David obliged with a picture of Neil, who, he explained, was his mother's boyfriend. He then revealed that Neil was using him for sex.

In a session about pets, a five-year-old girl announced, 'I have sex with our dogs in bed at night'. Commendably, the student teacher thanked the child for the information and continued with the lesson. A few minutes later, when the child was engrossed in drawing, the student took her on one side and encouraged her to talk about her pets but sensitive questioning was unproductive. She was about to move away when the child suddenly drew a picture of a sexually stimulated nude male. 'That's an interesting picture! Who is it?' the student teacher enquired. The artist replied that it was her older brother. 'Where do you see him like that?' the student asked. 'When he comes into my bedroom at night,' the artist replied.

The student then asked the child whether she would like to draw a picture of her brother coming into her bedroom at night. The child agreed on condition that she could use coloured markers and a larger sheet of paper. Now confident, she described what

Take note when children persistently use phallic symbols in drawings.
Marina was violently abused by her stepfather from age 7–12 years.
Her mother kept all of the drawings that she brought home from school
and police examined them after the disclosure. Many times during that
five-year period, Marina depicted herself as armless and her stepfather
as a penis. Neither her mother nor her teachers had taken note. When
police asked Marina about this picture, she replied she drew it because,
after refusing to be used for anal intercourse, the offender accused her
of not loving him and he threatened to withdraw basic care.

was happening as she drew her pictures and gave permission for
the dialogue to be recorded beneath the drawings. The result had
a comic strip effect which confirmed that the five-year-old child
hid under the sheets and pretended to be asleep when her brother
entered the room with one of the dogs. The bizarre nature of the
abuse suggested that the twelve-year-old boy was also a victim
who urgently needed therapy. When presented with the drawings,
the school administrator said, 'I'm not at all surprised. We've been
worried about those kids for ages.'

Sometimes drawings are vague but the verbal description is
sexual and constitutes a cry for help. The adult needs to ask:

- 'Who is this person in your picture?'

- 'What is this person doing?'
- 'What do you do?'
- 'Where does this happen?' and,
- 'Who else is with you when this happens?'

Questions should be designed to provide sufficient information to decide whether the suspicion of abuse is sufficiently strong to warrant a report being made and, if so, what level of urgency is involved. Is the child safe to return home at the end of the day? Relevant artwork and records of conversations should always be photocopied and the photocopies stored in a locked, safe place before the originals are handed over to child protection authorities. The officers receiving the drawings should be asked to provide a receipt.

RESPONDING TO CHILDREN WHEN SEXUAL ABUSE IS SUSPECTED

If a child is giving signals that he or she is distressed, talk gently and reassuringly, in private, pointing out that you are there to help.

- Reassure the child that it is good to talk about things that worry us and that you want to help: 'I'm really concerned about you. You haven't been your usual cheerful self lately. I think you'll feel much better if you can tell me about it. I'm sure I can help.'
- Locate the source of the distress: 'Someone is obviously upsetting you. Is it someone at home?' If the child responds 'No', enquire, 'Is it someone at school?'
- If the child says 'No' again, continue on the lines of, 'Okay, we know that someone is upsetting you. You say it isn't anyone at home and it isn't anyone at school . . . so where do you see this person who is bothering you?'
- Ascertain whether the child has been sworn to secrecy. 'Is it something that is really hard to talk about? Is it a secret? Is it a secret that makes you feel happy or a secret that makes you feel scared?'

Sometimes children give hints that they have a secret that can't be told. Please note that you should *never ask a child to disclose the secret.* However, you can find out whether the secret is harmless by asking, 'Who else knows this secret?' 'What will happen if you tell?' The responses to these two questions should tell you who is involved in the secret and whether it involves abuse. Has the child been threatened with 'big trouble' if the child talks about what is happening? Has someone suggested that an adult will go to jail, that the family may break up, that the mother will be angry (or will disbelieve the report) or that the child will be sent away to a place for 'bad kids'? The kind of response that you receive should indicate whether the matter needs to be reported.

Please note that when there is a strong suspicion of abuse, it is not the teacher's or caregiver's role to interrogate the victim about what happened.

DENIAL BY PARENTS

When children give out cries for help, these are often misinterpreted by adults as inconvenient aspects of normal development which, with time, will disappear. When mothers disclose concerns about children who have been victimised, staff realise that they too have been concerned.

From time to time, mothers confide in teachers or caregivers that they are worried about the inappropriate behaviour of relatives or acquaintances. Their concerns are usually justified but they hope for reassurance that their children are safe.

Quite often, mothers disclose their concerns to their partners who dismiss them as 'paranoid'. A typical husband response is, 'Don't be stupid! How could you think that? My brother/father/best mate wouldn't dare do that to my kids; and anyway, he loves them.' Few fathers are well educated about child sexual abuse or child protection; their 'knowledge' usually comes from the myths surrounding abuse. However, the strength of their response often makes mothers feel guilty, dirty-minded and foolish, deterring them from making the necessary reports.

Unfortunately, unless parents have already opened up channels of communication about sexual matters, children will not confide in them. Most children have been punished for 'rude' behaviour and they assume that their mothers will 'get cross' if they 'find out' what happened (Briggs 1991a). This belief is, of course, encouraged by offenders. Unfortunately, most victims are disbelieved or reprimanded and even punished for 'making up bad stories' about trusted adults (Briggs et al. 1994).

The reasons for parents' denial are complex. First, most parents lack education about child abuse and they imagine that their families are immune from the problem. Second, unless the offender is a stranger, the abuse is likely to have serious emotional if not financial implications for the parents. Third, few parents have done everything possible to protect their children and when abuse is confirmed they suffer enormous feelings of shame and guilt.

In addition, sexual abuse often involves a betrayal of the parent's trust as well as the child's trust. It is very hard for adults to come to terms with the fact that they could have misjudged another adult's trustworthiness. It is much easier to dismiss the allegation as a misunderstanding or a figment of the child's imagination.

The victim is least likely to be believed if the offender is the mother's spouse or sexual partner. She is likely to confront the accused who provides the denial that she wishes to hear. The child's predicament is ignored, the offender threatens to use violence if the child repeats the allegations and the abuse continues. The child is more psychologically damaged than before because events have provided further confirmation that he or she is helpless.

SUPPORTING THE PARENTS OF SEXUALLY ABUSED CHILDREN

Teachers and early childhood professionals often find themselves giving support and advice to shocked and bewildered mothers whose trusted partners are their children's abusers. The professionals often have to persuade parents of the need for specialist counselling for their children and for themselves so that they can provide better informed support. Parents often deny that therapy is necessary. It is a traumatic experience for them to have to take children to a therapy unit because each visit gives reminders of the abuse and their failure to provide adequate protection.

Sometimes, mothers of victims turn to staff for confirmation that they should ignore the abuse and accept their partner's explanation for what happened, for example that:

- the child misunderstood normal affectionate behaviour;
- it was a single offence which happened in a 'moment of weakness' and will not occur again;
- it happened a long time ago; and,
- the victim caused the offence by behaving in a sexually provocative way.

None of these explanations is valid and mothers should be urged to put the support and protection of their children first and foremost. To be effective, schools and preschools should have information readily available about specialist services for abused children and their families.

PROVIDING POSITIVE LEARNING ENVIRONMENTS FOR CHILD VICTIMS OF ABUSE

Schools and teachers have an important role to play in providing a supportive, stable environment in which victims of all forms of abuse and neglect can learn to trust others and feel safe. Young victims need:

- special programmes designed to develop their self-esteem, confidence and assertiveness;
- special programmes to develop personal safety skills;
- opportunities for therapeutic play, such as painting, finger-painting, water, clay and mud play, and play with wet and dry sand. These are soothing and there is no risk of failure associated with them; and,
- opportunities for success and praise for effort as well as for achievement.

Teachers and caregivers, through their normal daily contact with victims, have an opportunity to make a significant contribution to their adjustment. They can:

- maintain children's normal status in the group;
- provide consistency and structure and predictability in the daily routine until they can mobilise their own resources;
- respect and maintain children's privacy: a major fear of victims is that their abuse will become common knowledge among the whole school and staff;
- clearly define what is acceptable behaviour. Disruptive, antisocial or sexual behaviour should be discouraged by encouraging appropriate behaviour;
- encourage a sense of belonging by fostering new peer relationships;
- respect children's personal space, for example, find alternatives to touching;
- help them to verbalise sad feelings; and,
- model sound adult–child behavioural boundaries.

Most education authorities now accept responsibility for teaching assertiveness skills and personal safety skills to children. These programmes will be discussed in greater detail in chapter 13.

HOW TO HANDLE A DIRECT DISCLOSURE OF SEXUAL ABUSE

Children often disclose sexual abuse to before and after school caregivers and holiday programme leaders, as well as to parent-helpers and teachers. Non-teaching staff are chosen when they are perceived as approachable, non-authority figures. When children reveal sexual abuse, it is important to talk in private and tell them that they are strong and very sensible and have done the right thing. They need to know that by disclosing what happened they have helped protect other children from becoming upset and hurt by the offender. Acknowledge that it is hard to talk about this. Acknowledge that some adults misbehave with children. Abuse victims must also be told very clearly that children are never to blame when older children or adults behave this way. Explain that offenders know that what they are doing is wrong; that is why they use secrecy or threats or tricks.

Victims also need to know that what happened to them has happened to other children in that school or centre. They must be helped to realise that they were not abused because they are weak, stupid, naughty or different.

Victims must be told that abuse has to be reported to 'special people who help children when this happens. When people do this to children they must be told to stop it.' Explain that if the victim wants to tell you something more at another time, you will gladly listen. Finally, never assure the child that the abuse will stop; unfortunately that cannot be guaranteed.

Record everything that the child said.

Victims need to know that they are worthwhile human beings, are not helpless and powerless and that others will care for them without making demands on them.

It is sometimes helpful to acknowledge victims' unhappiness when they are having a bad day. Unhappiness occurs when the child sees the offender, has an interview about the abuse or is reminded in some other way of what happened. It is helpful to say, 'I can see that you're feeling sad today. You've had a really rotten time lately. Would you like to talk about it?'

Sometimes reports are made and nothing seems to happen. When teachers and early childhood professionals are dissatisfied with the responses of case workers they should contact the regional manager of their social welfare services and, if necessary, ask their seniors to call a conference of relevant parties. Always bear in mind that you will be working with victims long after case workers have closed their files and moved on.

Employers usually instruct staff not to question children when they have a 'gut feeling' that abuse is taking place. Although this advice is sound, the reality is that child protection services are unlikely to investigate any report based only on vague impressions.

There are many publications available for teachers, parents and children about child protection and child abuse. (Books for children are usually designed to minimise the guilt and self-recrimination which haunts victims of child sexual abuse.) Free booklets are available from child protection services and inexpensive books are available at personal growth and educational bookshops, many of which offer a postal service to rural customers. These publications should be readily available in all school and parent libraries.

THERAPY FOR VICTIMS OF SEXUAL ABUSE

It is important that schools, early childhood centres and residential institutions help all child victims to receive therapy following acts of sexual abuse. Treatment is necessary to:

- alleviate the victim's feelings of guilt engendered by the abuser;
- alleviate non-offending parents' feelings of guilt;
- explore issues of trust to help victims regain their trust in other people and themselves;
- provide basic information about normal sexuality and interpersonal relationships; this is vital because victims have already learned about abnormal sexuality and if we do not teach them about the normal range of appropriate behaviours, they cannot recognise the abnormal when they encounter it;
- discuss homosexual issues when necessary, assuring boys that they were chosen because they were children, not because they are effeminate, weak or homosexual; and
- explore victims' feelings about the abuse and the abuser.

Therapists explore, eliminate and rechannel secondary behavioural characteristics, such as inappropriate acting out of the sexual abuse, self-destructive behaviour and aggression. They reduce depression by helping victims to express their anger relating to their abuse, the abuser and the adults who did not protect them. In addition, therapists inform children about their rights.

Without support and therapy, child victims of sexual abuse are at high risk of serious emotional disturbance which often results in the reproduction of the abusive behaviour with other children. The victim becomes the offender and another generation of child sexual abuse victims is created.

When children undertake therapy, it is important that their teachers and parents maintain regular contact with therapists to ensure that there is continuity of treatment in the home and classroom. Teachers have prolonged contact with children and their observations can contribute substantially to the therapist's understanding of children's progress. Furthermore, they should always ask to be present at case conferences relating to children in their classes.

IMPEDIMENTS TO REPORTING

Acting to assist children who have experienced abuse or neglect is vital, but picking up the pieces after abuse has occurred is second best to preventing it from happening in the first place. We have shown that teachers are expected to report cases of suspected abuse (chapter 1). This will go some way towards assisting children in need. However, reporting abuse is a difficult task because of the inhibiting effects of denial or other emotional responses to abuse. Many child professionals nonetheless find the courage to report their suspicions, only to find that no action is taken to stop the abuse. In some cases the child has overcome reluctance and fear to share the terrible secret with a trusted adult. The adult has, in turn, overcome emotional barriers to pass the complaint to the relevant authorities but then nothing is done. This, of course, dissuades professionals from reporting again and confirms to victims that the adult world cannot be trusted and that the abuser is more powerful than teachers.

Statistics in many countries show substantial increases in reported and substantiated child abuse cases over recent years.

For example, in Australia there was an increase of 26 per cent in reported child abuse and neglect cases from 1992–93 to 1993–94 (to a total of 74 436 cases) (Angus & Woodward 1995). In Australia there has been a 75 per cent increase in reports over the last five years.

Naturally, the general public finds it difficult to believe that there has been such a dramatic, epidemic-like increase in child abuse. In addition, there have been some well-publicised cases in several countries of overzealous child abuse investigations and there are cases where parents or professionals have been falsely accused of abuse. As a consequence, some people have reacted against child protection attempts, believing that the problem has been overstated (Sinclair 1995). This reaction has been termed the 'backlash' and has been the subject of recent books (for example, see Myers 1994). The backlash is a cause for concern. Roland Summit, who is one of the most experienced and respected advocates of child protection, explains that since child abuse is such an emotionally difficult subject to face and since societies have historically been very good at maintaining secrecy and denial about the topic, the backlash may lead to a closeting-away of the problem once again (Summit 1994).

The prevalence statistics do not really show a new epidemic of child abuse. Rather they reflect responses to mandatory reporting legislation together with the relatively recent increase in public recognition of the problem (Clark 1995) which has led to some reduction in historical levels of denial and secrecy.

10

PROTECTING CHILDREN WITH DISABILITIES[1]

North American studies show that children with disabilities are at much higher risk of all forms of abuse than non-disabled children.

During pregnancy, parents often try to imagine the baby and their future family life. When a baby is born with a disability, the difference between reality and their expectations often results in shock, denial, guilt, depression, anxiety and anger which are the stages involved in the grief process. When the child has a severe disability, there is often a feeling of not being able to cope. Parents and even grandparents grieve for the loss of the child they might have had. What is less generally known is that, although the child may be dearly loved, guilt and grief often persist throughout life, especially when the disability is severe (Garbarino et al. 1987).

When a baby is born or becomes severely disabled, the parents and family often experience social isolation if not rejection. At the time when they need most support, parents tend to become isolated from former friends and even relatives avoid them.

Caring for a severely disabled child is often a full-time task. It is demanding, exhausting, frustrating and stressful. Dressing, feeding, bathing and toileting a heavy, incapacitated child requires considerable strength and patience. The mother often finds herself

---

1 Much of the content of this chapter has been adapted from Briggs, F. (1995a) *Developing personal safety skills in children with disabilities* (London: Jessica Kingsley Publishers), a book of curriculum ideas for teaching safety skills to disabled children. The suggestions are also appropriate for non-disabled children in mainstreamed classrooms.

housebound, concentrating on the physical and medical needs of her dependent offspring. Partners and siblings may eventually resent the loss of attention. Support agencies claim that 50 per cent of marriages fail under the strain of caring for these children.

Given that stress and social isolation are two major factors which contribute to child abuse, it is easy to see why children with disabilities are at much higher risk of physical and emotional abuse than their non-disabled peers. Apart from the risk of abuse in the home, there is, of course, a high risk of bullying and victimisation of all kinds in the school and social environment.

CHILDREN WITH DISABILITIES ARE AT GREATEST RISK OF SEXUAL VICTIMISATION

American and Canadian studies confirm that children with disabilities are up to seven times more likely to suffer sexual abuse than non-disabled children. Our own study involving eleven-year-old girls in New Zealand (Briggs & Hawkins 1996a) revealed that 80 per cent of those identified as having severe learning difficulties had already been multiply sexually abused by multiple offenders. Furthermore, when they attempted to report the abuse to their mothers or their primary school teachers, they were disbelieved because they were intellectually disabled.

Senn (1988) summarised a number of studies showing that up to 69 per cent of girls with developmental disabilities are victimised. Chamberlain et al. (1984, cited in Senn 1988) found that 25 per cent of girls in this category were raped or suffered attempted rape, one-third by their fathers or father figures.

British and American studies also show that more than half of all deaf boys (52 per cent) were sexually abused and that boys were more at risk than girls. The greatest risk for boys was in residential schools but 25 per cent of victims were abused both at home and at school. Between 80 per cent and 100 per cent of deaf boys identified as 'emotionally disturbed' had been victimised (Kennedy 1989; Mounty & Fetterman 1989; Sullivan, Vernon & Scanlan 1987).

Children with disabilities are at very high risk of sexual victimisation because they are:

- devalued and dehumanised by society as a whole (because they are imperfect);

- often touched by many different caregivers and professionals. When children cannot take responsibility for their own hygiene, this touching may involve intimate parts of their bodies;
- uninformed about their rights, their sexuality, the limits of acceptable social behaviour, the differences between acceptable and unacceptable touching and the need to reject and report sexual misbehaviour;
- inadequately protected by child welfare and education services;
- disadvantaged by communication barriers and often lack the skills to report sexual abuse;
- often overprotected, have a restricted social life and few opportunities for independence. Families often do everything for them because it is easier than teaching and letting them practise skills for themselves;
- lacking in self-esteem and the confidence and assertiveness needed to complain.

In addition, they are unprotected by the justice system; adult criminal courts rarely cater for child witnesses who lack the sophisticated communication skills needed to respond to prolonged cross-examination by defence lawyers. Offenders know that they are safe from prosecution if there are no non-disabled witnesses to their offences.

WHY THE PROTECTION OF CHILDREN WITH DISABILITIES IS IGNORED

Society's failure to protect children with disabilities can be explained in several ways. First, there are many misunderstandings about the nature of sexual abuse itself. Many people do not expect disabled children to be sexually abused because they are not perceived as sexually attractive by popular media standards. Parents, teachers and caregivers have often dismissed reports and suspicions in the mistaken belief that offenders only abuse 'attractive' children. The reality is that sexual abuse involves the manipulation of weaker and uninformed human beings. Children with disabilities are targeted for victimisation because they are the least knowledgeable, the least assertive, the least valued and the least protected members of society.

Unfortunately, many people, including the offenders, choose to believe that the abuse of disabled children is somehow less damaging and less serious than the abuse of non-disabled children.

This delusion enables them to ignore reports and signs of abuse without conscience. They tell themselves that developmentally disabled victims 'don't really understand what happened'. Margaret Kennedy's study of deaf victims showed that these assumptions are not only false but that the abuse of disabled children compounds the emotional problems associated with their disabilities (Kennedy 1990). Before the abuse, victims felt isolated, anxious, confused, powerless, angry, embarrassed, depressed, fearful, stigmatised and withdrawn because of their disabilities. Sexual victimisation exacerbated all of those feelings.

CHALLENGES FOR PARENTS AND TEACHERS IN DEVELOPING SAFETY SKILLS WITH DISABLED CHILDREN

Parents and teachers should not underestimate the difficulties involved in teaching safety concepts to young and intellectually disabled children.

- Many of the concepts involved in self-protection are difficult to grasp, for example, unsafe, trust, secret, sexual misbehaviour. They require thorough exploration using a variety of means. Reinforcement must be ongoing, catering for individual needs. Sessions should be repeated with minor modifications until there is evidence that they are understood.

  Intellectually disabled and young children may find it difficult to transfer information from one setting to another. For example, if taught to go to a Safety House for help, children will suggest the Safety House as the safe solution to all problems, even to the examples of being lost in a large store, at the beach, park or market where there are no Safety Houses. Parents and teachers should check children's learning after each session by asking relevant 'What if . . . .?' questions.

- Instructions and questions must be clear. Use short, simple sentences. Avoid using either/or questions and those which can be answered with 'Yes' or 'No'. Ask one question at a time.
- Remember that intellectually disabled children have a much slower rate of progress than non-disabled children of the same age. Information must be broken down into small segments

and opportunities for practice must be provided on a daily basis (Anderson 1982).

- Young and intellectually disabled children tend to be 'doers'. They need a variety of concrete activities including role plays and puppetry.
- Young children and intellectually disabled children are unlikely to grasp vague hints about unacceptable, sexual touching.

ADDITIONAL CHALLENGES WHEN WORKING WITH DEAF CHILDREN

To be successful, programmes for deaf children must ensure that the following are addressed.

- There are communication barriers between deaf family members and hearing school personnel. Some schools have found that deaf teachers are needed for deaf children because they can present material from a 'non-hearing' perspective. Mixed hearing and deaf teachers are desirable for workshops.
- Deaf teachers need sensitive training to teach personal safety skills, given that many members of the adult deaf population are also survivors of abuse.
- Because learning is predominantly visual, a range of visual materials (such as pictorial cards, puppet shows, role plays and, if possible, special videos) should be used to extend and reinforce children's learning.
- Children with communication problems often lack the means to communicate concerns about their bodies.

Teaching personal safety skills to deaf children requires a heightened awareness of the varied communication backgrounds of individual children whose access to communication has been restricted. Few deaf children will have had the opportunity to discuss sensitive sexual issues with reliable adults. Because shared communication is essential to the establishment of trust, extra care must be taken to create clear, open and safe communications between teachers, parents and children.

To adapt a personal safety programme for use with deaf children, we have to go beyond the translation of the text from print to sign language and change the perspective to a visual one.

157

We must bear in mind that there is a much higher tolerance of touch in the deaf community than in the hearing community. Touching is essential for attracting attention and transmitting information. Hugs and other touches are commonly involved in communicative interaction between deaf people. As a result, the acceptability of some touching behaviours may be different in children with hearing impairments. The differences between acceptable and unacceptable touching must be clearly illustrated and explained. This can be conveyed by using pictures, puppets, and role plays accompanied by subtle changes of facial expression and body movement to demonstrate unacceptable touching.

When reporting suspicions of sexual abuse involving deaf and non-verbal children, staff should request the child protection agency to employ the services of a qualified and suitably experienced interpreter. Problems arise when interviewers are inexperienced in translating information relating to sexual offences, feel uncomfortable with the children and fail to gain their trust. Children may feel more comfortable if the trusted staff member who received the report works in tandem with the interviewers. This is useful when assessment is urgent or when the interviewee has intellectual disabilities, multiple disabilities or a very idiosyncratic communication system which strangers may not understand.

ADAPTING PROGRAMMES FOR CHILDREN WITH COMMUNICATION PROBLEMS

Some children now have technical aids which give them access to telephones. However, deaf and non-verbal children may not be aware of resources such as Rape Crisis Centres and telephone help and crisis lines and, until introduced to child protection programmes, few parents realise the need for such information.

Schools catering for children with special communication needs should locate and contact the professionals or agencies capable of providing therapy for special needs children. Support networks should be created *before* cases of abuse are reported. If no specialist support workers are available, schools and parents should lobby their child protection authorities and politicians.

In common with intellectually disabled and non-verbal children, children with hearing impairment also need to be taught when and how to use other attention-seeking strategies, such as pulling alarms on trains, stopping buses, triggering fire alarms and writing simple requests for help. In addition, physical defence training is an important asset for all children with disabilities (Mounty & Fetterman 1989; Kennedy 1989).

WORKING WITH NON-VERBAL CHILDREN

When working with non-verbal children, it is advisable to consult a speech pathologist for the acquisition and use of the appropriate Blissymbols, Picture Communication Symbols (PCS) (Mayer-Johnson Co.), Picture Vocabulary System for Sexuality (BC Rehabilitation Society) or similar symbol system.

WORKING WITH CHILDREN WHO HAVE VISUAL IMPAIRMENTS

Children with severe visual impairments are likely to need extra help to develop body awareness. This is necessary to teach safe social behaviours that provide protection from the risk of abuse. Anatomically correct dolls with genitals, mouth, anus and breasts are a 'must' for sightless children. Dolls should be selected for their realistic 'feel'. Again, it is useful to involve an adult with impaired sight to ensure that teachers provide the appropriate cultural perspectives.

PROVIDE CURRICULUM TO DEVELOP SELF-ESTEEM

To keep children safe, we have to give them the knowledge, skills and confidence to reject sexual misbehaviour involving bigger, stronger and more powerful people. Developing a positive self-image is at the root of all confidence building and self-protection. Because of society's high valuation of physical perfection, it is difficult for disabled youngsters to acquire a healthy level of self-esteem. Curriculum planning must take this into account.

Schools, institutions, families and children should work together to provide an integrated approach to independence and protection. Home–school cooperation is vital but may be difficult to obtain when children are in residential situations or travel by special transport and there is little parent–teacher contact.

HELP CHILDREN TO DEVELOP INDEPENDENCE

The task of teaching personal safety skills to disabled children may appear daunting, especially when parents try to protect them by exercising total control over their lives. Overprotection has the opposite effect to the one desired. Children's dependence and ignorance increase vulnerability to abuse and they have no idea what to do when things go wrong. Parents indoctrinated with the myth of the dangerous stranger also believe, mistakenly, that if they act as taxi drivers, their children will be safe (Briggs 1988).

When children rely on others for getting in and out of bed, dressing, showering and toileting, staff and parents should explore opportunities to increase self-reliance. The keys to independence are choice and privacy. Disabled children are deprived of the most elementary choices, even the choice of flavours for ice-creams. They are also deprived of opportunities for privacy, including privacy for intimate tasks. Barriers to independent living can be summarised as:

- societal ignorance of how to relate to people with disabilities;
- pity for the disabled person;
- intrusive curiosity or benevolence.

The first task for teachers, parents and caregivers is, then, to explore their own attitudes to the disabled. The second task is to plan and implement curriculum that will help children to become more independent. This curriculum must, of necessity, involve parent participation.

TEACH CHILDREN HOW TO STAY SAFE

When teaching children with disabilities how to stay safe, we have to be open, honest and clear about what we mean. Many of the programmes intended for non-disabled children rely on vague hints about touching and having unsafe feelings; it would be safe to operate from the premise that developmentally disabled children are incapable of adapting vague hints to very complex abusive situations involving caregivers.

It may be useful for older children to meet professionals involved in child protection and other helping services so that they know who to contact if they need help. It is also important to ensure that children are capable of making emergency and collect telephone calls. Help them to learn about what an emergency is. Teach children how to report emergencies to services. Ensure that they know the circumstances in which the services should be used. Take children to public telephones to ensure that they can use them. Institutions should have public telephones at an appropriate height for children in wheelchairs. It is often argued that children with disabilities are handicapped by their lack of access to telephone communications. In a real emergency, they often do not know what to do.

TEACH CHILDREN HOW TO COMMUNICATE EFFECTIVELY

When children with disabilities need help, they are often handicapped by poor communication skills. It is beneficial if they can be taught how to talk, listen and look at people, establishing eye contact without staring. It is helpful if they can practise using an appropriate posture and stand at a suitable distance from those with whom they are communicating, in other words, neither too close nor too distant. They are more likely to be taken seriously if they use clear firm speech for communicating serious issues: children with intellectual disabilities often shout or mutter. They also need to know how to interrupt adults for emergencies.

USE ROLE PLAYS

Children with intellectual disabilities learn safety skills very effectively through role plays (Anderson 1982). Children act out scenes involving bullying or unwanted touches of a non-sexual nature. One person takes the part of the perpetrator and another acts as the victim. Children can also role play scenes involving tricks by potentially dangerous strangers. Participation should be limited to about five minutes and the role plays should focus on ways of staying safe. The teacher acts as coach, stopping proceedings at appropriate moments to ask participants how they felt about what took place. Teachers encourage the promotion of children's own ideas for role play after the discussion of a particular safety issue. Children usually have ideas but they may need guidance relating to their appropriateness.

The capacity for role play may be very limited in a group of children with profound intellectual disabilities. Scenes should be frozen at crucial points to enable the audience to suggest how participants feel and what they could do for bad feelings to stop. Brainstorming methods should be used to enable children to put forward their own ideas for staying safe. The coach may stop proceedings to ask the audience to help victims who are uncertain about what to do. The coach uses positive reinforcement for each appropriate example of assertiveness.

Role play offers an excellent technique for children with disabilities to learn and practise assertiveness skills. Since the techniques of role play need particular skills in order to be used effectively, and since role plays risk overlap with psychotherapy, the technique is best conducted by specialist drama teachers.

CASE STUDIES

1 Debbie, aged thirteen, a special needs child with Down syndrome, complains that her father insists on washing, bathing and undressing her. This makes her feel angry because she can do these things herself. Should you report this? Discuss.

2 The mother of an intellectually disabled child in your class says that she wishes to withdraw the child from your child protection and sex education curriculum. Plan your response to justify offering these curriculum subjects to a child with disabilities.

3 You are a new teacher on a one term contract which could be extended if you perform satisfactorily. During your first week of working with children who have moderate to severe disabilities, you return to the classroom at lunchtime and find a female voluntary helper fondling the genitals of a cerebral palsy child on the classroom floor. You are horrified by what you see and, forgetting your training, demand an explanation. The woman (who has an intellectual disability) replies, 'I was only changing her'. Again forgetting your training, you rush into the staffroom and tell others about the incident. The senior member of staff says 'You must be mistaken, that woman has been a voluntary helper for about eight years. She wouldn't do anything like that. She loves our kids. After all, you've only been here a week.'
What would you say? What would you do? Why?

11

UNDERSTANDING OUR FEELINGS ABOUT CHILD MALTREATMENT

One of the major barriers to protecting children from abuse and neglect is the priority we give to our own feelings.

A very common response to the whole issue of child abuse involves some form of denial of the problem. Denial is a self-protective mechanism which is normal and commonplace. Denial about child maltreatment may not be total, but may operate at some less-than-complete level. Partial denial is often referred to as 'discounting'. Unfortunately, discounting can interfere with an adult responding appropriately to the issue of child abuse. Discounters may say that:

- child abuse does not exist at all (this form of denial is uncommon given that reports of maltreatment are ubiquitous in newspapers and television news reports);
- the problem exists, but it is not a significant problem. It has been greatly overstated in general and is certainly not an issue where I live or work;
- child abuse is a problem but there is little that can be done about it; and,
- child abuse is a problem but it is not my problem and there is nothing I can do to help.

All too frequently teachers and early childhood professionals tell us of the disclosures of sexual abuse which they ignored because they were 'too embarrassed' and 'didn't know what to say'. The tragedy is that it takes a great deal of courage for child victims to report abuse to trusted adults and when their reports are ignored or rejected, the trusted adults increase the psychological damage caused by the abuse. Eventually, rejected children resign themselves to victimisation, convinced that they are helpless, hopeless and not worth helping. This has a devastating effect on their self-esteem and emotional and social development.

When we receive information which suggests that a child has been abused, it is in the child's best interests that we conceal our shock. We have to remind ourselves that the child is the victim and the child's needs must take precedence over our own needs, however uncomfortable and inadequate we may feel. Professionals in schools and preschools offer the child's best defence against abuse. If we ignore our responsibilities and victims' cries for help, we collude with the perpetrators of abuse. Sometimes teachers inform offenders of the allegations, imagining that the abuse will stop. It seldom does because the offender thinks, 'The school knows what's happening and they haven't reported it. I'm safe!' The abuse often becomes more frequent and more violent than before.

CHILD ABUSE AROUSES STRONG EMOTIONS

Child abuse is a highly emotional subject. The public outcries that occur when excessively violent cases are publicised demonstrate the spontaneous emotional reaction that takes place in individuals. The most commonly expressed emotions are as follows.

Shock

Shock is the first and most common reaction to evidence of child abuse. It is greatest when we are inadequately prepared for handling the visual or oral information suggesting that a child has been maltreated. It is also a powerful force when the abuser is someone we know and trust or someone who can influence our current or future employment.

Professionals who have worked with victims for many years are continually shocked by the inhumane ways in which some adults treat children. Modern technology has increased the variety of ways in which human beings inflict injury on their young. Who would not be shocked, for example, by two separate Australian cases in which men placed their partner's babies in microwave ovens and switched them on, ostensibly to 'stop the kid from crying'.

In the best of centres and the best of schools in the best of neighbourhoods there will be at least one abused child in every class or group. In other words, disclosures or suspicions of child abuse should not be so unexpected that we fall apart when we see signs or receive information about maltreatment. The incidence is so high that any caring professional should be prepared to receive disclosures at any time. Shock is dangerous when it is overwhelming because it inhibits us from taking appropriate action to stop abuse and help victims. Shocked adults tend to concentrate on their own emotional needs and, in that state, they forget about the feelings and needs of the children in their care.

Denial

When the implications of what we hear and see are horrendous, shock is followed by denial which results in statements such as, 'I don't believe it! It can't be true! They must be mistaken.'

Denial is a normal response. When information is unbearable, we want to distance ourselves from it. Reactions to child abuse can be explained in terms of selective perception; our emotions act as filters which screen and adjust our sensory and intellectual world to enable us to remain in control. In other words, to make life tolerable for ourselves, we may see only what we expect or want to see, believe or hear and we may deny the unacceptable either by telling ourselves that it did not happen or by accepting that it happened but discounting or minimising the seriousness of the behaviour.

Sympathy, pity and the desire to help victims

Teachers and caregivers feel sympathy and pity for children who are persistently neglected or physically abused. When parents fail to collect children from child care centres, staff often express the urge to 'take them home and look after them'. When children are dirty and undernourished, staff declare their desire to 'give them a bath and a good feed'. Some professionals do, in fact, provide food, showers and clothing for dirty children but this well-meaning intervention has no long-term benefits unless it is accompanied by a report to the authorities followed by support for the parents.

Frustration

Frustration is also felt because of our limited ability to protect children in our care. Teachers and caregivers are frustrated when they try to report suspicions of abuse to senior staff who either dismiss them or minimise their importance. We may be frustrated or outraged by the inadequacies of the justice system which, so frequently, appears to protect adults at children's expense. We may be frustrated by welfare authorities when they bend to the wishes of parents to the detriment of the needs of children. Frustration is dangerous if it deters us from acting in children's interests.

Anger

There is usually a great deal of anger surrounding child abuse. It becomes rage when young children die or suffer serious injury or the abuse is particularly vicious.

Anger is a normal and healthy response which can be channelled into a commitment to help children. Angry people are more likely than the indifferent to report suspicions of abuse. On the other hand, anger becomes destructive if it prevents us from fulfilling our professional roles sympathetically and efficiently. The professional who is angry with a negligent parent is unlikely to gain the desired cooperation from that parent and may even add to the parent's depression, low self-esteem, stress, inadequacy, helplessness and sense of isolation, placing children in greater jeopardy than before. Parents who view family services personnel as critical and punitive will avoid contact with the staff.

Anger will be felt when professionals reveal that they have been aware of child abuse but they have done nothing to stop it.

We also direct anger towards ourselves when we trusted the offender or fell for the tricks or ruses used to stop us from reporting our suspicions.

We feel angry with child protection authorities which dismiss a report as 'low priority' when we perceive the child's situation as in urgent need of intervention.

We feel angrier with the justice system when a child abuser is allowed to go free on the basis of a technicality or because the child is too immature to give testimony in court or because a short non-parole period, good behaviour bond or suspended sentence was handed down by a judge.

Distress and anxiety

When British university students were shown photographs of injured children, they found it difficult to record their reactions because of the inadequacy of the English language to express their strong feelings (Roberts & Carver 1980, p. 20). Most respondents became anxious immediately after being invited to look at the photographs.

Teachers and caregivers suffer enormous feelings of anxiety when they suspect that a child has been sexually abused. However, student teachers and child care students are increasingly receptive to the fact that child abuse occurs. They have been exposed to more than a decade of media coverage and many recent graduates studied the problem in secondary school projects with the result that, in general, they respond with less anxiety and distress than their older colleagues.

Guilt and self-recrimination

Guilt and self-recrimination are commonly associated with child abuse and sexual molestation in particular. When offences are confirmed relating to a child in our care, we invariably look back and realise that we have ignored or misinterpreted the child's cries for help for a very long time.

Blame

There is only one person to blame in a case of child sexual abuse and that is the offender. Because everyone who knows the victim, the family or the offender feels uncomfortable, blame is usually apportioned to everyone involved in the victim's social environment. Parents blame themselves for entrusting their children to relatives, registered childminders, babysitters, Sunday school teachers or whoever was responsible for the abuse. To reduce their feelings of guilt, they are also apt to apportion blame to the victims: 'Haven't I always told you to come straight home and not to walk through the park?' 'How many times have I told you not to talk to strangers?'; 'Why didn't you tell me what was happening?'

Child victims are attacked illogically and unreasonably because they did not behave as adults, albeit without the benefit of the adult's knowledge. Parents teach children to be obedient to adults and keep their secrets but, at the same time, they expect children to instinctively recognise sexual misbehaviour, avoid it or yell, fight, escape from it and report it to them (having received no information to facilitate this process).

Child victims are blamed by adults who do not understand the dynamics of sexual abuse and find it hard to believe that an intelligent adult would choose a child as a sexual partner. 'Why would a teacher risk his career for the sake of sex with a six-year-old?' asked a New Zealand defence counsel. The jury agreed that it was unbelievable. When a well-dressed defendant accused a twelve-year-old boy of seducing him, the jury believed him too, only to find (too late) that both men had previous convictions for child sexual abuse.

When adults try to find logical explanations for sexual abuse, they fail. Mothers of children in father–daughter incest cases often blame and even hate victims, perceiving them as competitors and mini harlots, albeit six or seven years old.

Teachers and early childhood professionals blame themselves when they realise that they inadvertently gave the offender access to victims; for example, when children are snatched from school grounds, abused in school toilets or when a voluntary helper or colleague utilised opportunities for privacy to commit offences. Staff then need a great deal of support and counselling.

Sadness or depression

Sadness or depression is inevitable when there is evidence that the world is a terrible place for some children.

Revulsion, horror and disgust

Revulsion, horror and disgust are intertwined with shock when we learn of the detail of offences against children. When we know that a child has been sexually abused, we may have to make a conscious effort not to think about what happened as this could affect the way we feel about the child. Mothers of victims often become obsessed with thoughts of the abuse and end up hating their children (Briggs 1993). It is vital that teachers and caregivers do not go down the same track.

For most professionals involved in child care and education, a key personal issue is the stress of working with a child whose early victimisation has resulted in sexualised behaviours. Such behaviours can be thoroughly sickening to onlookers. Reminders of sexual abuse are difficult to control when victims exhibit sexual behaviour. Staff find this upsetting and difficult to handle. Unfortunately, they often transfer their strong negative feelings to victims. It is stressful for teachers, foster parents and early childhood professionals who are under constant pressure to provide special care for these needy youngsters while keeping vigilance to ensure the safety of others in the group.

Revenge and the desire for punishment

Revenge and the desire for punishment are common reactions to all forms of child abuse because of the strong emotions that are aroused in caring individuals. Ironically, once punitive feelings are stirred, people often experience a desire to use violence in protest against the violence used by the abuser against a child.

There is always an unstated assumption that the abuser is quite different from anyone we know. Because human behaviour is so complex, we also find it difficult to understand how people who suffered abuse in childhood can grow up to betray the trust of other children, including their own sons and daughters or grand-children.

COPING WITH OUR FEELINGS RELATING TO ABUSE

To provide maximum protection for children, it is vital that involved professionals are aware of their feelings about child abuse and recognise how these feelings affect their behaviour. If we reconsider the common responses to child abuse, we will see that the emotions can be turned to advantage by a combination of education and a psychological technique called reframing.

Self-education is one very effective way to modify unhelpful emotional responses to abuse. By familiarising yourself with the literature, including case studies, you can become more prepared for the harsh realities of abuse. The shock of new cases, while never removed by education, can be reduced to a level where people are not immobilised.

In the case of denial, it is useful to be able to fall back on procedures dictated by policy. When professionals are covered by policies requiring reporting, they can, in effect, bypass the emo-tional response of denial by simply adhering to a standard practice of reporting indications of abuse. Professionals can then report because they are 'required to', even if they have not fully dealt with their tendencies towards denial.

Distress and anxiety can also be reduced to more acceptable levels by a process of self-education which has some desensitising effects. Tertiary training institutions have a responsibility to provide exposure to child abuse issues and in-service training is also essential to supplement and extend pre-service training.

Even feelings of guilt can be reframed. Reframing is a process used extensively in clinical psychology to modify a person's view of events from one which is limiting and restricting to one which allows fresh possibilities for action. When people feel guilty as a consequence of not recognising indicators of abuse in children in their care, there is a likelihood that they will be particularly skilled in detecting future cases. Guilt can serve the positive function of leading to improved skills in the longer term.

Blaming child victims is easy to do in ignorance but, again, when professionals inform themselves thoroughly about the dynamics of abuse, they understand much more fully and accept the reality that the power differential between adults and children absolves children of blame.

Revenge and the desire for punishment are very common feelings which can be reframed positively. When professionals consider that even severe punishment of offenders does not remove the trauma from the victim, resources and attention can be redirected towards prevention strategies.

The teacher or early childhood professional who reacts strongly to cases of abuse is, if you like, primed for action. The emotion-induced readiness to act can be usefully channelled into the education of self and others towards involvement in protection programmes.

The risk with sympathy, pity and the desire to help is that professionals may, in effect, collude with perpetrators if they simply adopt a strategy of 'being nice' to child victims in a compensatory way while avoiding the difficult but necessary step of reporting the abuse. It is important to show children that not all adults are prepared to be caught up in a conspiracy of secrecy.

Anger and frustration can lead to low morale and teacher burn-out but, paradoxically, they can become motivating factors resulting in a greater commitment to help children.

It is clear that emotional responses to child abuse can result in adult paralysis and inaction or even inadvertent complicity. To avoid this result, the following process is helpful:

- self-education—this helps in desensitisation and challenges inappropriate beliefs and attitudes;
- reframing—this takes a negative experience and reconstructs it so that a more positive perspective can lead to better future responses;
- staff development or informal networking.

These not only serve an educational role but they provide useful support for people grappling with their responses to child abuse.

WHAT IF I, TOO, WAS ABUSED IN CHILDHOOD?

Some uncomfortable feelings will relate to our own experiences. Almost all of us have experienced some form of abuse at some time in our lives. If we can recollect our own responses, we can begin to understand the traumatic stress of child victims and their need for support. If we deny our abuse, we are unlikely to be able to respond effectively to the needs of the children in our care. If reminders still produce strong feelings of anger, guilt, embarrassment or other powerful emotions, readers should seek specialist counselling to work through these feelings in a healthy way. This is important because when children's cries for help revive memories and feelings which have not been dealt with, we may freeze and become incapable of responding. Adult survivors of abuse often need frequent reminders that children are never responsible for what adults do (or did) to them. If we can work through our feelings in a constructive way, we are likely to emerge stronger, more committed and better able to help children than those who have had no abusive experiences.

THE EFFECTS OF EMOTIONS ON SENSORY AND INTELLECTUAL PERCEPTIONS

It is important to recognise the effects of our emotions on our sensory and intellectual perceptions for several reasons.

- They affect the way in which parents and children relate to us, making us approachable or unapproachable people.
- They affect the way in which we receive information, accepting or rejecting it, being judgemental or non-judgemental, appearing critical or uncritical, shocked or helpful.
- These behaviours are disclosed in our verbal expression and body language and they tell children and their parents whether we are likely to be helpful, or unhelpful, critical and punitive.
- They affect our perceptions of what we hear and see and affect our capacity to help.
- They affect our capacity to interpret and make sound judgements relating to real-life situations.

It is important that students and professionals identify and come to terms with feelings and past experiences which might influence the way they think, behave and feel about specific situations. It is perfectly reasonable to feel angry or even outraged when children have been maltreated. There is no virtue in 'turning the other cheek'. As teachers and early childhood professionals, we are not concerned with judgements, however; our responsibility is to protect children and keep them safe.

Few cases of child abuse and neglect are straightforward situations. The range of emotions they elicit is often contradictory and confusing. In marginal cases of neglect or physical abuse, we may find ourselves sympathising with the perpetrators as well as the victims. At this stage, 'at risk' families can be identified and helped.

When children are seriously injured or neglected, there has usually been a long history of maltreatment which preschools and schools have ignored.

CONFLICT IN SYMPATHY FOR MARGINALLY ABUSIVE PARENTS AND SYMPATHY FOR CHILDREN

Mature adults who are also parents are the ones most likely to identify with marginally negligent or physically abusive parents as fellow human beings, recognising that children can be exhausting and infuriating and, at times, unresponsive to affection and attention. They realise that, placed in certain circumstances, most of us are capable of hurting a child. Paradoxically, idealistic university students who have been sheltered from the harshness of the world are the ones most likely to hold hostile opinions towards abusive parents, regarding all forms of abuse as inexcusable and unforgivable. This has serious implications for professional services involving families.

If we view parents as substantially different from ourselves, it is difficult to accept and interpret information correctly. When teachers tell themselves that child abuse is committed only by the criminal classes and the mentally sick and 'none of our parents falls into those categories', they miss the signs of maltreatment.

Understanding is an emotional as well as an intellectual exercise involving the ability to empathise, sympathise and comprehend how situations arise. If we cannot accept that the majority of people who physically abuse and neglect children are people like ourselves, we are unlikely to be able to help abused children or relate to families at risk. In addition, we may deny the evidence that we see when it involves colleagues, acquaintances and people who have the capacity to influence the community in which we work.

Students and professionals who are parents tend to grade abuse and respond in order of their perceptions of severity. They create a judgement continuum of severity and acceptability with hand-smacking at one end of the line and deliberate burning or scalding at the other. They see a qualitative difference between the adult who hits too hard in a moment of stress and the one who deliberately dunks a child in a hot bath. They demand more information about the child and circumstances to judge levels of provocation and the motivation of the abuser. This suggests recognition of the fact that we are all capable of such things as reacting impulsively, vindictively and, in some circumstances, we too may resort to outbursts of violence. Few parents can honestly say that they have never 'taken it out on the children' when things have gone wrong. We usually hasten to add, 'Ah yes but we never injured them', indicating that we have drawn a fine intellectual or emotional line between which kind of abuse is admissible and which is inadmissible.

What happens with our emotional filters is that we can sympathise with abusers if we can relate to their circumstances. Readers who know from personal experience how exhausting it can be to nurse fretful, crying unresponsive infants will empathise with parents who find themselves in that situation. Can you imagine yourself being driven to the use of violence if sufficiently stressed or provoked? What might those circumstances be?

To help and protect children, we need to show a genuine concern for our fellow human beings. If our sympathy for children overrides concern for parents, we are unlikely to be successful as professionals in community support agencies. Conversely, if all our sympathy is with parents, we are unlikely to make reports to child protection authorities when reports are necessary, because we value our relationship with the adults more than we value the safety of the child.

COMMUNITY DISCOURAGEMENT TO LEARNING ABOUT CHILD ABUSE

Almost everyone has a strong opinion about the subjects of child abuse and child protection. There is often a spontaneous denial of the problem: 'I'm sure that it's exaggerated by the media' or 'I think kids make it up'. The latter is usually supported by at least one piece of anecdotal evidence to the effect that someone was falsely accused of incest by a daughter who later retracted her statement. No-one pauses to question the societal, family and court pressures that might have been placed on the girl to retract.

People deny the problem of child abuse because acceptance of the truth places an obligation upon members of the community to do something about it, especially when our work involves the care and development of young people.

Earlier in this chapter we advocated the importance of self-education in the field of child abuse. It is difficult to initiate self-education when barriers such as denial exist at both the intra-individual and community level. We recommend that the reader gives careful thought to the issues raised in this chapter. Your response will very much influence your effectiveness when confronted with the problem of child abuse.

TASKS FOR STUDENTS

1 To give readers some indication of their own conflicting attitudes to negligent and abusive parents, we have provided a list of statements commonly heard in staffrooms. Using the five point scale, work through the list as honestly as you can. There are no right or wrong answers. The aim of the exercise is to clarify your own complex feelings and assess how they will affect your relationships with abused children and their parents.

SA = Strongly agree; A = Agree; N = Neutral; D = Disagree; SD = Strongly disagree

Statement	SA	A	N	D	SD
I can't bear to look at pictures of children who have been hurt or neglected.					
I feel tense, anxious and uncomfortable when the conversation is about child abuse.					
I have to keep unhygienic children at a distance because the smell makes me feel sick.					
I can't believe that a parent would deliberately burn a child with a cigarette.					
We shouldn't have to clean up kids; it's the parents' responsibility.					
People shouldn't be allowed to have kids if they don't care for them properly.					

Statement	SA	A	N	D	SD
They should put child abusers in jail and throw away the key.					
Abusive parents should be sterilised.					
I feel really sorry for kids who are neglected or abused.					
The children who get into trouble at school are the ones most likely to be hit at home.					
There are times when I wish that I could take neglected children home with me.					
I am sorry for abused kids but it's not my responsibility: I'm not a social worker.					
Some people live like animals. They shouldn't be allowed to have kids.					
Most parents are capable of hurting their children when they're stressed.					
It must be awful having a fretful baby that never sleeps.					
It's okay for parents to smack children when all else fails.					
Some children provoke adults until they lose control.					
We tend to use the same methods of discipline that our own parents used with us when we were children.					
Few parents have been taught non-violent methods of resolving conflict.					
Few parents are taught positive child management techniques as an alternative to yelling and smacking.					
Abusive parents were probably abused themselves.					
Children seem to love and remain loyal to parents however badly they treat them.					
It must be difficult bringing children up when you're a sole parent.					
Abusive parents seem to have more than their fair share of problems.					
I wouldn't believe a report of abuse if it came from a child with intellectual disabilities.					

2 When you have completed all of the questions, take a close look at your responses.

  a How many responses show that you have strong negative feelings about people who abuse children?

  b How many show that you resent having the child protection role imposed on you? How might these negative feelings affect your capacity to relate to abused or neglected children?

  c How might your negative feelings affect your capacity to relate to negligent or abusive parents? For example, could you talk to them comfortably and non-judgementally about their problems? Could you make helpful suggestions relating to the support services that could help them? Could you welcome them sincerely and encourage their involvement in your centre or classroom? Look closely at your current parent-helpers: are they mostly middle-class women who think like you?

  d To what extent do you have conflicting feelings about abusive parents?

  e Could you create a supportive relationship with a negligent parent for the sake of the child? No-one expects professionals to approve of abusive or negligent behaviour but abusive parents were often victims caught in the abuse cycle. They are disappointed with parenting and may be childlike in their need for attention and approval.

  f Did your responses show that you are sympathetic to child victims and unsympathetic to parents?

  g Early childhood professionals sometimes work with physically abusive and negligent parents on behaviour modification programmes, teaching them how to play with and relate to their children in a positive and rewarding way. This valuable work requires a partnership. Could you work in such a partnership with such a parent to make a child safer or would your negative feelings and desire for retribution be uppermost in your mind?

3 When thinking of the parents of the children in your care (and being scrupulously honest):

  a What are the characteristics of the parents with whom you have an excellent relationship?

b What are the characteristics of the parents with whom you have no relationship (or a poor relationship)? How can this be rectified?

12

CHILD PROTECTION IN THE SECONDARY SCHOOL

Much of the information given in previous chapters applies to secondary schools as well as primary schools and early childhood services. Many of the problems are the same and there is the same need for specialist training for teachers to recognise and handle child abuse and neglect cases effectively.

The powerlessness of young children and the abuse of the power differential by adults are central to our definition of child abuse and our sympathy for victims. As children proceed through the secondary school, they gradually gain some power although they lack equality with adults. They develop an increased capacity to determine how their lives proceed. In cases of abuse, this power is often utilised to escape from or deal with abuse by running away from home. Some adolescents escape from their problems through drug and alcohol abuse which, in the ultimate attempt at problem solving, may lead to suicide.

Teenage years are particularly important for the development of sexual identity and sexually abused children have particular problems in this regard. It is during the developmental period too that children who were victims are most likely to become victimisers. Our Australian study (Briggs, Hawkins & Williams 1994; Briggs & Hawkins 1996b) showed very clearly that the vast majority of male sex offenders had not only been victimised as children but, more importantly in this context, they began offending during adolescence.

CHILD HOMELESSNESS

Worldwide, there are about 100 million homeless children (Davis 1993). In 1989, the Australian Human Rights and Equal Opportunity

Commission estimated that there were 20 000–25 000 homeless children in Australia.

In 1996, statistics on the number of homeless children in New Zealand were not available from the Office of the Commissioner for Children. In the United Kingdom too, data on homeless children are hard to find, although in England there were 169 966 homeless households in 1992 (Robinson 1996). The first Australian National Census of Homeless School Students (May 1994) revealed that 11 000 school aged children were homeless during the week of the census and new cases arose throughout the year; for example, a welfare coordinator at a senior secondary college in Melbourne recorded that there were 46 cases at the beginning of census week (1994), 18 of whom later left school. In the meantime, 12 other students became homeless (MacKenzie & Chamberlain 1994).

The study also showed that most chronically homeless teen-agers had their first experience of homelessness while they were still at school. Chronically homeless adolescents are often unemployable and their lifestyles make them highly vulnerable to sexual abuse, drug or alcohol abuse and ill health. Most homeless students drop out of the education system within a few months because it becomes too hard for them to maintain the expected standards of work and appearance when they are transient or living in difficult circumstances with no income.

It is estimated that up to 30 000 Australian secondary school students experience homelessness each year (MacKenzie & Chamberlain 1994). School counsellors believe that the incidence is very much higher than the census indicates. Even though between 98 per cent and 100 per cent of schools completed the forms in all states, some counsellors have revealed that, in middle-class schools, some principals submitted zero returns when in fact there were 20–25 homeless children enrolled. The reason for this deception was that it 'wouldn't be good for the school if this information was published' and 'parents might take their children away if they knew that we had those kinds of problems here'.

For the purpose of the census, homelessness meant living in:

- a vehicle, tent, shop doorway, cardboard box, park shelter, charity clothing bin, cave, under a bridge, in a drainpipe or similar place;
- temporary accommodation with or without friends;
- a refuge or crisis accommodation;
- a youth housing programme or hostels;

- a room in a lodging house.

A significant number of schools submitted returns which indicated that they also had homeless students living in shared households.

WHY SCHOOL AGED STUDENTS LEAVE HOME

The media often present adolescent homelessness as an attractive option for rebellious teenagers who refuse to comply with parents' reasonable expectations and rules designed to protect them. At times, the media also encourage the public perception that homelessness is fostered by state-employed social workers who provide overgenerous government handouts too easily. They argue that more resources should be invested in returning children to dependence on their families.

School counsellors agree that some teenagers do rebel against reasonable limits and leave caring homes voluntarily but they constitute a very small minority of the homeless population. As the Brotherhood of St Laurence (1994) has shown, the income provided for homeless secondary students is extremely low and inadequate for continuing their education.

The vast majority of homeless young people would dearly love to be able to return home and live peaceably with their families but, in most cases, they have been abandoned, the doors are firmly shut or they have escaped from long-term sexual and/or physical abuse at the hands of parents or step-parents.

Most homelessness is triggered by family breakdown. There are several commonly experienced scenarios, the most common of which result from the build-up of tension when the custodial parent takes another partner. In some families, the stepmother is only marginally older than her stepdaughters. The less mature woman who tries to wipe out her husband's past life may view the adolescent daughter as a threat. The oldest daughter is the most vulnerable because she is likely to have been in a mother-replacement role during the period between the departure of her own mother and the arrival of the new partner. She often has responsibility for cooking, shopping and cleaning the house, is used as the family babysitter and may also have a part-time job in a supermarket or hamburger restaurant. When the new partner moves into the home, she often takes over responsibilities very selectively, leaving the daughter with the childminding and other onerous chores. The girl eventually complains that the arrangement is unfair and that she has a much less attractive social life than her peers. Typically, she refers to the fact that the children were much happier before the stepmother arrived. The stepmother then uses the complaints to drive a wedge in the father–daughter relationship. Without counselling, the situation deteriorates.

Another common scenario is that of the unsupported mother whose new partner says, 'I want you but I don't want your kids'. This is understandable when children make it very clear that they do not want a father-replacement figure. Connolly (1983) showed how easily children can destroy their parents' new and unwanted relationships. Children do not perceive their parents as sexual beings and they are highly embarrassed by their parents' flirtatious and sexual behaviour with other people (Goldman & Goldman 1988).

A great deal of discord is likely to have occurred prior to the issue of the ultimatum which requires the mother to choose between her lover and her children. The mother with a difficult parent–child relationship is unlikely to find parenting rewarding. Teenagers' threats to 'leave home' merely confirm that they are unlikely to 'be around' for long. Torn between responsibility for their recalcitrant teenagers and the opportunity to satisfy their own emotional (and possibly financial) needs, some mothers choose the latter and move in with their new partners. Teenagers typically adopt an 'I don't care' attitude and say that their friends will look after them. The scene is then set for the first stage of homelessness.

Many young people leave home following arguments about sexual matters. Student counsellors confirm that 'lots of children of twelve and thirteen years are now engaging in short-term heterosexual relationships'. Intelligent middle-class children are aware of the need for 'safe sex' and they take responsibility for contraception. Parents often have difficulty in viewing their daughters as sufficiently mature to be entering into sexual relationships. Children in this age group often lack privacy at home and when parents find contraceptives, 'the balloon goes up'. Fathers in particular find it difficult to cope with their daughter's sexuality: 'She's only a baby,' they protest.

According to school counsellors, too few parents understand adolescent development or handle it well. The common response is to become critical and restrictive at the very time that children are moving towards independence.

Escape from physical abuse

Some secondary school students leave home because the level of violence is no longer tolerable. First, there are those who have always lived in households where violence is a way of life, often associated with alcohol or drug abuse. In secondary schools, however, there is often a new group of victims who have never been abused before; they tend to be the ones who express opinions and expectations which are substantially different from those of their parents. The parents find it difficult to cope with their children's struggles for independence. They become increasingly authoritarian and the children, in turn, become increasingly rebellious. As the tolerance threshold diminishes, the children come to school with black eyes and bruises where they have been held and punched for being 'cheeky', defiant and 'answering back'. Girls try to conceal bruised arms by wearing longsleeved clothing, regardless of weather conditions. They make excuses to miss swimming, sports and games sessions because they know that their secret will be revealed if they get undressed.

Escape from sexual abuse

Large numbers of boys and girls leave home when they are no longer prepared to tolerate sexual abuse by parents or step-parents. Student counsellors confirm that very few are prepared to initiate court proceedings because they know that the justice system is on the side of the perpetrator.

> They are very cynical about the adult world . . . and who can blame them. In recent years, I've been involved with victims in six separate court cases involving prolonged sexual abuse by stepfathers, fathers and grandfathers. All of the accused men were found not guilty or they successfully appealed against their conviction on the basis of a technicality. Before the trial, the families were divided into two camps . . . those who believed the kid and those who believed the perpetrator. When he was found 'not guilty', for whatever reason, the victims lost the support of all family members. They had to leave home to avoid further victimisation of all kinds. Word soon got around that the court victimises the victim. We get reports of sexual abuse almost daily but the kids don't want to go to court when it's a close relative . . . they just want to get away from it all (school counsellor, Paralowie, South Australia, 1994).

Unwanted pregnancies and terminations

School counsellors in the affluent suburbs encounter unwanted pregnancies just as frequently as those in disadvantaged areas but the handling of these situations varies markedly according to the socioeconomic status of the family.

Middle-class families are the ones most likely to arrange a 'termination' soon after the pregnancy is revealed. Girls in disadvantaged areas are more likely to keep their babies and give them to their mothers to be reared. The grandmother may pretend that she is the child's mother while the real mother pretends to be a sister. This results in huge emotional and behaviour problems when the children realise that they were deceived.

Counsellors confirm that girls in disadvantaged schools are more likely to have conceived as a result of sex or rape while drunk. They often do not know the identities of their children's fathers. They continue their schooling, sometimes in classes specifically for unsupported teenage mothers.

In middle-class families, a teenage pregnancy is much more likely to be viewed as a disgrace. After the abortion, family relationships often deteriorate and the girls leave home, then school.

Although comparatively few in number, some teenagers regard pregnancy, the provision of state housing and welfare benefits as a more attractive option than unemployment, financial dependence on parents and completing school.

WHERE DO YOUNG PEOPLE GO WHEN THEY LEAVE HOME?

During census week, there were 810 Australian school students who had no roof over their heads: 130 were living in streets and derelict buildings and 680 were 'moving from place to place'. An additional 1800 were in government-funded short-term placements, 600 more were in emergency youth refuges, 4500 were in temporary accommodation and 2400 were living in their friends' homes. An additional 1900 had moved in with relatives as a temporary measure.

When children become or are about to become homeless, they usually tell their best friends, a trusted teacher or school counsellor. Their predicament is revealed in many different ways:

• tearfulness and distress;

- failure to hand in homework;
- they reveal that they don't have access to their books;
- they wear the same clothes all week;
- they are unclean; and,
- other children group together and gossip about 'what happened'.

In their paper to the International Year of the Family Conference in Adelaide, MacKenzie and Chamberlain (1994) confirmed school counsellors' findings that, if young people are homeless for more than two weeks, they start to move from place to place on a downward spiral. They descend on their best friends with the expectation of returning home 'when things have settled down' or promising to leave 'when I get somewhere to live'. 'Can you let me stay for a few days?' often stretches to several weeks and the friendship becomes strained. The parents in the host family eventually become weary of the drain on their emotional and financial resources and, when there is an argument, they issue the edict that they are no longer prepared to provide free board and lodgings for 'someone else's kid'.

The student finds another friend and then another, moving from place to place until the support networks and the friendships have all run out. Without assistance from a counsellor, the homeless student then seeks out others in a similar situation and chronic homelessness begins.

THE SCHOOL AS A SITE FOR INTERVENTION

There is no national coordinated policy on how Australian schools should deal with homeless students and the report by MacKenzie and Chamberlain (1994), argues that prevention and early intervention policy should focus on schools as the major site for early intervention. This is because most homeless students are not in the hard-core homeless subculture and it is much easier to help them before they make the transition to chronic homelessness. Unfortunately, the evidence is that most secondary schools do not intervene sufficiently quickly. Homeless children leave school because, without the support of a family, attendance becomes very difficult.

The most supportive schools tend to be those in the disadvantaged suburbs where teachers have a holistic approach to education and 'care and protection' is well established in the school culture. Because the primary school has usually built up a good home–school relationship over the years, it is relatively easy for children and parents to talk to counsellors about their problems. There is often an 'open door policy' and counsellors are recognised as non-judgemental resources.

By contrast, professional families feel a greater need to keep their problems secret. Their children often feel ashamed of having the need to talk to a counsellor. Some parents instruct them that they must 'never to talk to that counsellor again', after a problem has been revealed. In these circumstances, victims of abuse often have to rely on their friends to seek help on their behalf.

It takes a long time and a lot of effort for a counsellor to build up trusting relationships in a mixed or middle-class school because there is a much greater concern for 'appearances'.

The administrators of Ravenswood High School, Melbourne, created a highly effective interventionist welfare policy to deal with the problem of student homelessness. As a result, the school has only a 'small' homeless problem of around eight students per week. This low figure is attributed to:

- effective leadership in a school which recognises its protector role;
- a dynamic full-time counsellor who works effectively with the local community and with senior staff, especially in raising staff awareness of the problem of homelessness and child maltreatment;
- clearly defined practices for identifying and assisting homeless and 'at risk' children with an established procedure that if anyone suspects that a student has serious problems, the school counsellor must be informed;
- careful attention to records of attendance, for example, truancy is monitored and parents receive a telephone call if students are absent for three days, which helps to identify 'high risk' children;
- a well-developed pastoral care programme. When students enrol, they are given a pastoral teacher who remains with them throughout their school life. They are with the teacher for a short time each morning and have two pastoral lessons weekly which concentrate on issues relating to human relationships and personal development;
- the school counsellor is responsible for knowing, on a daily basis, which children are homeless, where they are sleeping that night and what is happening to them;

- the counsellor and deputy principal meet parents when family difficulties arise;
- the school has introduced a 'buddy system' involving other staff. The 'buddy' is attached to the homeless student and acts as friend, confidante and provides on-going support; buddies have regular meetings with the school counsellor to share information and receive support for handling difficult cases;
- the counsellor and deputy principal know where to find resources outside school and they have developed good working relationships with trusted social workers (MacKenzie & Chamberlain 1994).

Student counsellors emphasise the need to locate and maintain contact with competent social workers employed in statutory family and community welfare services. They also stress the need to provide in-service education for secondary school teachers in academically focused schools.

Many secondary school teachers are unsympathetic towards neglected children. They believe that adolescents should be able to change their parents' ways or, alternatively, take responsibility for laundering and repairing their uniforms and organising a chaotic household. Counsellors refer to 'one liners' which secondary school teachers use to 'put neglected children down'. Sarcasm such as, 'I see you've condescended to join us today' can be very hurtful to a child who could not attend school for want of the appropriate clothing or equipment. 'Isn't it time your mother took your pants to the cleaners?' or 'You don't seriously expect me to accept work in this condition?' is distressing to the boy who struggled to complete his homework while living in a drainpipe.

Students sense this lack of empathy and they leave school, convinced that they no longer fit into the school environment. In most cases, they join the chronically unemployed and unemployable.

Education is one of the most important escape routes out of poverty. School involvement is an extremely important way, often the only way, for homeless children to maintain contact with normal society (Sykes 1993, p. 5). It is widely thought that, if all schools are to help, then some will have to change. O'Connor (1988) showed that homeless children do not currently regard schools as a source of help; indeed, they often see them as part of the problem.

TEACHERS HELPING: AN OPTIMISTIC STORY

Reading material in the area of youth homelessness and child abuse is depressing, demoralising and leads to cynicism about society. However, there is some good news. A book by Helen Sykes (1993) described a case study which shows how schools can help. The story about Ardoch-Windsor Secondary College in Melbourne, Australia, is a superb antidote to the pessimism engendered by the endless reports about youth homelessness. We recommend that anybody who doubts their ability or the ability of a school-based team to change the system should read Sykes' book. It is a story of how a dedicated team faced a problem, saw that the system was failing and enlisted community support to provide real assistance for young people. It has some lessons for others wanting to emulate their approach.

The Ardoch story began with one homeless adolescent and one compassionate and resourceful teacher. This led to the introduction of a small student support programme (1988) which in the first year assisted twelve homeless children. This number increased to 102 in 1992. The programme has since been transferred to Prahran Secondary College as the Ardoch Youth Foundation Inc. The foundation now offers funding to schools throughout Australia for the purpose of extending programmes modelled on their homeless youth support programme. Sykes (1993) lists other funding sources for interested schools.

The Ardoch programme began slowly with the provision of lunch for homeless children. The school encouraged the children to shower and launder their clothes at school. The school then networked with the Brotherhood of St Laurence and the Salvation Army. From there the programme developed to include: 'housing, health care counselling advocacy with government departments, lunch and breakfast programs, curriculum support, pantry of food, store of second hand clothing, store of toiletries, store of furniture, a crisis fund, a part time holiday employment project and a public relations program' (Sykes 1993, p. 36).

The developers of the Ardoch project soon found that existing bureaucratic responses to the problems of the homeless were inadequate. By working with government representatives (who were well intentioned even though official responses to the problem were inadequate), innovative and more appropriate solutions began to emerge. Kathy Hilton, one of the architects of the Ardoch project, described her frustration with the government system: 'we had to deal with seven different departments. There was a definite lack of coordination. It was obvious to me that the government needed to take a new approach to youth homelessness' (Sykes 1993, p. 38).

The school rented a flat for the use of its homeless students and initiated rent subsidies. The education authority soon stopped the school from signing rental leases but community support developed and the homeless programme flourished.

Helen Sykes identified several factors which will help others who want to repeat their success.

- There is a lack of awareness of the problems of youth homelessness and of contributing factors. Most teachers are uninformed. The topic is neglected during their professional training.
- It is important to develop partnerships between schools, government agencies and the community. It is not the responsibility of governments alone.
- The school is an ideal place to base solutions to the problem of youth homelessness. The school can and must offer a supportive environment. Basic physical needs, including food, must be available if a homeless programme is to succeed.
- Community support is crucial.

One of the major difficulties is the level of teacher resistance. Some say that their responsibility is limited to teaching a particular academic subject, not acting as counsellors, social or health workers. They point to the fact that they were not trained for these roles and, furthermore, time spent on welfare issues is at the expense of academia. Sykes does not dismiss these arguments but suggests some selected schools could offer similar programmes. In the meantime, awareness levels about the problems of homelessness should be raised in all schools.

TASKS FOR STUDENTS

1   To what extent do you believe that it is the role of teachers and caregivers to assist in the problem of child homelessness?

2   If you became aware of a homeless child in your class, what action might you take to intervene?

3   Compile a list of resources which could be utilised in assisting 'at risk' or homeless children.
4   Raise the issue of student homelessness at a school meeting for discussion.
5   Do you know how many students enrolled at your school are homeless or at risk of becoming homeless?
6   What would you do if a child came to tell you that she was homeless? How would your actions and reactions differ according to whether she had:

- left home voluntarily;
- left home as a result of physical abuse;
- left home as a result of sexual abuse;
- left home as a result of conflict with parents;
- been abandoned by parents.

7   If you became aware of delinquency or substance abuse in children in your care, do you have any mandate or responsibility to intervene?
8   Compile a list of resources to help with problems of delinquency, substance abuse and suicide risk.
9   A twelve-year-old boy tells you that he can't communicate with his parents, he hasn't any friends and he has thought of killing himself. What would you say? What should you do?

CASE STUDY

Rene, aged thirteen, has been 'off-colour' for several weeks. Eventually, she tells you that she is pregnant, her stepfather is the father of the child, you must keep it secret because her mother will kill her and there are four young children in the family.

a   What are your responsibilities?
b   How could the school support Rene through the reporting and assessment process?
c   Who would support Rene's mother in this crisis?

13

THE NEED FOR PERSONAL SAFETY EDUCATION PROGRAMMES

In recent years public awareness of the problem of child abuse has grown and responses to abuse have emphasised school-based initiatives.

SCHOOL-BASED CHILD PROTECTION PROGRAMMES

Schools and preschools have long been involved in safety education. They teach children how to stay safe in traffic, how to stay safe from fire, water and electricity. It is logical that schools should also teach children how to stay safe with people. Hundreds of different child protection programmes have been developed in schools in the United States and Canada (Berrick & Gilbert 1991). These programmes have the common objective of equipping children to prevent or stop abuse. Johnson (1994) has reviewed the concepts commonly taught in prevention programmes which are designed to help children to:

- identify their intuitive danger signals, in other words, they are taught to identify when they feel 'uncomfortable', 'mixed up', 'yukky', or 'unsafe', in a variety of situations but especially those involving touching;
- understand and assert their rights, for example, to reject unwanted touching, bullying and harassment;
- identify their 'private parts', in other words, children are taught that there are parts of their bodies that, in general, should not be touched by others. Programmes vary in their level of

explicitness about what constitutes 'private parts' ('the parts covered by a swimsuit' through to direct identification of genitals, anus, breasts/chest and mouth);

- enlist adult support—children are taught to 'tell someone you trust' if they feel unsafe;
- not keep 'bad secrets'—children are taught to identify the difference between 'bad or scary' secrets and other secrets, and are encouraged to tell adults about bad secrets; and,
- not blame themselves for their victimisation—children are taught that 'it is never your fault when a bigger person/adult does something wrong' (Johnson 1994, p. 261).

Programmes also need to teach about:

- risks to boys—boys are made aware that they too are at risk;
- stranger awareness—children are taught that potential perpetrators cannot be identified by looks;
- perpetrator/child relationships—children are taught that offenders can be people they may know;
- how to escape from potential danger—children are taught verbal and physical responses to abuse; and,
- tricks—children are warned of tricks used by perpetrators. (Perniskie 1995).

Schools in the United States and Canada have offered child protection education for more than a decade. For about the same length of time, New Zealand has had a national school-based curriculum which provides step-by-step, developmentally appropriate modules including videos, games, stories and suggestions for homework to be undertaken by children with their parents. The Education Department for the state of South Australia adopted an American generic 'empowerment' programme, *Protective Behaviours*, in 1985. The same and a similar programme are in use in schools in the state of Victoria while the state of New South Wales produced its own age-appropriate school curriculum including a module for children with intellectual disabilities. No similar national effort has been made in the United Kingdom and Ireland. Michelle Elliott's *Kidscape* was made available in 1986 to provide 'good sense defence' for 5–11 year olds. Although it avoided controversy by concentrating on safety from bullies and dangerous strangers, there has been no widespread adoption of this or any other safety programme.

Interestingly neither sex education nor safety education have been incorporated in the National Curriculum for England and

Wales, omissions which will inevitably leave British children vulnerable to the risk of sexual abuse.

WHY SCHOOLS AND PRESCHOOLS SHOULD ACCEPT RESPONSIBILITY FOR TEACHING SAFETY SKILLS TO CHILDREN

There is international evidence to show that children who lack access to a personal safety programme are at high risk of sexual abuse for a variety of reasons.

Parents do not teach their children how to stay safe

Surveys of Australian, American and New Zealand parents have confirmed that children are usually not taught safety skills at home. At best, some parents advise children not to talk to strangers although it has long been realised that most child molesters are known and trusted by their victims. Parents avoid their responsibilities in child protection because they:

- trust their friends, relatives and neighbours, children's teachers, priests and so on, and think that their families and neighbourhoods are immune from sexual abuse; like road accidents, abuse is seen as 'something that only happens to other people';
- believe that abusers are readily identifiable because they are 'mentally ill' and 'as we don't have anyone like that in our family, we don't need child protection programmes';
- underestimate the damage caused by sexual abuse;
- survived their own abuse by denying that it was harmful; and
- want to repress their own abusive experiences.

In most cases, parents do not discuss safety with their children because they only know about dangerous strangers and 'don't know what to say'. Parents fear that protective education will involve talking about deviant and frightening sexual acts and, rather than talk about sex of any kind, they leave their children unprotected (Briggs 1988).

The authors' recent research in New Zealand also showed that safety education needs to be introduced when children are young; at eleven to twelve years, parents found that it was difficult to talk to their sons because, having kept matters relating to human sexuality a taboo subject for so long, both parties were too embarrassed to open up channels of communication.

Without safety education young children do not realise that abusive behaviour is wrong

If young and developmentally disabled children are not taught the limits of acceptable and unacceptable social behaviour, they usually regard sexual abuse as 'normal'. This is especially likely when boys socialise in highly sexualised peer groups or offences involve older children, siblings and caregivers. Young children are least likely to identify genital fondling as wrong if they find it (or the relationship) pleasurable.

Without personal safety education, children are vulnerable to dangerous strangers

Paradoxically, although young children are terrified of strangers, they do not know what strangers are. Before the age of eight, they imagine that strangers are part monster, part human, always male and are readily identified because they wear black masks, balaclavas, black clothing and they drive old black cars. When asked if they had ever seen a stranger, hundreds of Australian and New Zealand children told the authors that they had not but they would recognise one instantly if they saw one. They assured the senior researcher, who had just arrived on an international flight, that she could not possibly be a stranger because she:

- is a woman (and 'ladies aren't strangers');
- looked nice like their grannies (and strangers look evil and leer through the slits in their masks);
- sounded nice (and strangers sound cruel);
- carried a briefcase (and, therefore has a job); strangers don't work, they merely 'steal kids' and other things; and,
- was on school premises (and teachers 'would never allow strangers to come to our school').

So strong is the stereotyping of the male stranger as an imaginary creature that, without a child protection programme, class after class of children indicated that if they were lost in a busy store or street, they would accompany the first kindly looking adult who offered to take them home.

It soon became clear to us that the very concept of stranger is too difficult for young children to understand and information about dangerous strangers merely causes anxiety. If an adult refers to children by name or pretends to be a neighbour or a friend of the family, children believe that the adults are trustworthy and truthful. As a result, whole classes of five year olds said that they would accompany a stranger who met them outside school and claimed to be representing their parents.

Without personal safety education, children will keep sexual misbehaviour secret

Child sexual abuse thrives on secrecy. Offenders often tell victims that there will be terrible punishments if they tell anyone about their behaviour. Most parents teach their children to keep adults' secrets. Children of five years already know that the disclosure of family secrets is a heinous crime which is guaranteed to result in the withdrawal of love if not punishment (Briggs 1991a).

When children try to disclose abuse they often start out with the announcement, 'I've got a secret I can't tell' or 'Is it okay if I tell a secret?' Countless adults respond with, 'Secrets must be kept'. They should be enquiring whether the secret is a nice secret or a worrying one, who else knows about it and 'What will happen if you tell?'

Australian and New Zealand children told us that they would keep an adult's secret for fear of getting into trouble with their parents. Furthermore, they would keep all sexual misbehaviour secret whether told to do so or not because:

- sexual behaviour is naughty;
- naughty means that you're bad; and,
- bad means that you're unlovable, will be punished and it's all your fault.

An additional trap for children aged seven years and upwards was the fear that, if they told a parent or teacher, other children would eavesdrop and taunt them with jibes such as, 'You're yucky! Fancy being so stupid as to let someone do that to you'. Without safety education, fear of embarrassment at the hands of siblings and peers would keep older children silent.

Parent participation is vital

At age five years, most children have complained to a parent about the too-tight hugs and sloppy kisses of relatives, the tickling that lasts too long and becomes painful or the grandfathers who think it's amusing to rub their bristly chins on children's faces. At age five, children know that 'adults stick together' and 'they don't listen to kids' or 'don't believe kids' when they complain about other 'grown-ups'. On the contrary, when children turn to parents to stop unwanted and uncomfortable touching, the parents defend the perpetrators, explaining that 'grandpa just does it for fun', 'aunty will be upset if you tell her you don't want to be kissed' or 'she only does it because she loves you'. Some children are even reprimanded for protesting. In other words, parents teach children that they have to tolerate unwanted and uncomfortable touching to please the adults and they must not protest. This message makes children vulnerable to sexual abuse.

Unfortunately, Australian and New Zealand research (Briggs & Hawkins 1994; Briggs & Hawkins 1996a) shows quite clearly that when children report sexual abuse to their mothers, they are unlikely to be heard or believed and may even be punished for telling bad lies about trusted acquaintances or relatives. Some Asian and South Pacific children believed that they were particularly disadvantaged because parents are powerless to stop abuse by a senior member of the family hierarchy.

Children's distrust of their parents confirms the importance of parent involvement in school-based child protection programmes. When parents are involved, they are taught the importance of helping children to stop (and escape with dignity from) unwanted touching and teasing. This gives children the clear message that their parents can be relied upon to protect them.

Most parents want to help but they are reluctant to attend school information sessions about child protection. In the United States, United Kingdom, Australia and New Zealand, only a third of parents attend these meetings. The main reasons given for non-attendance are 'pressure of work', 'family pressures' and 'I didn't think it was necessary because we've told him/her about strangers, it's safe around here and I'm very happy for the school to get on with it'.

WITHOUT SAFETY EDUCATION, VICTIMS DO NOT KNOW HOW TO REPORT SEXUAL MISBEHAVIOUR

Because the human body is a taboo subject in most homes and classrooms, few children have been taught the correct biological names for their genitals, anus and breasts. Without an appropriate vocabulary, children are unable to report sexual misbehaviour. Children who have been deprived of safety education give hints of abuse which are usually incomprehensible to the listener (see table 1).

Table 1 Responses to child indications of potential abuse situations

What the child says	What the adult says	What the adult should say
I don't like the way he teases me.	We all have to learn to put up with teasing.	What does he do?
Is it alright if he does funny things?	Yes if he makes you laugh.	What does he do?
I've got a secret I can't tell.	We have to keep secrets.	What will happen if you tell it? Who said so?
I don't like his ice-cream.	But you like ice-cream.	Tell me about it.
I don't want to go to grandpa's/uncle's any more.	Grandpa/uncle will be upset.	Has something happened to upset you?
The babysitter wanted me to get undressed.	You have to get undressed to go to bed.	What happened?
I don't like that babysitter.	You'll have to put up with her.	Why? What did she do?
I don't like his magic stick.	Um! really!	What does he do with it?

People who have not been involved in personal safety education unwittingly reassure children that what is happening is harmless. They are devastated when, much later, they realise that they failed to respond to children's cries for help. More knowledgeable adults listen to children and ask a few strategic questions to find out why they are worried.

HANDLING PARENTS' CONCERNS ABOUT PERSONAL SAFETY EDUCATION

Parents who have had no previous experience with safety education may be concerned about:

- the relevance of the programme to the developmental level of the child;
- possible effects on family relationships and parenting styles;

- the possibility that it might encourage children to challenge the parents' authority;
- the appropriateness of teaching children the names of body parts ('I don't think he's (or she's) old enough to know the word penis');
- fears that safety education might make children fearful or spoil their innocence;
- whether the programme will teach children about sex before they are old enough to understand;
- whether teaching children about safety might encourage them to make false allegations to get even with people who discipline them.

First, personal safety education is not sex education although we recommend that age-appropriate sexuality education should be taught alongside safety, in other words, providing children with information about their bodies. Second, international studies show that young children are not alarmed by education for child protection; to the contrary, parents have found them to be more confident when they understand the limits of acceptable and unacceptable behaviour. Third, if false allegations are made, they usually involve adolescents who are well aware of sexual matters.

When parents adopt negative attitudes about safety education, their views are often based on myths about child abuse and child protection. Although fathers are usually the complainants, studies consistently show that fathers leave safety and sex education entirely to mothers and don't bother to check whether they have accepted that responsibility. When programmes were in their infancy, some fathers feared that they would upset family relationships and place them at risk of being reported. They were afraid that, if they tapped their children on the buttocks for fun and the children told the teacher, they might be accused of sexual molestation. Parents can be assured that teachers do not make, and social workers do not investigate, frivolous reports. The response to fathers should also involve an assurance that, if they become involved in the programme, they will have an important role to play in their children's support network.

When complaints occur, they invariably come from parents who neither attended information sessions nor talked to staff about what was being taught. A New Zealand father complained to the national media that his preschool child had been taught to distrust parents in a programme entitled *Feeling Safe*. The evidence for his complaint was that his daughter had announced that she no longer wished daddy to wash her genitals in the shower, she wanted to do it herself. Any early childhood educator would have rejoiced that the child had the confidence to assert herself and, furthermore, that she felt capable of attending to her own hygiene. However, the parents interpreted this as preschool paranoia about sexual abuse and they demanded the banning of the programme. What became clear in the subsequent radio interviews was that the parents had not discussed the programme with the child or the teacher but had taken their concerns to a sensationalist media.

Criticisms of child protection programmes come from three sources:

- well-meaning but misguided conservatives who believe that we can maintain children's innocence and keep them asexual by depriving them of knowledge about their rights;
- those who refuse to accept the seriousness of the child abuse problem; and,
- offenders who have a vested interest in maintaining children's ignorance.

STRATEGIES FOR HOLDING PARENT INFORMATION SESSIONS

When planning to hold parent information sessions, take account of local customs and ensure that the meetings do not clash with late night shopping or popular community activities. In disadvantaged areas, some parents may feel more comfortable meeting at the local community centre rather than the school.

Invite a social worker or suitably experienced educator or police officer to provide basic information relating to child sexual abuse, the extent of the problem and the difficulties associated with child protection. Introduce local child protection officers to parents and ask them to explain how they help families and how they can be contacted. For the first meeting, it is best to seek the involvement of experienced educators. Also, seek advice from multicultural educational services and community representatives on cultural aspects of child protection.

Send written invitations which indicate that staff and many parents are concerned about the safety of children and, for that reason, a safety education programme will be introduced. Impress on parents that schools cannot teach safety skills in isolation; children need to be protected by both their fathers and their mothers, and dads have an important contribution to make. Ensure that invitations are clearly written in jargon-free language. Use community languages in correspondence and posters.

Use community radio and ethnic media to publicise what the school is doing. For best results, offer a child care facility so that fathers cannot use babysitting as an excuse to stay at home. If necessary, have separate sessions for men. Where there are large numbers of unemployed or shift workers, it may be possible to meet during the day. Some schools offer both day and evening sessions to cover everyone's needs. It is best to use tear-off slips which ask parents to provide an alternative date to meet the class teacher or senior staff if they are unable to attend the meetings. For best results, telephone parents who fail to return the slips.

Further strategies for parent information sessions could include the following.

- Provide refreshments to make the meeting enjoyable.
- Involve interpreters as necessary.
- Outline the programme to be used, giving examples of sessions.
- Discuss ways of improving the protection of children.
- Enquire whether parents would like to attend workshops relating to the most sensitive parts of the programme. Will they participate in joint homework with their children? Do they want, week by week, information on what has been taught at school and how they can reinforce the teaching at home?
- Create a parent group which will develop and implement strategies to increase parent interest.
- Ensure that the work of all the children is displayed in a classroom when parents are visiting.

WHICH CHILD PROTECTION PROGRAMMES ARE MOST EFFECTIVE?

While all of the prevention programmes are well intended there has been a general lack of evaluation of the effects of the programmes. The few evaluation studies which have been performed showed some major weaknesses. The lack of evaluation studies for these programmes has made it difficult to choose between models. However, recent evaluation research experience (Briggs & Hawkins 1993b; Briggs & Hawkins 1994) allows a description of the attributes of two quite different approaches.

The two models to be described are the American *Protective Behaviours* programme, used in some Australian schools, and *Keeping Ourselves Safe,* which is the national New Zealand school-based child protection curriculum designed and supported by New Zealand Police in partnership with the Ministry of Education.

In 1985, Victoria Police (Melbourne) became concerned by the high proportion of reports (96 per cent) of child sexual abuse involving perpetrators who were known and trusted by their victims. This made a mockery of the traditional school safety programme which concentrated exclusively on dangerous strangers. Victoria Police adopted and engaged in a national promotion of *Protective Behaviours,* a relatively unknown Wisconsin (USA) 'empowerment' programme. This had the appeal of requiring no books or expensive kits, it claimed to be generic and did not refer to human sexuality (a supposed advantage). The programme revolves around two themes: 'We all have the right to feel safe all of the time' and 'Nothing is so awful that we can't talk about it to someone'. Seven or eight sessions aimed to teach children to identify 'early warning signs' (unsafe feelings), confide in a member of their previously identified 'support network', and persist in 'telling' until safety is restored.

Protective Behaviours assumes that sexual abuse will cause 'unsafe' feelings which will result in child resistance. Thus it takes no account of the context of child sexual abuse which may well occur in an affectionate relationship. Nor does it acknowledge the fact that sexual touching may feel exciting and pleasurable rather than 'unsafe'.

The New Zealand approach was quite different. They rejected the 'empowerment' model per se on the grounds that there was no empirical support for its effectiveness with children, it lacked an appreciation of the principles of learning theory in child development and involved misconceptions of the dynamics of child sexual abuse.

The New Zealand Police and Ministry of Education took the expensive step of creating a national, culturally appropriate, step-by-step curriculum using teams of teachers and curriculum designers at every stage of programme and materials development. The designers aimed for an 'open and honest' approach, accepting that some children encounter sexual misbehaviour. The kit combines instruction, videos, stories, games and problem-solving exercises. Parent evaluation was built into the programme.

Our evaluation of the two programmes involved interviews

with 378 South Australian and New Zealand children (5–8 years old). A single questionnaire was used to discover whether children could suggest safe strategies for handling a wide variety of potentially unsafe situations. Unsafe situations included: being separated from parents in an unfamiliar or crowded place and a stranger offers to take you home; a babysitter wants to play an undressing game and insists that it should be kept secret; a stranger meets you outside school and asks you to accompany him/her after providing a plausible rationale; or an adult kisses, hugs or touches you in a way that feels 'yucky'.

Data were collected before the introduction of the programme and the children were re-interviewed after a one-year interval. Although all of the Australian children had been exposed to *Protective Behaviours* between the two interviews, there was little improvement in the quality of the children's responses. Only 30 per cent of children provided 'safe' answers to the questions. The remainder asserted that:

- children cannot stop bigger people from touching them, even if the behaviour is 'rude';
- children have to keep all adults' secrets because they get into 'big trouble' if they tell;
- adults who look kind and sound kind are trustworthy and can be accompanied, especially if they are women; and,
- children cannot report 'rude' behaviour because they will get into trouble and be punished.

Teachers, disappointed with the results, admitted that they had taught the programme selectively and spasmodically, selected the general safety issues that appertain to the classroom and playground and avoided aspects involving adult misbehaviour and issues to do with sexuality.

In marked contrast to the Australian findings, the New Zealand children showed substantial gains after their programme. Three-quarters of the children had learned that secrets must never be kept if they involve 'rude' behaviour. More than two-thirds of children gained the ability to offer several safe strategies in the event of becoming lost in crowded places. More than half now realised that some people might use tricks to persuade them to do things that they would not otherwise do. More than half also gained knowledge about their right to reject inappropriate touching, and were confident that they could report and stop 'rude' behaviour without getting into trouble. Least development occurred in their ability to recognise feelings associated with being safe and unsafe. These concepts were clearly difficult for the 5–8 year age group although the success of the alternative *Protective Behaviours* programme depends on them.

The two variables which significantly affected children's initial gains were teacher commitment and socioeconomic class. Teachers classified as 'highly committed' achieved twice the number of 'gains' as those with 'average commitment'. The highly committed teachers used the programme conscientiously, often alongside curriculum to develop self-esteem and assertiveness skills. They integrated safety concepts into their day-to-day teaching strategies, provided parents with reports of children's progress and indicated how the parents could help. Children in these classes were confident of their rights and confident that their teachers and parents would help them if they were concerned about someone's behaviour. They knew that they were not obliged to keep uncomfortable secrets, least of all those about 'rude' behaviour. This group of children could suggest several safe strategies for handling potentially dangerous situations.

We found that prior to the *Keeping Ourselves Safe* programme, children from low income families were relatively disadvantaged in all of the personal safety knowledge and skills we measured. For example, compared with middle-class children, the children from lower income families were:

- less likely to believe that their parents would protect them from other adults who behaved inappropriately;
- more likely to have already sought help from parents to stop unwanted touching from relatives and been rejected;
- more likely to believe that they have to keep all adults' secrets and would be punished if they 'told', especially if the secrets involved 'rude' behaviour; and,
- at higher risk from truly dangerous strangers because their understanding of a 'stranger' only related to males with a stereotypical appearance (mean or ugly looking, leering, wearing masks, balaclavas and black clothing and driving old black cars).

While the *Keeping Ourselves Safe* programme led to gains across all social classes, it was clear that middle-class children made more frequent gains than their classmates from lower income families.

It is important to remember, however, that middle-class children are not immune from sexual victimisation and their superior knowledge was not acquired by virtue of their status but by a successful combination of teacher–parent effort.

THE IMPORTANCE OF PARENT PARTICIPATION IN THE PROGRAMME

Socioeconomic status proved to be important in both pre-programme differences and benefits obtained from the programme. Why should the income level of parents make such a difference to children's safety skills?

Parent involvement in protective education proved to be a key mediating variable. Parents of middle-class children were much more likely to have used personal safety books and reinforced safety concepts at home. Since parents were significantly more likely to have attempted home teaching where the teacher was rated as highly committed regardless of socioeconomic class, it seems possible that the limiting effects of low socioeconomic class may be mitigated by increased parental involvement induced via high teacher commitment. Research by Wurtele, Kast and Melzer (1992) confirms that children who are taught personal safety skills by parents and teachers in a cooperative effort are much more likely to remember them than children who are taught only by their teachers.

The results show the superiority of the *Keeping Ourselves Safe* programme and highlight the importance of parental involvement, socioeconomic status and teacher commitment to a successful result.

In a survey of South Australian parents, Hunt, Hawkins and Goodlet (1992) found that child abuse came fourth on a list of twenty-two issues which concerned them. While 46 per cent of parents were concerned about child abuse, they were also reluctant to attend parenting courses on prevention and they regarded professionals with scepticism. Briggs (1990) has also shown that the majority of parents were content to leave the responsibility for safety education entirely to teachers. None of the schools in the present study found it easy to involve parents in its programme.

Professional parents often explained that they were 'too busy' to attend meetings and due to a false belief that sexual abuse wasn't likely to happen in their family, they regarded their own attendance as unnecessary.

Successful schools attracted parents by arranging day and evening meetings with child care facilities and refreshments. They emphasised the importance of participation by both parents because fathers otherwise tend to disassociate themselves and leave all aspects of child protection to mothers.

A COMPARISON OF THE PROGRAMMES

Our comparison of the two distinctly different programmes suggests that young children make better progress in the acquisition of personal safety knowledge when:

- the programme is adopted by the whole school and has a place in the timetable;
- there is a strong network of support for teachers using the programme;
- teachers use prescribed materials which are designed with children's developmental levels in mind;
- parent participation is built into the programme and parents reinforce the concepts at home;
- teachers use the programme conscientiously and enthusiastically, modelling safety concepts and incorporating them in their teaching strategies across the curriculum;
- programmes use children's own language and reflect their thinking;
- there is a continuity of teaching and scope for the reinforcement of concepts;
- programme designers acknowledge children's difficulties in grasping complex concepts and therefore use concrete examples;
- the content includes references to the more common sexual misbehaviours experienced by children;
- curriculum designers acknowledge children's sexuality.

Without parent participation in child protection education, children may learn of their rights but the knowledge remains academic unless they have evidence that their own parents will be supportive and protective (without blaming them) if they need help.

It is also clear that parent participation in programmes is especially important in low socioeconomic areas. International research suggests that, while child sexual abuse occurs across all social, economic, educational, racial, ethnic and religious groups, there is a higher risk for children in low income families (Finkelhor 1984). Our New Zealand study (Briggs & Hawkins 1996a) confirmed that these children had least safety knowledge before programmes were introduced and they made fewer gains than middle-class children when the curriculum was in place.

Since our comparison of the New Zealand and Australian programmes, independent research in both New Zealand (Perniskie 1995) and Australia (Johnson 1994, 1995) has supported our findings.

TEACHERS HAVE ULTIMATE POWER OVER THE SUCCESS OF PROTECTION PROGRAMMES

It might be reasonable to assume that once schools have initiated a prevention programme they have made a significant contribution to children's protection. Some fascinating work by Bruce Johnson (1994, 1995) shows that this is not always the case. Johnson interviewed very experienced teachers who had been trained to teach the American *Protective Behaviours* programme. His results were startling. About two-thirds of the teachers used it very selectively. The sections not taught were the most important relating to sexual touching and domestic violence. These were omitted as a way of resolving personal dilemmas presented by the programme. Johnson found that inadequate attention was given to teachers' personal beliefs, attitudes and feelings during implementation of the programmes. Sabotage was the result.

Johnson was not critical of the teachers for their behaviour. He found that they had a deep concern for their pupils, yet their own personal sensitivity to child abuse, even after a minimum of six hours of training, made them too uncomfortable to be able to teach the most relevant parts of the curriculum. In trying to understand why teachers failed to cover the required curriculum, Johnson identified several key factors.

- The training of teachers included permission to avoid aspects of the programme that they found upsetting or difficult during their training, by leaving the room or by mentally 'tuning out'. Teachers extended this permission to their own non-teaching of such aspects.
- Teachers questioned the accuracy and truth of claims about the prevalence of child abuse. This phenomenon, called 'dis-

counting', is a form of denial which affected motivation to teach. Some of the discounting took the form of admissions that abuse was a problem in general, but in the particular teacher's own locality it was not a serious problem.

- Teachers inaccurately perceived the programme as relevant at the level of tertiary prevention (dealing with abuse after the fact) rather than as a primary prevention strategy (preventing abuse).

Johnson's work helps us to understand why a well-intentioned programme using competent and experienced teachers failed to work as well as it might. His analysis provides a checklist of factors which teachers can use to help determine whether their own training and support are appropriate to enable them to make a positive contribution to child welfare.

As 'guardians' of the curriculum, teachers are very powerful. They are also, in general, very well motivated to ensure the well-being of children. There is no doubt that teachers who are convinced of the merits of a primary prevention programme can be powerful agents of social change. Teachers can be assisted in this endeavour if:

- programmes are well designed;
- teachers are well trained, not only at the technical tasks of teaching curriculum, but also in dealing with the psychological underpinnings of the curriculum; and,
- teachers are well supported by their organisational structure in terms of ongoing staff development.

TASKS FOR STUDENTS

1 If you are a professional working with children and families, plan a child protection session for parents. Invite a representative from your local welfare agency or authority responsible for receiving child abuse reports to come to your school or centre to address staff and parents on the mechanisms for reporting abuse and to explain what the authority then does with these reports.

2 How would you respond to an angry or disbelieving parent or principal who says that claims about the frequency of abuse and neglect are exaggerated and that your school should direct its efforts away from prevention attempts back to educational basics?

3 Have you ever deliberately not reported a suspected or known case of child abuse or neglect? If so, describe your reasons. If the same circumstance presented itself again, would you now act differently? Explain why.

4 Given the evidence suggesting that parent–teacher cooperation leads to improved results in school-based child protection programmes, what strategies could be used to encourage parent participation? What can be done to encourage parents who initially do not respond to invitations for involvement?

5 If your school already teaches a prevention programme for child abuse, how does it rate in comparison with the description given of the *Protective Behaviours* and *Keeping Ourselves Safe* programmes?

6 Consider the concept of 'discounting' as used by Johnson (1994). What are your own views about the incidence of abuse in the area in which you teach? Do you discount?

7 If you already teach a prevention programme, do you teach it as designed or have you been selective in presenting the curriculum? If you have been selective, what factors have influenced your choices? Did your own discomfort with some topics influence you?

14

DEVELOPING A CHILD ABUSE PREVENTION POLICY[1]

Because of the extraordinary responsibility placed on people who work with children (voluntarily or otherwise), it is important that the administrators and staff of schools, early childhood centres, before and after school care, holiday programmes and their management boards develop child protection and abuse prevention policies and ensure that these are both communicated to and implemented by teaching and non-teaching personnel and parents. This is a Ministry of Education requirement in New Zealand.

This chapter was written to assist schools, early childhood education and care services to develop and implement their own child abuse prevention policies. To do this, it is necessary for staff to understand, think about and discuss some of the issues and dilemmas involved in child protection in their own particular establishments before policies are developed.

The following sections provide a step-by-step discussion of the process of developing a policy for the prevention of child abuse and the protection of staff.

The general aims of child abuse prevention policies are:

- to protect children from child abuse;

---

1 This chapter has been adapted from *Prevent Child Abuse. Guidelines for Early Childhood Education Services* (Ministry of Education, Wellington, New Zealand, 1993) with the kind permission of the Secretary for Education, Dr Maris O'Rourke.

208

- to respond in ways which will make children safe when abuse is suspected or identified;
- to reduce stress on staff by providing guidance;
- to protect staff from the risk of wrongful accusation; and,
- to reassure parents by involving them in policy development.

The specific aims are to:

- identify and make public the underlying philosophy and commitment of a care and/or educational service which accepts its responsibilities for the protection of children and the prevention of abuse;
- develop and maintain a knowledge of and trust in agencies with statutory power to respond effectively to reports of child maltreatment;
- develop and maintain a knowledge of support services for parents;
- ensure that staff respond to all cases and suspected cases of child maltreatment in supportive ways;
- ensure that thorough checks are made into the backgrounds of new personnel before they are employed in an education and/or child care service;
- protect children from the risk of abuse by other students, employees or voluntary assistants;
- protect staff from the risk of unfounded allegations by establishing boundaries of staff roles and maintaining high professional standards;
- protect children by teaching and practising personal safety skills;
- protect children by involving parents in protective education programmes;
- protect children by responding to concerns sensitively.

Schools and early childhood centres need policies about the prevention of child maltreatment because prevention and responding to abuse raises issues which are difficult for adults to handle. Clear policies and procedures should aim to increase adult awareness of child abuse and that, in turn, increases the likelihood of abuse being identified and stopped in the early stages.

STEP 1: ESTABLISHING BASIC PRINCIPLES

The first step involves discussion with staff and parents to establish the basic principles which underlie the school or centre's child abuse prevention policy. These principles can then be set out in a clear statement in which the commitment of the service to child protection is clear. They should establish the attitudes and actions which underlie policy in other sections.

This statement must be available to all parents at times of enrolment, to all staff, students on field experience and others working in either a voluntary or paid capacity in the school or early childhood centre setting.

Each school or centre should nominate a staff member to take overall responsibility for ensuring that the policy is developed and implemented. This will encourage commitment to the philosophy of the service.

Objectives for step 1

Objectives should be specific, measurable, limited in time, achievable and challenging. They might include:

- how a basic set of principles for child abuse prevention will be developed;
- when this will start and finish; and,
- who has responsibility for the introduction, implementation and maintenance of the policy.

Example of a policy statement on basic principles:

Consider this example for guidance when developing and writing your own basic principles.

BASIC PRINCIPLES

This school (or centre) is committed to the prevention of child abuse and the protection of children. This commitment means that the interests and welfare of children are our prime consideration when any decision is made about suspected cases of abuse or neglect. The school [or centre] supports the role of the statutory child protection service [name] in the investigation of suspicions of child abuse and neglect and will report suspicions to that agency. We are committed to giving support to families. We maintain knowledge of and relationships with agencies and individuals in the community available to support and counsel families.

STEP 2: STAFF IN-SERVICE TRAINING

The second step involves staff training. Learning about abuse necessitates discarding some of the long-held myths about child abuse and accepting new and sometimes distressing facts. Child abuse is now widely researched and, for this reason, it is important that the topic is discussed frequently so that knowledge can be updated.

Teachers and early childhood personnel, including 'relievers', need to be thoroughly aware of children's emotional needs and the damage that abuse (of all kinds) can cause. To increase staff awareness, it is important that everyone who works in a school or preschool centre is given the opportunity to attend training seminars.

Staff with initial training in child protection and abuse prevention need regular updating.

Objectives for step 2

Objectives for this step might include being able to demonstrate knowledge in the following areas:

- legislation, policies and guidelines relating to the reporting of child abuse and neglect;
- recognition of the signs and symptoms of child abuse and neglect;
- how to respond to children when abuse or neglect are suspected;
- how to respond to children when they tell you about abuse;
- how to recognise and deal with your own feelings;
- what resources are available for children and their families in the local community;
- how to support an abused child in your care; and
- how to get support for yourself.

In towns and cities there are usually agencies experienced in the delivery of workshops and seminars for teachers including early childhood professionals.

Administrators must undertake several leadership tasks that focus on developing reporting procedures, educational and training programmes and community linkage mechanisms (McClare 1990). In developing procedures, it is advisable for administrators to involve local specialists, such as social and health workers, psychologists and child development experts.

Example of a policy statement on staff training:

Consider this example as a guide to develop and write your own policy on staff training.

STAFF TRAINING

This school [or centre] is committed to maintaining and increasing staff awareness of how to prevent, recognise and respond to child abuse and neglect. This school [or service] ensures that all staff attend at least one whole day workshop or training session annually relating to child abuse and neglect. As part of their induction, new staff will familiarise themselves with the centre's policies relating to child protection and will be encouraged to read the resource material.

STEP 3: RESPONDING TO CHILD ABUSE AND NEGLECT

Training and consultation offer the best means of identifying abuse and helping abused children.

Suspicion versus certainty

Because the symptoms of abuse often resemble the symptoms of other forms of stress or developmental delay, all members of staff need to have a sound understanding of the signs and symptoms of all forms of abuse and neglect. However, we cannot all be experts in identification, least of all in cases where the signs are vague. If in doubt, staff must consult the child protection authority.

Fear of being wrong

Staff often fail to act when they suspect or when children disclose abuse because they are afraid of making a mistake. When teachers or early childhood professionals are uncertain, they should always consult with the child protection authority. It is obviously much easier to do so if the social workers are known by name. Consultation and reporting are quite separate. In the consultative process, the inquirer does not have to name the child or the institution.

Minimisation and hope

Reporting abuse is distressing. It is easier to ignore it or minimise the seriousness of what was seen or heard. A child who has been abused once is at high risk of being abused again and again unless there is expert and comprehensive intervention. Never approach the abuser with your suspicions.

Fear of repercussions

Some individuals allow abuse to continue because they fear that the parents or the abuser will be angry and that the child or the reporting staff or the institution will suffer. However, the safety of the child cannot be ensured without reporting. If violent repercussions are feared, seek an assurance of confidentiality when making the report to the social worker and share your fears relating to the violence.

Confidentiality

The child's safety must always take precedence over confidentiality. It is inappropriate to promise a child, a parent or anyone else that you will keep a secret if it involves abuse. Your job is to convince the informant that help must be obtained to stop the abuse.

Confidential records

Detailed records must be kept when abuse is suspected. Records are valuable to child protection authorities when they have to make a decision about a child. Safe, locked storage facilities are vital for these records. The key should be kept by the administrator or deputy and no-one else.

Questioning children when abuse is suspected

Only ask the minimum number of questions required to ascertain whether the suspicion is justified and should be reported. It is not the staff's responsibility to find out the details of what happened. There may be a temptation to question excessively through fear of making a mistake. If child victims sense that there is something seriously wrong they may 'clam up'.

If children spontaneously disclose abuse, thank them for the information and follow the instructions in chapter 9. Do not allow other adults to question the child.

Responsibilities for reporting

In countries or states which lack mandatory notification legislation or reporting procedures dictated by the department responsible for child protection, the school or centre should decide on internal procedures for reporting. This should rest with the person who is most competent to handle reports rather than the most senior member of staff. *Make clear policies about what should be done if a staff member is suspected of child abuse.* This is quite the most stressful situation that staff in a school or centre may have to face. Policies and procedures need to be very clear from the outset because of the not uncommon desire of staff to protect the reputation of the institution at the expense of child victims.

Objectives for step 3

Objectives should be specific, measurable, time limited, achievable and challenging. They could include, for example:

- how, where and by whom reports about suspected cases will be safeguarded;
- whom staff will consult when suspicions arise;
- in what circumstances reporting to police or the child protection authority will take place;
- how, when and by whom suspicions of abuse involving a member of staff, volunteer, student or other visitor should be reported;
- how and by whom the details of support services for parents and victims will be obtained, maintained, updated and made available for staff and parents; and
- how and when local child protection officers can be invited to meet staff and parents.

Example of a policy statement on responding to child abuse and neglect

Consider this example as a guide to develop and write your own policy for responding to child abuse.

RESPONDING TO SUSPICIONS OF ABUSE AND NEGLECT

This school [or centre] will record observations, communications and impressions which cause concern.

When abuse or neglect are suspected, voluntary and employed staff will consult a senior administrator who will be committed to taking action and arranging consultation with the child protection authority.

Where we suspect that abuse has occurred or is about to occur and the child is unsafe, we are committed to reporting the matter to [the statutory authority].

Where we suspect that the abuse has been perpetrated by someone close to the family, the child protection social worker will be asked to inform that family.

When a child has been recently abused and the perpetrator is still in the neighbourhood, we will inform police.

If we suspect that an employed or voluntary worker in the school [or centre] has abused a child, we will report the matter promptly to management AND the statutory authorities. Staff under suspicion will be suspended while the matter is investigated and they will be informed of their rights.

We believe that children, families, staff and others involved in an investigation of child abuse should receive support and we will maintain knowledge of agencies which will provide support.

Basic principles of responding to suspected child abuse

1 Believe what children tell you and accept what you see and hear.
2 Record your observations, impressions and concerns.
3 If there is an immediate risk of the child being re-abused, take action to ensure the safety of the child. This may mean contacting police as well as the child protection service. If the abuser is unknown and is still in the vicinity, contact police.
4 Trust your own judgement and act on your concerns: do not leave it to other people. If you have reported serious concerns to a senior member of staff and no action has been taken, take action yourself.
5 If there is no immediate urgency and you have doubts, seek advice from the department's duty officer. Consult with a more experienced member of staff who may have additional evidence

to support your suspicion. If there is no short-term risk, take the time to consult thoroughly in order to make a well-informed decision.

6 Obtain support for yourself. Reporting child abuse is always stressful. You need to be able to talk to a counsellor or someone who understands the situation about how you feel.

STEP 4: EMPLOYMENT

The suitability of job applicants must be thoroughly checked. There are dangers in making informal and casual appointments to positions involving the care of children. Children's centres should *never* be used by criminal courts as community work placements for criminals, whatever the nature of their offences. Extra care must be taken when voluntary workers or the relatives or friends of staff are on the premises. Particular care is necessary when helpers are adolescents or adults with developmental disabilities. Care is necessary because of the unfortunate fact that so many disabled people are themselves victims of violence of all kinds (see Sobsey 1994).

Although it may embarrass us, checks must be made on all applicants for employment. Checks can be made with a few telephone calls. Unfortunately, in the past, institutions have resolved the problem of abusive staff by asking them to resign when their offences were disclosed. History shows that, without being reported and treated, they move on to other centres or schools and continue offending.

Most people have histories which can be validated. This can be done by asking for documentary evidence of claims and by making contact with training institutions and past employers. Telephone calls to past employers are most useful because, if applicants have left under a cloud, the employer is unlikely to disclose this in a written report. It is important not to rely on written testimonials. With the applicant's knowledge, ask questions such as:

- Did you ever have any reason to be concerned about this person's behaviour with children?
- Have there ever been any complaints from staff, parents or children about this person?
- To your knowledge, has the applicant had major personal

difficulties which interfered with his/her ability to behave responsibly with children or adults?

- Did the applicant form appropriate relationships with the staff, children and/or parents?

Any adolescent or adult suspected of or having a history of sexual offences against adults or children should not be employed in any role which provides access to children. Those who have received treatment are advised as part of their rehabilitation that they should avoid contact with children.

Employers should question applicants who have had frequent changes of residence and employment or, alternatively, have significant gaps in their work history. Gaps sometimes indicate that they have been in prison or a psychiatric hospital. There are often charitable motives for employing former residents of these institutions but our prime responsibility is the safety and protection of children. Safety can be compromised if rehabilitation is the motive for employing someone with a dubious history. Crimes of violence, major dishonesty or a history of substance abuse could indicate that the applicant is not safe around children. Persistent offenders may have a lack of conscience and poor impulse control. It is very difficult for an expert, least of all an employer, to make a judgement about whether someone has overcome major difficulties sufficiently well to be trusted with children.

If it is possible to have a police check on an applicant, this facility should be used. However, such checks are not enough because few offenders are prosecuted and convicted, least of all if they offend against preschool aged children.

If applicants happen to be friends or relatives of staff members, they should be subjected to the same rigorous checks as other applicants.

If employers find that any information presented by applicants is misleading or dishonest, they should not be employed.

Caution should be used in engaging temporary staff and voluntary helpers. Make use of a pool of tried and trusted relievers and check them as thoroughly as you check permanent staff. If there is no way of checking the history of temporary staff, volunteers or students, limit the duties they perform with children and ensure that they are always supervised.

Students are accountable to their training organisation and to the staff member in the service responsible for their supervision. Students should be made aware of the child protection policy of the centre as part of their introduction to the field experience. In addition, where there is legislation relating to reporting, staff should check with course supervisors that students have been trained for mandatory notification and have a knowledge of the signs, symptoms and procedures for handling suspicions or disclosures of child abuse and neglect.

Finally, employers should not protect former employees about whom they have had concerns. Children's rights to protection should always be our priority and, in an age of litigation, we expose ourselves to the risk of civilian action if an offender gains access to and abuses a child as a result of our negligence.

Objectives for step 4.

Objectives should be specific, measurable, achievable, challenging and time limited. They could include, for example:

- how, by whom and when an applicant is informed about pre-employment policies;
- how, by whom and when an applicant's previous work history and references are checked;
- by whom and how an applicant is interviewed.

Example of a policy statement on employment

Use this example as a guide to develop and write your own policy on employment.

EMPLOYMENT

This school's [or centre's] employment procedures include a thorough checking of applicants' work histories, making personal contact with referees and past employers. This is done with the applicant's consent. Our prime considerations when choosing staff are ensuring that they have the skills and attributes which contribute to the children's safety and to their physical, emotional, intellectual and social development.

STEP 5: SUPERVISION

Staff may fear they will be constantly watched and constantly suspected of maltreating children. However, not all adults are safe and it is important to limit opportunities for children to be abused while they are in our care. Good policies and procedures help to protect staff and visitors from unfounded allegations. While the example here is general, individual services should develop a specific policy for their situation.

Limit opportunities for staff and other adults to be alone with children. Staff should be invited to identify and examine the opportunities for adults and adolescents to be alone with a child or with small groups of children.

International research shows that most sexual abuse in early childhood services occurs in connection with toileting, in sleep rooms or when there are few adults around. If it is not practical to have two staff members available in each situation, other measures should be put into place to protect staff and minimise risks to children. These can include an open-door or no-doors policy. Supervisory staff should make regular 'safety rounds' in child care centres.

Design of buildings

Buildings for young children should be designed in such a way that while some privacy is available, children are always visible to staff through adult-level windows.

Taking children away from the premises

Given that abuse involving paedophile groups and pornography occurs predominantly when children are removed from kindergartens and child care centres by senior staff and director-owners, a clear policy should apply to children taken on outings. Except in an emergency, children must not leave a service without a parent's or guardian's permission. Blanket permission should not be allowed; for example, clergy and owners of private centres should not remove children for any reason without being accompanied by a member of staff with written parental consent.

Tasks performed by parents and visitors

Parents should not be allowed to perform caretaking (personal hygiene) tasks with children other than their own. Visitors and volunteer helpers should not be allowed to perform these tasks or be alone with children.

Rules about touching children

The care of young children involves physical contact. This is normal, natural and desirable. Staff may already have fears that their contact with children could be misinterpreted. It is natural to touch children to show affection, to comfort, to reassure and give them praise as well as for taking care of personal needs. However, there must be some protection for both adults and children in the development of guidelines about appropriate touching. The following examples are suggestions only and service personnel should discuss these matters with management to develop mutually acceptable rules.

1   If a child initiates physical contact in seeking affection, reassurance or comfort, it is appropriate to respond. It is not appropriate to force unwanted affection or touching on a child.
2   The physical contact of children during personal hygiene procedures must be at the minimum level for the purpose of the task. Encourage children to take care of themselves. It is not appropriate to tickle or fondle children's bodies, however innocent the intent.

In making physical contact with children, staff should be guided by the principle that they will do so only to meet the child's physical or emotional needs. Touching should never be initiated to gratify adults' needs.

Objectives for step 5

Objectives should be specific and measurable, achievable, time related and challenging. They could include, for example:

•   how, when and by whom staff and other adults are supervised when they are with children;
•   how, why and when staff and other adults should be alone with children;
•   how, when and with whom children may be taken from the centre (with parental approval for that occasion);
•   how, when and with whom rules about acceptable touching of children will be discussed, implemented and updated;
•   what action should be taken and by whom if, after accepting the policy, staff fail to keep to the rules.

Example of a policy statement on supervision

Consider this example as a guide in developing and writing your own policy on the supervision of staff and others who have access to children.

SUPERVISION OF STAFF AND ACCESS TO CHILDREN
MISSION STATEMENT

This early childhood centre is committed to children's safety. To that end, we ensure that staff and visitors to the centre are well supervised and visible in the activities they perform with children. This includes an open-door policy, especially for private spaces where intimate caretaking of children is required.

Opportunities for staff and visitors to be alone with children are kept to a minimum. Except in an emergency, children are not taken from the service without parental approval in writing. This early childhood service has established rules about the acceptable touching of children which are discussed with staff and other adults who have contact with children at the centre.

STEP 6: RELATIONSHIPS WITH PARENTS

Parental access

A useful strategy in the prevention of sexual abuse by staff or visitors to an early childhood centre is to encourage parents to drop in at any time. In cases of child sexual abuse involving privately owned kindergartens and child care centres in Australia and the United States, parents were instructed not to call between midday and 2 pm because children were asleep during that time and should not be disturbed. Some were asleep but others were removed for sexual abuse involving pornography.

Visible policies

Making the school's or centre's policy known to parents is very important. Policies should be printed in a pamphlet and given to the parents of enrolled children and those about to enrol. Parents should be encouraged to participate in the development of policies.

Complaints procedure

Parents sometimes tell staff of concerns about certain procedures or about sexual misbehaviour by other children, staff or visitors at a school or centre. Typically, in the past, parents have been reassured or their complaints have been discounted.

Later, additional concerns have led to further investigations and, occasionally, action has been taken in relation to a member of staff. If parents had been taken seriously when they expressed their concerns, additional abuse might have been prevented. Although some parents can be overprotective and unduly demanding, all concerns relating to sexual behaviour must be taken very seriously. Take time to sit down and listen to them. Never minimise their concerns or offer reassurance prematurely. If appropriate, ask parents to put their concerns in writing. Include another staff member (other than the accused perpetrator) if the complaint involves an employee at the school or centre.

Schools and early childhood centres should have an established procedure for hearing parents' concerns and complaints. Parents should be made aware of the procedures, a copy of which should be displayed on the noticeboard.

If a complaint involves sexual abuse, inform parents that you will have to report the matter to the statutory child protection authority for further investigation. It is not your responsibility to conduct an investigation.

If the complaint involves inappropriate behaviour which does not constitute an offence, tell the parent how the matter will be dealt with. This will involve informing the individual concerned and, if necessary, changing procedures and practices, and monitoring them. When there is an allegation of abuse involving a staff member, the accused should be informed of his or her rights and suspension should be immediate.

If you disagree with the complainants about the outcome of an investigation, it is recommended that you use the services of an outside mediator such as an adviser from the government department responsible for your service.

While the matter complained about may not be child abuse, it may be that the appropriateness of the employee working with children needs to be examined. Parents should have confidence in management's willingness to hear them.

Keeping parents informed

If there is an unusual amount of sexual play on the part of children in a class or centre there may be a reason to suspect that one or more of the children is being sexually abused. Parents have the right to know of management's concerns about such behaviour and they should be told how the problem is being investigated and dealt with. However, the administrator should consult with the child protection authority about the timing of this information and the way in which it should be given so that an investigation into the abuse is not compromised. It is also important that parents are made aware of the importance of introducing a child protection programme at home when there is a risk that young children are being sexualised prematurely by one of their peers.

Objectives for step 6

Objectives should be specific, measurable, time related, achievable and challenging. They could include, for example:

- how, when and by whom parents will be informed about the school's or centre's child protection policies;
- who will respond to parents' concerns and complaints and how.

Example of a policy statement on relationships with parents

Consider this example as a guide for developing your own policies about relationships with parents.

RELATIONSHIPS WITH PARENTS

This school [or centre] encourages parents to visit at any time. Our child protection policies are available to all parents and prospective users of the centre/school. If parents have concerns about the treatment of a child or the behaviour of a member of staff or visitor, they are encouraged to make these concerns known to the [senior member of staff] who will ensure that the matter is investigated and that action is taken, using an adviser from the department if necessary.

STEP 7: EDUCATION FOR CHILD PROTECTION

Children rarely know how to tell adults that they have been sexually abused. They are often not believed when they try to inform their parents about sexual offences. Parents do not always know the signs and symptoms of abuse nor do they have enough information about their children's needs and the effects of abuse. Furthermore, parents may not know where to turn for help when a child has been abused.

Education and child care services have a role in encouraging parents to attend courses, receive training and have access to written material. Families with difficulties should be advised of support agencies.

Schools and centres will organise parent education programmes for child protection. If staff are not confident to address parents, experts can usually be contacted through the child protection authority. Parent libraries should stock child protection books for parents, as well as books for parents to use with children.

Schools and centres have a duty to inform parents of the family's importance in child protection. Children will not disclose sexual abuse to their parents unless parents have already shown that they can talk about the human body without becoming overemotional and punitive. They will not confide in their parents if those parents have created a taboo around genitals.

Objectives for step 7

Your objectives should be specific, measurable, time related, achievable and challenging. They might include, for example:

- how, when and which staff will initiate and encourage parents to attend education programmes about child protection;
- the purchase of books on child protection for the parents' lending library;
- how and when child protection books and resources will be introduced and maintained for use by staff with children;
- how, by whom and when staff will be trained to provide child protection education programmes for children and answer their questions.

Example of a policy statement on education for child protection.

Consider this example as a guide for developing your own policies about education for child protection.

EDUCATION FOR CHILD PROTECTION

This centre/school believes that personal safety education for children and parents is important for the prevention of child sexual abuse. We encourage parents to make use of education programmes available in the community. We use the [name] programme with children. This carries the endorsement of the Department of [name]. We invite parents to participate and reinforce the safety concepts at home. Parents are encouraged to borrow books on child protection for their own reference. Books about personal safety for young children are available in the parents' library and book corner. Regular training ensures that staff are comfortable about responding to questions and disclosures from children.

WHAT HAPPENS WHEN YOU REPORT CHILD ABUSE OR NEGLECT?

Although legislation varies in different states and countries, the procedures are broadly similar.

When a suspicion or disclosure of abuse is reported, the duty officer receiving the call has to decide whether it involves an emergency and warrants immediate investigation or, if the child is now safe, whether it can be given a lower level of priority.

If an investigation is deemed to be necessary, the case is assigned to a social worker who will gather information from you and, if appropriate, from other community members and professionals. The social worker will also interview the child and the parents. If the child has disclosed sexual abuse at the school or centre and the abuser is in the family home, some staff request that the child be interviewed at the school or centre.

The social worker's first concern is whether the child is safe. If the parent is unwilling or unable to take action to make the child safe, emergency care becomes necessary. The worker has the power to remove the child and place him or her in a hospital, a temporary foster home or other safe place. Children are rarely removed from their homes. This happens only when the child is seriously injured, the parent is suffering from psychiatric illness or clearly cannot cope or the mother insists on supporting the perpetrator of sexual abuse who continues to live in the family home. This often happens when the offender is an older son or her sexual partner who supports her financially.

A case conference will be held to decide:

- what action to take if the child remains at home and is not deemed to be in need of care and protection by the authority;
- which support services are needed by the parents, for example, subsidised child care, respite care, a home intervention (child management or behaviour modification) programme, budget advice, a loan, rehousing, treatment for drug, alcohol or gambling addiction, the provision of domestic help or referral to an early childhood and family centre. Protection may involve making a contract with the parent;
- when to hold a family meeting as a measure in itself or in conjunction with other services to set up family support;
- whether emergency action is necessary and whether court proceedings should be initiated.

Teachers and early childhood professionals can make a useful contribution to case conferences because they know the children and they may be the only people present who have a strong child development background and a focus on children's, rather than adults', emotional needs.

In some of the more enlightened countries, such as New Zealand, police and social workers work together in a coordinated team to investigate complaints of sexual abuse. This reduces the trauma of multiple interviews for the child and increases the chances of apprehending the offender. Interviews are also video-recorded and children may give evidence via video from an adjacent room. This spares them the ordeal of seeing the offenders and their supporters in court. Child victims should always be referred to specialist therapeutic programmes to give them the opportunity to work through their feelings about the abuse. Parents should also be referred to parent support groups which will help them to cope with the crisis.

DEALING WITH THE EMOTIONAL AND ANGRY RESPONSES OF PARENTS

Staff in schools and centres should be prepared for the times when they face parents who are emotionally upset due to circumstances which may include:

- their child being bullied or abused in the school;
- their child being involved in a school inquiry;
- the parents being denied access to a child because of a court order;
- the child being reported as a victim of physical or emotional abuse or neglect;
- the child being reported as a suspected victim of sexual abuse. (Betts 1994)

Parents who are investigated as a result of a report of child abuse or neglect experience a wide range of emotions. They sometimes seek external sources of blame or the opportunity to vent their anger. The staff of the child's school or centre are often the target of these intense emotions and blame.

It is important to understand that the school environment may be the only outlet for the parents' response to their crisis and the response should not be viewed as a personal attack. Regardless of the social workers' investigations, the school or preschool is likely to continue serving the family and it is important for staff not to alienate parents if this can be avoided (Betts 1994).

If the report of abuse or neglect was made by the school, that information does not have to be revealed to a parent. Although confidentiality is usually assured, those making a report can specifically request that their identities remain confidential. The important issue is the protection of the child and the crisis within the family, not the source of the notification. The risk of a parent's angry reaction should never deter professionals from undertaking their responsibility of responding to suspicions of abuse or neglect.

Angry, distressed parents will find it difficult to absorb information correctly. They may also find it difficult to express their feelings coherently. Inarticulate parents may use alcohol to give them the courage to take action. Some will inevitably use foul language. The recipient of the anger should let the parents have their say and attempt to calm them down with messages such as, 'I'm glad that you came to see me. I can see that this is a worrying time for you. I'd like to hear what is concerning you but would you care to come into the office where we can talk in private?' Calmly indicate that you are listening. Being heard is often the major concern for a parent at this time. When appropriate, involve the school principal, senior staff member or school counsellor.

It is often helpful to remove 'no smoking' signs when parents are in crisis. These situations can be defused by a calm and concerned professional. Parents who display anger may have many different concerns. A quiet, controlled response may reduce the possibility of our own overreaction to parents' hostility and increase opportunities to respond sensitively to their real feelings and concerns.

When a child has been sexually abused, parents should always be referred to counselling services. It helps if the members of staff can be involved in the referral as parents are often too embarrassed to make the telephone call.

TASKS FOR STUDENTS

1   How might a sensitive check be kept on children thought to be at risk of abuse?

2   In what ways would you want staff to be vigilant when there are several children from one high-risk family in the same school?

3   What are the likely feelings of a child who senses that his or her welfare is being monitored?

4   Who is the most appropriate person to make home visits—the class teacher, a teacher's aide, another parent, a school nurse?

5   How could staff organise a consultation and support structure for responding to child abuse and neglect?

6   What is the present policy of your school or centre relating to record keeping for child abuse and neglect? Is it adequate? Who has access to the records? Should information about 'at risk' children be given to new teachers or schools?

7   Are parents told if records are kept about their children? Discuss the implications of telling or not telling parents when child abuse is suspected.

REFERENCES

Abel, G.G., Becker, J.V., Mittelman, M.S., Cunningham-Rathner, J., Rou-leau, J.L., Murphy, W.D. 1987, 'Self-reported sex crimes of non-incar-cerated paraphiliacs', *Journal of Interpersonal Violence*, vol. 2, no. 6, pp. 3–25.

Alston, P. & Brennan, G. (eds) 1991, *The UN Children's Convention and Australia*, Human Rights and Equal Opportunity Commission, ANU Centre for International and Public Law, Australian Council of Social Service, Canberra.

Ammerman, R. T. & Hersen, M. (eds) 1990, *Treatment of family violence*, John Wiley & Sons, New York.

Anderson, C. 1982, *Teaching people with mental retardation about sexual abuse prevention*, Illusion Theater Guide, Minneapolis.

Angus, G., Wilkinson, K. & Zabar, P. 1994, *Child abuse and neglect Australia 1991–92*, Australian Institute of Health and Welfare: Child Welfare Series No. 5, AGPS, Canberra.

Angus, G. & Woodward, S. 1995, *Child abuse and neglect Australia 1993–94*, Australian Institute of Health and Welfare: Child Welfare Series No. 13, AGPS, Canberra.

Barber, D. 1995, 'NZ's forgotten children', *Bulletin,* 28 March, p. 50.

Bastick, S. 1995, *Lateline*, Australian Broadcasting Commission, 25 May.

Bean, P. & Melville, J. 1989, *Lost children of the Empire: The untold story of Britain's child migrants*, Unwin/Hyman, London.

Beitchman, J.H., Zucker, K.J., Hood, J.E., DaCosta, G.A. & Akman, D. 1991, 'A review of the short-term effects of child sexual abuse', *Child Abuse and Neglect,* vol. 15, pp. 537–56.

Beitchman, J.H., Zucker, K.J., Hood, J.E., DaCosta, G.A., Akman, D. & Cassavia, E. 1992, 'A review of the long-term effects of child sexual abuse', *Child Abuse and Neglect,* vol. 16, pp. 101–18.

Bentovim, A. 1991, 'Evaluation of a comprehensive treatment approach to child sexual abuse within the family', *Proceedings of the Third European Conference on Child Abuse and Neglect*, Prague.

——1994, Unscheduled report on the current research project undertaken at the Hospital for Sick Children, Great Ormond Street, London, 10th International Congress on Child Abuse and Neglect, Kuala Lumpur.

Berrick, J.P. & Gilbert, N. 1991, *With the best of intentions: The child sexual abuse prevention movement*, Guilford Press, New York.

Berridge, D. & Cleaver, H. 1987, *Foster home breakdown*, Oxford, Blackwell.

Betts, R. 1994, *Child Abuse: A teacher's response*, Melbourne, CPECG.

Birchall, E.M. 1989, 'The frequency of child abuse: What do we really know?' in O. Stevenson (ed.), *Child abuse: Professional practice and public policy*, Harvester Wheatsheaf, Hemel Hempstead, UK.

Blanchard, A. 1993, 'Violence in families', *Family Matters*, May, 34, pp. 31–6.

Blanchard, A., Molloy, F. & Brown, L., 1992, 'I just couldn't stop them', *Western Australian Children Living with Domestic Violence: A study of the children's experiences and service provision*, Curtin University School of Social Work for the Western Australian Government Office of the Family, WA.

Bowlby, J. 1953, *Child care and the growth of love*, Pelican, London.

Brassard, M.R., Germain, R. & Hart, S.N. 1987, *Psychological maltreatment of children and youth*, Pergamon Press, New York.

Briere, J. 1984, The effects of childhood sexual abuse on later psychological functioning: Defining a post-sexual-abuse syndrome, 3rd National Conference on Sexual Victimisation of Childhood, Washington DC.

Briere, J., & Runtz, M. 1989, 'University males' sexual interest in children—Predicting indices of "pedophilia" in a non-forensic sample', *Child Abuse and Neglect*, vol. 13, no. 1, pp. 65–76.

Briggs, F. 1988, 'South Australian parents want child protection programmes to be offered in schools and preschools', *Early Child Development and Care*, vol. 34, pp. 167–178.

——1990, *Evaluation of 'Keeping Ourselves Safe' curriculum used with children of 5–8 years in New Zealand schools*, University of South Australia report to the Commissioner of Police, New Zealand.

——1991a, 'Child protection programmes: Can they protect young children?' *Early Child Development and Care*, vol. 67, pp. 61–72.

——1991b, 'Keeping ourselves safe: A personal curriculum examined', *NZCER/ACER Set*, Item 7, 1991, Reproduced in *Best of Set*, 1994.

——1993, *Why my child?*, Allen & Unwin, Sydney.

——(ed.) 1994, *Children and families: Australian perspectives*, Allen & Unwin, Sydney.

——1995a, *Developing personal safety skills to children with disabilities*, Jessica Kingsley, London.

——1995b, *Victim to offender*, Allen & Unwin, Sydney.

Briggs, F. & Hawkins, R.M.F. 1993a, 'Children's perceptions of personal safety issues and their vulnerability to molestation', *Children Australia*, vol. 18, no. 3, pp. 4–9.

——1993b, 'Follow-up data on the effectiveness of New Zealand's national school based child protection program', *Child Abuse and Neglect*, vol. 18, no. 8, pp. 635–43.

——1994, 'Follow up study of children of 5–8 years using child protection programs', *Early Child Development and Care*, vol. 100, pp. 111–17.

——1996a *Keeping ourselves safe: A survey of New Zealand children aged 10–12 years and their parents*, report for the New Zealand Police & Ministry of Education.

——1996b, 'A comparison of the childhood experiences of convicted male child molesters and men who were sexually abused in childhood and claimed to be "non-offenders"', *Child Abuse and Neglect*, vol. 20, no. 3, pp. 221–33.

Briggs, F., Hawkins, R.M.F. & Williams, M. 1994, 'A comparison of the early childhood and family experiences of incarcerated, convicted male child molesters and men who were sexually abused in childhood and have no convictions for sexual offences against children', University of South Australia report for the Criminology Research Council, Canberra.

Briggs, F. & Lehmann, K. 1989, 'Significance of children's drawings in cases of sexual abuse', *Early Child Development and Care*, vol. 47, pp. 131–47.

Briggs, F. & Potter, G.K. 1995, *Teaching children in the first three years of school*, Longman Australia, Melbourne.

Broadhurst, D.D. 1986, *Educators, schools and child abuse*, National Committee for Prevention of Child Abuse, Washington DC.

Brotherhood of St Laurence 1994, *Inquiry into aspects of youth homelessness: submission to the House of Representatives Standing Committee on Community Affairs,* Fitzroy, Victoria.

Brown T. 1979, 'Putting down kids', *Journal of Canadian Society for Prevention of Cruelty to Children*, vol. 2, no. 11–13, Winter.

Browne, K. & Finkelhor, D. 1986, 'Impact of child sexual abuse: A review of the research', *Psychological Bulletin,* vol. 99, pp. 66–77.

Browne, K. 1993, 'Question time', *Australasian Conference on Child Abuse and Neglect*, Brisbane, Queensland.

Browne, K.D. 1993, 'Violence in the family and its links to child abuse', *Bailliere's Clinical Paediatrics*, vol. 1, no. 1, pp. 149–64.

Browne, K.D. & Herbert, M. 1993, *Preventing family violence,* John Wiley & Sons, Chichester, UK.

Butterworth, M. & Fulmer, A. 1990, *The effect of family violence on children: Implication for intervention*, a report to the Australian Association of Early Childhood Educators Inc., December.

Carey, S.E. 1986, *The risk of educational disadvantage for children in substitute care*, a report to the Children in Residential Care Task Force, Adelaide, South Australia.

Carlson, B.E. 1984, 'Children's observations of interparental violence', in A.R. Roberts (ed.), *Battered Women and their Families*, Springer, New York, pp. 147–67.

Ceresa, M. 1995, 'Religions denounce female mutilation', *Australian*, 7 June, p. 5.

Chamberlain A., Rauh J., Passer A., McGrath M. and Burket R. 1984, 'Issues in fertility control for mentally retarded adolescents: I. Sexual activity, sexual abuse and contraception', *Pediatrics*, vol. 73, no. 4, pp. 445–50.

Church, J. 1994, 'Family violence: Its effects on children and schools—A New Zealand Study', *Best of Set*, NZCER/ACER, Wellington.

Clark, R. 1995, 'Child protection services in Victoria', *Family Matters*, vol. 40, Autumn, Australian Institute of Family Studies, Melbourne.

Connolly, J. 1983, *Step families: Towards a clearer understanding*, Corgi Books, Sydney.

Cook, M. & Howells, K. 1981 (eds), *Adult sexual interest in children*, Academic Press, New York.

Creighton, S.J. & Noyes, P. 1989, *Child abuse trends in England and Wales, 1983–1987*, NSPCC, London.

Cumming, E.N., Zahn-Waxler, C., Radke-Yarrow, M. 1981, 'Young children's responses to expression of anger and affection by others in the family', *Child Development* vol. 52, no. 4, pp. 1274–82.

Dale, P. 1984, 'The danger within ourselves', *Community Care*, 1 March, pp. 20–4.

Davies, K. 1994, *When innocence trembles*, Angus & Robertson, Sydney.

Davis, N.J. 1993, 'Systemic gender control and victimisation among homeless female youth', *Socio-Legal Bulletin*, vol. 8, pp. 22–31.

Daw, M. & Male, A. 1992, 'Home truths on violence, Adelaide', *Advertiser*, 2 April, p. 13.

Department of Health (England and Wales) 1995, *Child protection: Messages from research*, HMSO, London.

DHSS (Department of Health and Social Security) 1974, *Report of the committee of inquiry into the care and supervision provided in relation to Maria Colwell*, HMSO, London.

——1982, *Child abuse: A study of inquiry reports 1973–1981*, HMSO, London.

Dobash, R.E & Dobash, R. 1979, *Violence against wives: A case against patriarchy*, Free Press, New York.

Dougherty, L.B. 1986, 'What happens to the victims of child abuse?' in M. Nelson & K. Clark (eds), *The educator's guide to preventing child sexual abuse*, Network publications, Santa Cruz.

Douglas, J.W.B. 1964, *The home and the school*, Macgibbon and Kee, London.

Drotar, D., Eckerle, D., Satola, J., Pallotta, J. & Wyatt, B. 1990, 'Maternal interactional behavior with nonorganic failure-to-thrive infants: A case comparison study', *Child Abuse and Neglect*, vol. 14, pp. 41–51.

Dube, R. & Hebert, M. 1988, 'Sexual abuse of children under 12 years. A review of 511 cases', *Child Abuse and Neglect*, vol. 12, no. 3, p. 321.

Duke, R. 1995, 'Children's and adults' attitudes towards parents smacking their children', *Children Australia*, vol. 20, no. 2, pp. 24–7.

Edgar, D. 1988, 'Family disruption and violence', *Family Matters*, Australian Institute of Family Studies, 22 December, pp. 12–16.

Family Violence Professional Education Taskforce 1991, *Family violence, everybody's business, somebody's life*, Federation Press, Annandale, NSW, pp. 210–13.

Farber, A. & Egeland, B. 1987, 'Invulnerability among abused and neglected children', in E.J. Anthony and B.J.J. Cohler (eds), *The Invulnerable Child*, Guildford Press, New York.

Farmer, E. & Owen, M. 1995, *Child protection practice: Private risks and public remedies*, HMSO, London.

Finkelhor, D. 1984, *Child sexual abuse: Theory and research*, Free Press, New York.

Finkelhor, D., Williams, L.M. & Burns, N. 1988, *Nursery crimes: Sexual abuse in day care*, Sage Publications, Newbury Park.

Garbarino, J. 1979, 'The role of the school in the human ecology of child maltreatment', *School Review*, vol. 87, no. 2, pp. 190–213.

Garbarino, J., Brookhauser, P. E., Authier, K.J. & Associates 1987, *Special children, special risks: The maltreatment of children with disabilities*, Aldine D.E. Gruyter, New York.

Garbarino, J. & Gilliam, G. 1980, *Understanding abusive families*, D.C. Heath and Co., Lexington.

Garbarino, J., Guttman, E. & Seeley, J.W. 1986, *The psychologically battered child*, Jossey Bass, San Franciso.

Gayford, J.J. 1975, 'Wife battering: A preliminary survey of 100 cases', *British Medical Journal*, vol. 25, no. 1, pp. 94–7.

Gilmour, A. 1988, *Innocent victims*, Michael Joseph, London.

Goddard, C.R. & Hiller, P. C. 1993, 'Child sexual abuse: Assault in a violent context', *Australian Journal of Social Issues*, vol. 28, no. 1, pp. 20–33.

Goddard, C. & Liddell, M. 1993, 'Child abuse and the media: Victoria introduces mandatory reporting after an intensive media campaign', *Children Australia*, vol. 18, no. 3, pp. 23–7.

Goldman, R. & Goldman, J. 1988, *Show me yours*, Penguin, Melbourne.

Good, T.L. & Brophy, J.E. 1978, *Looking in classrooms*, Harper & Row, New York.

Harper, G.F. 1980, 'Teaching and child abuse', *Educational Forum*, March, pp. 321–7.

Hart, S.N., Brassard, M.R. & Germain, R.B. 1987, in Brassard, M.R.,

Germain, R. & Hart, S.N. (eds) 1987, *Psychological maltreatment of children and youth,* Pergamon Press, New York.

Herman, J.L. 1986, 'Histories of violence in an outpatient population: An exploratory study', *American Journal of Orthopsychiatry,* vol. 56, pp. 137–41.

Hetherington, E.M & Parke, R.D. 1986, *Child psychology: A contemporary viewpoint,* McGraw-Hill, New York.

Hilberman, E. & Munson, K. 1977–78, 'Sixty battered women', *Victimology: An International Journal,* vol. 2, pp. 460–71.

Hollows, A. & Armstrong, H. 1992, *Children and young people as abusers: An agenda for action,* National Children's Bureau, London.

Hopwood, N.J. & Becker, D.J. 1979, 'Psychosocial dwarfism: Detection, evaluation and management', *Child Abuse and Neglect,* vol. 3, pp. 439–47.

Hughes, H. 1986, 'Research with children in shelters: Implications for clinical services', *Children Today,* vol. 15, no. 2, pp. 21–5.

Human Rights and Equal Opportunity Commission 1989, *Our homeless children,* AGPS, Canberra.

Humphreys, M. 1995, *Empty cradles,* Doubleday, London.

Hunt, G., Hawkins, R. & Goodlet, T. 1992, 'Parenting: A survey of community needs', *Children Australia,* vol. 17, no. 3, pp. 9–12.

Hyman, I.A. 1985, Psychological abuse in the schools: A school psychologist's perspective, paper presented to the annual convention of the American Psychological Association, Los Angeles.

ISPCC (Irish Society for the Prevention of Cruelty to Children) 1996, personal communication.

ISPCC Irish Marketing Surveys 1993, *Childhood experiences and attitudes—an Irish marketing survey,* Dublin.

Iwaniec, D., Herbert, M. & McNeish, A.S. 1985, 'Social work with failure-to-thrive children and their families: Part I. Psychosocial factors', *British Journal of Social Work,* vol. 15, pp. 243–59.

Iwaniec, D., Herbert, M. & Sluckin, A. 1988, 'Helping emotionally abused chidren who fail to thrive', in K. Browne, C. Davies and P. Stratton (eds), *Early prediction and prevention of child abuse,* John Wiley & Sons, New York.

Jackson, S. 1989, 'Education of children in care', in B. Kahan (ed.), *Child care research: Policy and practice,* Hodder & Stoughton, London.

Jackson, S., Sanders, R. & Thomas, N. 1994, *Protecting Children in Wales: The role and effectiveness of area child protection committees,* Department of Social Policy and Applied Social Studies, University of Wales, Swansea.

Jaffe, P., Wolfe, D. & Wilson, S.K. 1990, *Children of battered women,* Sage Publications, Beverley Hills, California.

James, M. 1994, 'Child abuse and neglect: Incidence and prevention', *Family Matters,* International Year of the Family Priority Issue, vol. 37, April, pp. 80–5.

Johns, M. & Baxter, R. 1986, Academic intervention for children in residential care, paper presented to the Australian Association of Special Education, 11th National Conference, Adelaide.

Johnson, B. 1994, 'Teachers' role in the primary prevention of child abuse', *Child Abuse Review*, vol. 3, pp. 259–71.

——1995, *Teaching and learning about personal safety: Report of the review of 'Protective Behaviours' in South Australia*, Painters Prints, Adelaide.

Johnson, R.L. & Shrier, D.K. 1985, 'Sexual victimization of boys', *Journal of Adolescent Health Care*, vol. 6, pp. 372–6.

Johnson, T.C. 1988, 'Child perpetrators—children who molest other children: Preliminary findings', *Child Abuse and Neglect*, vol. 12, pp. 219–29.

Jouriles, E.N., Murphy, C.M. & O'Leary, K. 1989, 'Interspousal aggression, marital discord and child problems', *Journal of Consulting and Clinical Psychology*, vol. 57, pp. 453–5.

Kempe, C.H., Silverman, F.N., Steele, B.R., Droegamueller, W. & Silver, H.K. 1962, 'The battered child syndrome', *Journal of the American Medical Association*, vol. 181, pp. 17–24.

Kennedy, M. 1989, 'The abuse of deaf children', *Child Abuse Review*, Spring, pp. 3–7.

——1990, *The deaf child who is sexually abused—Is there a need for a dual specialist?* National Deaf Society, London.

King, R. 1978, *All things bright and beautiful?* John Wiley & Sons, Chicester.

Kitzinger, J. 1994, 'Challenging sexual violence against girls: A social awareness approach', *Child Abuse Review*, vol. 3, no. 4, pp. 246–59.

Klaus, M. & Kennell, J. 1976, *Maternal infant bonding*, CV Mosby, St Louis.

Kolko, D.J. 1988, 'Educational programs to promote awareness and prevention of child sexual victimisation: A review and methodological critique', *Clinical Psychology Review*, vol. 8, pp. 195–209.

Korbin, J.E. 1977, 'Anthropological contributions to the study of child abuse and neglect', *Child Abuse and Neglect*, vol. 1, pp. 7–12.

——1991, 'Cross cultural perspectives and research directions for the 21st Century', *Child Abuse and Neglect*, vol. 15, Supplement 1, pp. 66–77.

Kosky, R. 1987, 'Is suicidal behaviour increasing among Australian youth?' *Medical Journal of Australia*, 47, 17 August.

Krugman, R.D. & Krugman, M.K. 1984, 'Emotional abuse in the classroom: The pediatrician's role in diagnosis and treatment', *American Journal of Diseases of Children*, vol. 138, pp. 284–6.

Leighton, B. 1989, *Spousal abuse in metropolitan Toronto*, report no. 1989–02. Solicitor General's Office, Ottowa, Canada.

Levin, P. 1983, 'Teachers' perceptions, attitudes and reporting of child abuse/neglect', *Child Welfare* vol. 62, no. 1, pp. 14–19.

Lewis, D. & Green, J. 1983, *Your children's drawings: Their hidden meaning*, Hutchinson, London.

Lewis, J.R. 1985, *The parents handbook: Understanding child sexual abuse*, Governor's Office, Salem, Oregon.

McClare, G. 1990, 'The principal's role in child abuse', *Education and Urban Society*, vol. 22, no. 3, pp. 307–13.

MacKenzie, D. & Chamberlain, C. 1994, The national census of homeless school students, International Year of the Family National Conference, November, Adelaide, South Australia.

MacLeod, L. 1980, *Wife bashing in Canada: The vicious circle*, Canadian Advisory Council on the Status of Women, Ottowa.

——1987, *Battered but not beaten: Preventing wife bashing in Canada*, Canadian Advisory Council on the Status of Women, Ottowa.

Maher, P. (ed.) 1987, *Child abuse: the educational perspective*, Basil Blackwell, Oxford.

Mathias, J., Mertin, P. & Murray, B. 1995, 'The psychological functioning of children from backgrounds of domestic violence', *Australian Psychologist*, vol. 30, no. 1, pp. 47–56.

Mayes, G.M., Currie, E.F., MacLeod, L., Gillies, J.B. and Warden, D.A. 1992, *Child sexual abuse: A review of literature and educational materials*, Scottish Academic Press, Edinburgh.

Ministry of Education New Zealand 1993, *Prevent Child Abuse. Guidelines for Early Childhood Education Services*, Wellington.

Minty, B. & Pattinson, G. 1994, 'The nature of child neglect', *British Journal of Social Work*, vol. 24, pp. 733–47.

Mounty, J.L. & Fetterman, R.J. 1989, *An abuse prevention program for deaf and hard of hearing children*, CAID Convention, San Diego, California, June.

Mugford, J. 1989, *National Committee on Violence, No 2. Domestic Violence*, Australian Institute of Criminology, Canberra, April.

Myers, J.E.B. (ed.) 1994, *The backlash: Child protection under fire*, Sage, Thousand Oakes, California.

National Centre for Child Abuse and Neglect 1988, *Study findings: Study of national incidence and prevalence of child abuse and neglect*, Department of Health and Human Services, Washington.

National Children's Home 1992, *The Report of the Committee of Enquiry into Children and Young People who Sexually Abuse Other Children*, London.

Nesbitt, W. 1991, 'Emotional abuse: Vulnerability and developmental delay', *Developmental Disabilities Bulletin Special Issue*, vol. 19, no. 2, pp. 66–80.

New South Wales Child Protection Council, *Child Protection in non-English speaking background communities. Culture—No excuse*, Sydney.

Newell, P. 1995, *Lateline*. Australian Broadcasting Commission, 25 May.

NSPCC 1993a, Annual Report, London.

NSPCC 1993b, *Children Act Report*, London.

O'Connor, I. 1988, *Our homeless children: Their experiences*, report to the Human Rights and Equal Opportunity Commission, AGPS, Canberra.

O'Donnell, C.R. 1995, 'Firearm deaths among children and youth', *American Psychologist*, vol. 50, no. 9, pp. 771–6.

O'Hagan, K. 1993, *Emotional and psychological abuse of children*, University of Toronto Press, Toronto.

O'Neill, M. 1994, 'Dangerous families' in Briggs, F. (ed.), *Children and families: Australian perspectives*, Allen & Unwin, Sydney.

Oates, K. 1982, *Child abuse: A community concern,* Butterworths, Sydney.

——1985, *Child abuse and neglect: What happens eventually,* Butterworths, Sydney.

——1990 (ed.), *Understanding and managing child sexual abuse,* W.B. Saunders/Bailliere Tindall, Sydney.

Office of the Status of Women 1988, *Community attitudes towards domestic violence in Australia*, Department of the Prime Minister and Cabinet, Canberra.

Osofsky, J.D. 1995, 'The effects of exposure to violence on young children', *American Psychologist*, vol. 50, no. 9, pp. 782–8.

Pahl, J. 1985, 'Violent husbands and abused wives: A longitudinal study', in J. Pahl (ed.), *Private violence and public policy*, Routledge & Kegan Paul, London, pp. 23–94.

Perniskie, L.M. 1995, Child protection programmes: What do children learn and remember? 'Keeping Ourselves Safe'—An evaluation with follow up, Master of Arts in Psychology thesis, Victoria University of Wellington.

Peters, S.D. 1988, 'Child sexual abuse and later psychological problems', in G.E. Wyatt and G.J. Powell (eds), *Lasting effects of child sexual abuse,* Sage, Newbury Park, pp. 101–17.

Piaget, J. 1965, *The moral judgment of the child,* Free Press, New York.

Price, J. & Armstrong, J. 1978, 'Battered wives: A controlled study of predisposition', *Australia and New Zealand Journal of Psychiatry,* vol. 12, no. 1, pp. 43–7.

Queensland Domestic Violence Task Force 1988, *Beyond These Walls*, report of the Queensland Domestic Violence Task Force to the Minister for Family Services and Welfare Housing, Brisbane, Queensland.

Roberts, B. & Carver, V. 1980, 'Personal attitudes to child abuse', in V. Carver (ed.), 1980, *Child abuse: A study text*, Open University Press, Milton Keynes.

Robinson N. 1996, compiles of the refugee and homeless homepage, UK (http://sl.cxwms.ac.UK/Academic/AG-n/interest/homeless/homepage.html.), personal communication.

Roy, M. 1977, *Battered women: A psychological study of domestic violence,* Van Nostrand, New York.

Russell, D.E.H. 1984, 'The prevalence and seriousness of incestuous abuse: Stepfathers vs. biological fathers', *Child Abuse and Neglect,* vol. 8, pp. 15–22.

Scottish Office 1989, *Effective intervention: Child abuse. Guidance on co-operation in Scotland. Annex 5,* HMSO, p. 46.

Senn, C.Y. 1988, *Vulnerable: Sexual abuse and people with an intellectual handicap,* G. Allan Roeher Institute, Downsville, Ontario, Canada.

Sinclair, K. 1995, 'Responding to abuse: A matter of perspective', *Current Issues in Criminal Justice,* vol. 7, no. 2, pp. 153–75.

Sobsey, D. 1994, *Violence and abuse in the lives of people with disabilities,* Paul H. Brookes, Baltimore.

Strang, H. 1996, *Trends and issues in crime and criminal justice,* Australian Institute of Criminology, Canberrra.

Straus, M., Gelles, R. & Steinmetz, S. 1980, *Behind closed doors: Violence in the American family,* Anchor Books, New York.

Sullivan, P. M., Vernon, M. & Scanlan, J.M. 1987, 'Sexual abuse of deaf youth', *American Annals of the Deaf,* October, pp. 256–62.

Summit, R. 1994, 'The reluctance of adults to respond to the crisis of disclosure', *10th International Congress on Child Abuse and Neglect,* Kuala Lumpar.

Swain, P. A. 1993, 'Mandatory reporting and child protection', *Children Australia,* vol. 18. no. 3, pp. 20–2.

Sykes, H. 1993, *Youth homelessness: Courage and hope,* Melbourne University Press, Carlton.

Szur, R. 1987, 'Emotional abuse and neglect', in P. Maher (ed.), *Child abuse: The educational pespective,* Basil Blackwell, Oxford.

Tomison, A. 1995a, 'Update on child sexual abuse', *Issues in Child Abuse Prevention,* vol. 5, pp. 1–12.

——1995b, 'New measures for combating sexual assault', *Family Matters,* vol. 42, pp. 36–41.

Wahl, C.W. 1960, 'The psychodynamics of consummated maternal incest', *Archives of General Psychiatry,* vol. 3, p. 138.

Walker, L. 1979, *The battered woman,* Harper & Row, New York.

Weekes, P. & Westwood, M. 1993, 'Parents deluded on teen sex lives', *Australian,* 31 August, p. 3.

Welsh Office 1994, *Child Protection Register.*

Welsh, L.P. 1990, *The Bindoon file. Boys Town, Bindoon 1947–1954,* P&B Press, Como.

Widom, C.S. 1992, 'The cycle of violence', *Research in brief,* National Institute of Justice, Washington DC, October (cited in James 1994).

Wilson, C. & Dupuis, A. 1994, 'Poverty and performance', *NZCER/ACER Best of Set: Families & School,* Item 3.

Wolfe, D. A. 1991, *Preventing physical and emotional abuse of children,* Guilford Press, New York.

Wolfe, D. A., Zak, L., Wilson, S. & Jaffe, P. 1986, 'Child witnesses to violence between parents: Critical issues in behavioural and social adjustment', *Journal of Abnormal Child Psychology*, vol. 14, no. 1, pp. 95–104.

Wolock, I. & Horowitz, B. 1984, *Child maltreatment as a social problem: The neglect of neglect*, National Clearinghouse on Family Violence. Ottawa.

Wurtele, S.K. & Miller-Perrin, C.L. 1992, *Preventing child abuse: Sharing the responsibility*, University of Nebraska Press, USA.

Wurtele, S.K., Kast, L.C. & Melzer, A.M. 1992, 'Sexual abuse prevention education for young children: A comparison of teachers and parents as instructors'. *Child Abuse and Neglect*, vol. 16, no. 6, p. 877.

Wyatt, G.E. 1985, 'The sexual abuse of Afro-American and White-American women in childhood', *Child Abuse and Neglect*, vol. 9, pp. 507–19.

Wyatt, G.E., & Powell, G.J. 1988, *Lasting effects of child sexual abuse*, Sage, London.

Yates, A., Beutler, L.E. & Crago, M. 1985, 'Drawings by child victims of incest', *Child Abuse and Neglect*, vol. 9, pp. 183–9.

Yule, V. 1985, 'Why are parents tough on children?' *New Society*, 27 September, pp. 444–6.

INDEX